Urban Politics
a political
economy approach

WILLIAM A. SCHULTZE
San Diego State University

Prentice-Hall, Inc.   Englewood Cliffs, New Jersey 07632

Library of Congress Cataloging in Publication Data

Schultze, William A.
  Urban politics.

  Includes bibliographical references and index.
    1. Municipal government—United States.   2. Urban
policy—United States.   3. Right and left (Political
science)   I. Title.
JS341.S36   1985   320.8′0973   84-18072
ISBN   0-13-937517-1

Editorial/production supervision: Linda Benson
Cover design: Wanda Lubelska Design/Wanda Siedlecka
Manufacturing buyer: Barbara Kelly Kittle

Printed in the United States of America

10 9 8 7 6 5 4 3 2 1

ISBN   0-13-937517-1   01

Prentice-Hall International, Inc., *London*
Prentice-Hall of Australia Pty. Limited, *Sydney*
Editora Prentice-Hall do Brasil, Ltda., *Rio de Janeiro*
Prentice-Hall Canada Inc., *Toronto*
Prentice-Hall of India Private Limited, *New Delhi*
Prentice-Hall of Japan, Inc., *Tokyo*
Prentice-Hall of Southeast Asia Pte. Ltd., *Singapore*
Whitehall Books Limited, *Wellington, New Zealand*

To Blair, David, and Carol

Contents

Contents

Preface

Everyone was concerned for the American city in the 1960s and 1970s. From ghetto riots to the fiscal crisis, urban problems were front page news and rich sources of funding for academic research. The rise of the social and political forces that eventuated in the election of Ronald Reagan in 1980 corresponded with the decline in our interest in cities. More precisely, the formulation of the public agenda for cities shifted from an emphasis on remedies for physical and social squalor to protecting the economic base. Human problems, so evident in our cities, attracted less attention than did concern for business and industrial health.

Dramatic changes such as these call for new perspectives and provide opportunities for deeper insight. This book aims to contribute to our understanding of the American city with a new synthesis of recent materials from a variety of contributing disciplines—political science, economics, sociology, public administration, finance, and history, for example. My highest ambition is to make a modest contribution toward some ambitious goals.

1. *To establish the study of urban politics firmly in general theory.*

As Kurt Lewin long ago observed, there is nothing so practical as a good theory. By that standard, studies of urban politics have tended toward limited practicality. Scholars of urban politics have grown accustomed to noting the inadequacy of theory or "theoretical malaise" in the field. Surely, it has been lack of theoretical sophistication that accounts for the tendency of both scholars and citizens to view urban concerns as provincial.

2.   *To put the study of American cities into an international context.*

The effort to understand American city politics fully, systematically, and theoretically inevitably leads one to examine the international context in which they are set. In fact, the forces that are at work creating what some call the "new world economy" are the ones that are fundamentally transforming our cities. Corporate flight to the "Sunbelt" is the domestic counterpart to corporate multinationalism. Life in our cities is not isolated and apart from the most important issues of the day but, rather, is a proximate crucible in which to examine, test, and understand the effects of these complex forces.

3.   *To sketch the main features of urban political economy.*

Consistent use of a political economy focus will enable urban scholarship to advance toward a more theoretical and broadly relevant body of accumulated knowledge.

Political economy had in the recent past become nearly the exclusive preserve of economists. There is no reason to denigrate the substantial contributions that economists have made, but what has slowly been lost is the "political" emphasis. This book aims to redress that balance, not by overemphasizing the political, but by emphasizing the common context of both academic specialties. My vehicle for doing this is to examine political economy in terms of the prevailing worldwide ideological formulation, that is, as conflict among systematically stated neoconservative, liberal, and radical perspectives.[1]

This formulation emphasizes what has been missing in both the scholarly and the common public discussion of city politics: the fact of systematic, fundamental conflict. Most Americans tend to view the fundamental assumptions of capitalism as simply "truths," not as articles of faith. A more accurate, fair, and scholarly approach requires that we move back a mental step or two to see contemporary life—internationally, nationally, and locally—as a continuing struggle of differing political economies. Each ideology offers its own perceptions of facts, modes of analysis and understanding, truth, and prescription. So, rather than assume the position of advocate of any one of these positions, I have strained to present each ideology as fairly and fully as possible. My assumption is that mature and intelligent people who would continue to call their form of government "democratic" must make their own choices.

[1]This formulation appears in David M. Gordon, ed., *Problems in Political Economy: An Urban Perspective* (Lexington, Mass.: D. C. Heath, 1971).

4. *To raise the level of understanding of city politics so as to avoid simple partisanship in thinking, discussion, and research.*

It has been my own feeling that most of the available treatments of urban political economy are best understood as partisan pleas—although usually unintended—for one or another ideology, even many of those that claim the value neutrality of science. Science must begin with assumptions to test, and it is a strikingly different corpus of findings that a scholar makes when testing only capitalist assumptions than would be made if, say, Marxist assumptions were tested too. This is not to say that scholars intend to propagandize but, rather, to recognize that ideological reinforcement may easily become the effect of an inadequately introspective research tradition.

I have taken the liberty of classifying individuals, the bodies of their writings, and individual pieces of research in terms of these three ideological perspectives. That will inevitably prove offensive or simply wrong to some. As with all the material in this book, I take full responsibility for having done so. What I would hope is that more of us might become aware of the legitimacy and importance of recognizing the ideological congruence of our working knowledge. It need not be offensive, for example, for me to recognize that while I have no intention to reinforce, say, a liberal position, that a separate intellectual effort that aims to square my findings with liberalism is a legitimate and useful concern.

5. *To make the more esoteric concerns of academics readily understandable to introductory students and practitioners.*

Most non-specialists find it easier to connect their personal experience and common understanding to ideologically based formulations than to the less widely known frameworks of analysis that social scientists have more often used—such as the "systems" framework.

The effort to advance these goals is pursued here by first introducing the fundamental perspective and terms (Chapter 1), saving the central concepts of the ideologies of political economy—neoconservative, liberal, and radical—for a fuller treatment in Chapter 2. The remainder of the book traces the systematic conflicts among each of these ideologies on the usual topics of urban politics. Chapter 3 examines the differing formulations of the urban environment, particularly comparing the neoconservative "convergence" explanations with the more politically grounded explanations of liberals and the preferred "uneven peripheral development" formulation of radicals. Parallel conflicts are discussed as they surface in connection with describing the social and political environment of American cities. The major political actors are then located within this environment and are discussed in terms that also vary systematically by ideology, as they develop their consciousness and resources and formulate strategies (Chapter 4).

Chapter 5 carefully examines the patterns of coalition and conflict in American cities.

We move inside the institutions of city government in Chapter 6 and find that ideological conflict remains with us as struggles to shape the form of local institutions and determine what kinds of people take the leadership positions. Particularly important has been the transition from an ''old reform'' pattern to the ''new reform'' occasioned by the fiscal crisis of the American cities of the late 1970s.

The output of urban institutions—policy—is given relatively brief treatment in Chapter 7. There we focus on urban ''performance'' by comparing American cities with other cities of the world on a variety of indicators. Once again, we find that the performance levels are systematically interpreted differently from each ideological perspective. And, finally, in Chapter 8, I seek to summarize and trace the leading trends in contemporary urban politics.

There are always more people involved in a book than the author. In this ruggedly individualistic capitalist culture, I, of course, want my credit. But at moments, a latent socialism causes me to formulate myself more as a cooperative synthesis of the ideas and actions of others. The liberal in me causes me to walk the line here and just make a list of people who have in one way or another contributed to this book. Colleagues at San Diego State University, especially C. Richard Hofstetter, Woodrow Jones, Kathy Bulmash, Tae Jin Kang, Charles Andrian, Brian Lovemen, Louis Terrell, E. Walter Miles, Paul Strand, K. Robert Keiser, and James Conniff have, often without knowing it, recommended many of the materials that appear here.

I would like to thank the following reviewers who contributed a great deal to the improvement of the book: Gary L. Crawley, Ball State University; Lawrence G. Flood, University College at Buffalo; Nichola P. Lovrigh, Jr., Washington State University; Steve J. Mazurana, University of Northern Colorado; and Robert F. Pecorella, New York University.

I would also like to acknowledge the help of Veva Link and the support of San Diego State University. I appreciate too the able assistance of the many fine people at Prentice-Hall, especially Stan Wakefied and Linda Benson. In addition, several others contributed—including Sharon Schultze, Lela Prewitt, and Sandra Sutphen.

Desiree Scott deserves special thanks, most simply for her participation in all the phases of the creation of this book—from discussion of the central concepts to diagnosing the peculiarities of the word processor. But more important, she has been emotional support in some difficult times.

Finally, I dedicate this book to my three extraordinary children. Each in their own way is contributing to a better synthesis. Their very existence is proof enough to me that the universe is benign and that there is reason for optimism.

CHAPTER 1

*Introduction
to the Politics
of Urban
Political Economy*

Urban scholars are addicted to analogies. The American city has been called a sandbox, a reservation, an ecology of games, heavenly and unheavenly, and a cemetery, among other things. While analogies are not to be taken as seriously as careful observation of the thing itself, they offer some dramatic guidance. Personally, I prefer to think of cities as the children of civilization. They are the result of indulging natural passions without thinking carefully about the consequences. When their reality is incontrovertible, we have strongly mixed emotions—sometimes proud of our miracles, sometimes fearing that they are the new Frankenstein. If conception and birth are difficult, teenage is traumatic. Douglas Yates has applied our favorite epithet for teenagers to our cities—that is, "ungovernable." Parents and urbanists tend to one of two basic orientations to teenage problems: "Indulge the kid, he'll grow out of it" or "I'm going to kill that boy."

Many critics of Lyndon Johnson's "War on Poverty"—a cluster of federal policies aimed at alleviating the social and economic conditions that presumably caused poverty—argued that "war" was not toughness, but indulgence. As those critics of the War on Poverty gained political power, even some of those influential urbanists who had helped create it, Daniel Patrick Moynihan, for example, began to re-examine their child-raising practices. By the time he joined the Nixon administration, Moynihan was urging "benign neglect." Although it displeased liberal city-raisers, benign neglect was still not tough enough for many conservative critics. Some began to talk darkly about killing the kid.

Certainly the New York *Daily News* was exaggerating, as it occasionally does, when it headlined, "Ford to New York City: Drop Dead," during that city's fiscal crisis in 1975. But serious conservative critics were not just kidding around. William C. Baer challenged us to "admit that older cities and neighborhoods can die."[1] He detects our unrealism: "Cities may be 'sick' or 'deteriorating' but the belief is nevertheless held by experts and politicians alike that with proper treatment, these areas will recover and live forever."[2] Instead we must learn to think the unthinkable: "Urban death is very much in the natural order of things, to be taken in stride."[3]

Roger Starr, the administrator of the Housing and Development Administration of the City of New York, saves the interpretation from sounding like Jonathan Swift's modest proposal of infanticide by helping us to see that such a solution is benign when the killing is done by the increasingly ubiquitous Invisible Hand. Starr explains, "Part of the city's problem is that its exports have lost their attraction; in some industries like beer, the city's once thriving production has shrunk to exactly nothing. In others, like apparel, printing, and baking, the city's production for export and even for its own use has diminished drastically. Even much of the nighttime television production, once a New York monopoly, has moved to California."[4]

This perspective has gained sufficient currency to find its way into the self-proclaimed "objective . . . nonpartisan" President's Commission for a National Agenda for the Eighties Report that observed, "Whatever else they are, cities are economic entities; first and foremost they are the settings where great *this isn't* wealth is produced and distributed."[5] Noting the decline of the older northeastern *totally true.* cities and the rise of the Sunbelt to economic prominence, the Commission warned its urban children not to forget that "Contrary to conventional wisdom, cities are not permanent."[6]

Precisely where "politics" fits into this discussion is as difficult to see in this analogy to the daily conduct of urban affairs as it is in the family. We all know that it is there, but it hides under other labels like "truth," "rationality," respect for authority and submission to versions of a "higher order" expressed in various

---

[1] "On the Death of Cities," *The Public Interest*, Vol. 45 (Fall 1976), pp. 3–19.

[2] Ibid.

[3] Ibid.

[4] Roger Starr, "Making New York Smaller," *New York Times Magazine*, November 14, 1976, p. 33.

[5] President's Commission, *A National Agenda for the Eighties, Summary Report* (Englewood Cliffs, N.J.: Prentice-Hall, 1980), p. 66

[6] Ibid., p. 65.

ways, ranging from the Will of God to the Invisible Hand of the Marketplace. First, then, if we are to understand politics in any setting, we will have to decode common usage. People, be they parents, mayors, or business people, sometimes use language to assure compliance to their will. The words themselves are part of a political strategy. It is our opening need, therefore, to uncover the essence of the term "politics."

A DEFINITION OF POLITICS

It makes matters a bit more complicated that political scientists have no single agreed-upon definition of the term "politics." Traditional political scientists solve the problem by focusing on governmental institutions, on the specific content of constitutions and laws, and occasionally on "reform." In the post–World War II era, there emerged a challenging group, behavioralists, who wanted an alternative focus of study.

The behavioralists rebelled against traditionalism in a variety of ways, but particularly important to us, they felt the need for a careful differentiation of "politics" so that political behavior might be systematically observed.[7] Behavioralism also drew our attention to a need for more careful observation of the canons of science. Behavioralism, according to Robert Dahl, one of the pioneers in applying its tenets to the study of urban politics, exhibits (1) a decided preference for quantitative analysis of objectively selected data, (2) an insistence on the need for an explicit conceptual framework, (3) a demand for a research design that permits replication, and (4) a strong emphasis on the need to evolve theories of political behavior.[8]

During the 1960s, a number of criticisms of behavioralism occurred to political scientists. New Left Scholarship, as it was sometimes called, found much of the research of the behavioralists irrelevant to the real needs of both politicians and citizens. They argued that (1) substance is more important than technique, (2) behavioral science often masks an ideology of conservatism, (3) behavioral science is often apolitical, and (4) behavioral science in no way makes it clear that those with a specialized knowledge of politics have an obligation to take action,

---

[7]See particularly Harold Lasswell, *Politics: Who Gets What, When, How* (New York: McGraw-Hill, 1936); Charles E. Merriam, *A Study of Power* (Glencoe, Ill.: The Free Press, 1950); George E. G. Catlin, *The Science and Method of Politics* (Hamden, Conn.: Archon Books, 1964); and Robert A. Dahl, *Modern Political Analysis*, 4th ed. (Englewood Cliffs, N.J.: Prentice-Hall, 1984).

[8]Robert Dahl, "The Behavioral Approach in Political Science: Epitaph for a Monument to a Successful Protest," *American Political Science Review*, Vol. 55 (December 1961), pp. 763–772.

when necessary, to protect and promote humane values.[9] To a degree, the extraordinary concern with the analysis of public policy that characterized the research of political scientists in the 1970s and 1980s was stimulated by such criticism.

Each of these three perspectives on the study of politics—traditional, behavioral, and critical—offers us different conceptions of politics. Among the several definitions that have been offered and used are the study of legal government,[10] power,[11] decision making,[12] the system that authoritatively allocates values in society,[13] communications control in organizations,[14] and a number of others. In this book I use a conflict definition of politics. Not that I am claiming something as simpleminded as truth in definition. Simply, it is the definition that most clearly focuses on the causes of concern for our cities, does not arbitrarily rule out consideration of important elements of our public life, makes it easy to draw upon the research of other academic disciplines, and makes quickly intelligible the structure of the situation.

Definition 1. Politics: The most inclusive process by which social conflicts are managed.

Such a conception will encompass the range of phenomena from value or ideological conflict to those interpersonal conflicts that affect more than the parties to the dispute. To a large extent, a conflict definition subsumes the much more common "power" definition. As a tradition of explanatory theory, the conflict conception should be associated with that form of social theorizing running from Machiavelli and Hobbes to Marx, Smith, and Weber that explains the behavior of individuals in terms of their pursuit of self-interest in a material world of scarcity, threat, and potential violence. As Randall Collins has summarized it, these social theorists see "Social order . . . as being founded on organized coercion."[15] As a

[9]David Easton, "The New Revolution in Political Science," *American Political Science Review*, Vol. 63 (December 1969), p. 1052, is the source of this formulation. It is a distillation of the critique of a large number of political scientists, a few of whom are Ira Katznelson, Lewis Lipsitz, Alan Wolfe, Peter Bachrach, Henry Kariel, David Kettler, and Michael Parenti.

[10]Charles Hyneman, *The Study of Politics* (Urbana: University of Illinois Press, 1959).

[11]Merrian, *A Study of Power;* Catlin, *The Science and Methodology of Politics;* Laswell, *Politics;* and Dahl, *Modern Political Analysis.* Also see Ira Katznelson and Mark Kesselman, *The Politics of Power: A Critical Introduction to American Government* (New York: Harcourt Brace Jovanovich, 1975).

[12]Richard C. Snyder, *Foreign Policy Decision Making* (New York: The Free Press, 1962); Donald Matthews, *The Social Background of Political Decision Makers* (New York: Random House, 1954).

[13]David Easton, *A Systems Analysis of Political Life* (New York: John Wiley & Sons, 1965); Gabriel Almond and G. Bingham Powell, *Comparative Politics: A Developmental Approach* (Boston: Little, Brown, 1966).

[14]Karl Deutsch, *Nerves of Government* (London: Free Press of Glencoe, 1963).

[15]Randall Collins, *Conflict Sociology: Toward an Explanatory Science* (New York: Academic Press, 1975).

result of this understanding, we are asked to recognize two basic realms of important conflict: "There is an ideological realm of belief [religion, law] and an underlying world of struggles over power."[16]

To make an important, but difficult, matter explicit, this conception treats ideas and morals as though they are socially created—not transcendent—and assumes that they are in the service of the interests of the most powerful. Before you either relax with a feeling of security that the book will not challenge your fundamental commitments or throw it down with the righteous fervor of the believer scorned, let me remind you that definitions are meant not so much for belief as they are to be hypothetical assumptions by which we sort out the complexity of reality. Let me make explicit the most important additional assumptions that will be made as we use a conflict conception.

First, we assume conflict. Conflict is a fundamental fact of human existence. Whether we are talking about differing budgetary priorities, busing to achieve racial balance in the schools, or economic competition for a larger share of a market, we are still talking about conflict. Obviously, the effort is to make this observation without prejudging whether conflict is, in itself, either good or bad.

Then, we assume that politics involves an effort to manage or otherwise to resolve certain conflicts peacefully. Governments exist to resolve conflicts on matters of societalwide concern.

Next, we assume that in a democratic political process the right to present conflicting positions is protected, even promoted. Historically, Americans in particular have preferred to believe that any position should be able to be represented no matter how incredibly deviant or apparently unacceptable that position might be.

Finally, we assume that conflict is structured. Conflict is some hypothetical state of nature may appear a random war of each against all, but in established societies, it comes to take on a pattern. Social roles and statuses develop, as does an economic division of labor, to provide a certain degree of order. These provide a degree of consistency and stability, but their existence does not eliminate conflict so much as structure it. That is, as people press to change their role or job or to get a different result from what they do, they often meet opposition. The subjects of multiple conflicts within any society index its sore spots, calling attention to the need for adaptive response. So, in the 1960s the conflicts that multiplied in the United States, and indeed throughout the world, tended to be cries from people who felt disadvantaged by their social position. Their insistence was on social justice. The pattern of conflicts shifted in the 1970s and 1980s. Growing concern for resource and economic scarcity, and inflationary pressure on the buying power of governments, businesses, and individuals, generated pressures to cut back on governmental activity and expenditures and to stimulate investment in the private sector. "Get government off the backs of the people" and "Keep your eye on the

---

[16]Ibid., p. 57.

bottom line'' became the cries of the time, with the loudest voices belonging to those who wanted economic freedom. Patterns of conflict, then, shift over time.

POLITICS AND IDEOLOGY

But patterns of conflict do not shift in response to abstract impersonal forces. Such shifts need to be understood as themselves the result of conflict brought by those political groups and individuals who desired such a formulation. The stork did not bring the demand for economic freedom. It was consciously formulated and strategically sought. Most formulations are. It is not easy to get on the public agenda.[17]

Isolated conflicts usually have little effect on the public agenda. It is when there emerges a cluster of conflicts that are articulated in terms of a general program, explanation, or set of philosophical precepts that agenda building, or agenda shifting, becomes possible. Here I will call such a cluster of beliefs an ideology.

Definition 2. Ideology: A cluster of beliefs that is elaborate, integrated, and relatively coherent and that connects thought with a program of action.

It was popular among certain intellectuals during the 1950s and early 1960s to deny that ideological conflict underlay the profusion of American politics.[18] The rise of the political right, culminating in the election of Ronald Reagan to the presidency in 1980, has raised ideological differences to public consciousness once again. In my view, that is in itself an important contribution to American political discourse. Whatever were the virtues of New Deal liberalism, philosophical clarity was not one of them.

There are those academics who would prefer to keep ideology out of both public discourse and the scientific analysis of politics. They would point to a long series of survey research findings that suggest that Americans are not coherent enough in their belief patterns to be called ideological. Further, they would argue that a scientific research process should do all possible to avoid the intrusion of the kind of value judgment that ideological discourse has at its core. Finally, they

---

[17]For a careful and useful discussion of the concept ''public agenda,'' see Roger Cobb, Jennie-Keith Ross, and Marc Howard-Ross, ''Agenda Building as a Comparative Political Process,'' *American Political Science Review*, Vol. 70 (March 1976), pp. 126–138. In their formulation, the public agenda consists of all issues that (1) are the subject of widespread attention or at least awareness; (2) require action, in the view of a sizable portion of the public; and (3) are the appropriate concern of some governmental unit in the perception of community members.

[18]The so-called ''End of Ideology'' debate was occasioned by Daniel Bell, *The End of Ideology* (Glencoe, Ill.: The Free Press, 1960).

would press us to recognize that ideological debate is religious in its character—an exchange between true believers who accept their positions as a matter of faith. No accommodation is possible for the true believer. These and the other arguments made against ideological formulation of our public discourse and scholarly work are correct but insufficient reason for avoiding so useful a concept. Citizens may not be conscious of an ideology, or even have latent ideologies, but they will respond to cues from leaders acting out of ideological consistency. Research can be conducted using ideology as an operational construct without seeking to validate one or another ideology. And, finally, it is focusing unnecessarily on a perverted form of ideology to suggest that it must lead to insoluble conflict. European democracies, for example, have long exhibited a history of ideological conflict short of internal religious war.

More recently, scholars have found that "constructive handling of ideology" is possible and even a necessary antidote for some of the deficiencies of both contemporary discourse and analysis of politics.[19] The average citizen more quickly recognizes and understands political discussion framed in terms of ideology than in terms of political systems or some other artificial construct more familiar to political scientists. More important, focusing on ideology helps us to see the connections between the more concrete issues of the day and the overarching system of political thinking and strategy of which they are a part. Thereby, ideological thinking is an aid to philosophical and systematic thinking about politics—surely a high value in a democratic order. The overall effect of ideological thinking at its best, then, may stimulate individuals to move beyond ideological rigidity by encouraging what Charles Hampden-Turner called the attempt to integrate the feedback from such introspection into "'mental matricies of increas-complexity.'"[20] In other words, it is a step needed to help us become more politically mature.

Careful political analysts also may profit from conscious use of ideological perspectives. One of the most common criticisms of the social scientific tradition of the study of politics is that its findings are disassociated and fractured. Theory building attempts that seek to avoid ideological formulations often appear painfully contorted by the effort. It is precisely this need within a scientific tradition to find ways to unite intelligibly "clusters of more or less interconnected theories," which Imre Lakatos calls "scientific research programs" (SRPs).[21]

And, finally, scholars will find it easier to deal fairly with opposing points of view and research findings when they raise ideological disputes to explicit con-

[19]See, especially, William E. Connolly, *Political Science and Ideology* (New York: Atherton, 1967); Charles Hampden-Turner, *Radical Man* (Garden City, N.Y.: Doubleday, 1971); Philip L. Beardsley, *Redefining Rigor: Ideology and Statistics in Political Inquiry* (Beverly Hills, Calif.: Sage Publications, 1980); and also by Beardsley, *Conflicting Ideologies in Political Economy* (Beverly Hills, Calif.: Sage Publications, 1981).

[20]Hampden-Turner, *Radical Man*.

[21]Imre Lakatos, "The Methodology of Scientific Research Programs," in J. Worrall and G. Currie, eds., *Philosophical Papers* (Cambridge, Eng.: Cambridge University Press, 1978).

sciousness. All too often serious scholars try to dismiss other serious scholars with a foreclosing wave, as when the economist Bruno Frey dismisses a large and diverse body of thinkers, those I will define later as radicals, with a steretotype: "utopians and religious dreamers whose ideals are characterized by absence of conflict."[22]

POLITICS AND ECONOMICS

Because the most pressing urban problems of the day are connected to the economic base, this book focuses on conflicting ideologies of urban political economy.

Definition 3. Political Economy: The relationship between the political and the economic institutions of a culture.

You will note that this definition does not seek to make either political or economic institutions most important from the outset. Each political ideology that will be discussed here will make such assertions, but it is not proper to make that decision by definition. Whether economic institutions are more important than political institutions is a subject to be discussed and researched, not defined off the agenda. Also, some grasp of the fundamentals of economic thinking will be required. Political science as an academic discipline has always felt free to jump across disciplinary boundaries to borrow research findings, theories, even whole "scientific research programs." The barrier is particularly high when it comes to borrowing from economics, however. That field has developed in surprising insularity from the other social sciences and, more than most of its proximate disciplines, has consensus on its fundamental (or paradigmatic, if you prefer) assumptions. As a result, it has proceeded to a much greater extent with mathematical formulation and axiomatic theorizing. The literature of economics is impressive in its clarity and technical competence. But in important ways, the approach and product of economics is maladapted to the study of political economy. Why that is so is too elaborate a question to answer here. Bruno Frey, one of the pioneers among economists working to ground solidly a modern version of political economy, makes the same point. Largely because modern economics emerged quite properly as the science of the price system, it "does not concern itself with the political area."[23] The political process tends to be treated as an "institutional given," not studied as a complex set of forces, but reduced to a simple stereotype—usually appearing to be a "benevolent dictator" that has complete

[22]Bruno Frey, *Modern Political Economy* (New York: John Wiley & Sons, 1978), p. 44.
[23]Ibid., p. 5.

information about public wishes, no preferences of its own, always capable of achieving its will, and operating outside the economic sphere. Such a creature is fine so long as it remains benevolent. When it is good, it is very, very good. But when it's bad. . . . Frey, too, is critical of this caricature. "This constitutes, " he concludes "a basic breakdown in methodology."[24]

Still, there is a strong and growing research tradition, partly within economics and partly within political science, that begins to create the groundwork for an adequate political economy. I will introduce that research tradition now by describing three approaches to systematic political economy. Before that, one final definition is necessary.

CITY DEFINED

Political economy can be examined in any setting. Here our focus is considerably narrowed to American cities. Not everyone agrees that this is proper or even possible. Certain political scientists have argued that cities are not distinguishable in operational terms from the larger society. They would have us study political processes irrespective of geographical setting. There is certainly an important point to be made here. Without much doubt, cities simply manifest the tendencies of the society, although they may write them larger. But where does urban leave off and rural begin? Visiting relatives on an eastern Nebraska farm recently disabused me of the notion that rural and urban are different in kind. They were just as familiar with the most recent problems facing the "General Hospital" soap opera staff as were their urban counterparts. As we plowed in our fully enclosed, air-conditioned tractor that was complete with well-stocked bar, I vowed to rethink the problem.

This, too, is an important problem that should be studied and not foreclosed by prematurely restrictive definition. Cities and rural areas are, together, being integrated into a larger politicoeconomic unit. What will be the nature of that system is as yet unclear. Meantime, the classical definition of Louis Wirth will serve for general guidance:

Definition 4. City: A relatively dense human population concentration on the land, the members exhibiting heterogeneity.[25]

This definition contains three major elements. (1) It emphasizes that cities contain large numbers of people. And if that is not obvious enough, (2) it adds that

---

[24]Ibid.

[25]Louis Wirth, "Urbanism as a Way of Life," *American Journal of Sociology*, Vol. 44 (July 1938), p. 18.

they are located close together. A bit less obviously, (3) the city is distinguished by its heterogeneity; that is, people are different from one another in ways that are important to them and that affect how they relate to one another. Most generally, such differences are characterized as social, economic, and political, but the cleavages are much more minute.

So far this definition produces no great problems. It begins to bother us when we seek to use this or any other commonly used verbal description to pin down precise urban boundaries, so that city can recognizably end and noncity begin. This is particularly a problem when we construe the city to be a cultural phenomenon. For certain purposes, we would like to know whether certain patterns of social relations are peculiar to cities. Classical sociologists such as Durkheim and Tonnies suggested that personal, face-to-face relations gave way to impersonal, role-related interaction as part of the transition to urban culture, for example. Other scholars have found this proposition either untrue of the subpopulations they have examined or vastly overgeneralized. So it is not altogether clear that viable distinctions can be made between urban culture and rural culture in contemporary America.

Nonetheless, for practical purposes, the problem of defining a city's boundaries has been solved—not by recourse to a cultural definition but to (1) a legal definition and (2) a Bureau of the Census definition.

The City in Law

Legally, the American city does not exist unless the state creates it. A city or "municipal corporation" comes into being through an act of the legislature of the state in which it is located; thus the old axiom, "The city is a creature of the state." A municipal corporation is a

> body politic and corporate, established by public law, or sovereign power, evidenced by a charter with defined limits and a population, a corporate name and a seal . . . and perpetual succession, primarily to regulate the local or internal affairs of the territory.[26]

For particular cities, this may mean that they lack the legal authority to deal with new conditions or problems that arise until the state legislature specifically says they can. So-called "home rule" cities are presumed to have more local autonomy, but they too often find their actions constrained by lack of legislative authorization.

The disability of the legal definition of a city is that the city limits seldom

[26]Eugene McQuillan, in Clark A. Nicholas et al., eds., *The Law of Municipal Corporations*, 3rd ed. (Chicago: Callaghan, 1949), p. 451.

correspond to what most of us mean by the total city. Suburbs may be separate incorporations or unincorporated, but clearly a part of the social and economic sphere of influence of the city, and yet not embraced by the legal boundary. It was partially to meet the need for a boundary that embraced an entire metropolitan area that the Bureau of the Census provided a more accurate definition.

The Census Definition: The SMSA

The Standard Metropolitan Statistical Area (SMSA) is, in concept, a large population nucleus together with adjacent communities that have a high degree of economic and social integration with that nucleus. SMSAs and their larger relative, the Standard Consolidated Statistical Area (SCSA), are designated and defined following a set of official published standards presided over by the Interagency Federal Committee on SMSAs. As currently defined, each SMSA has one or more central counties containing the area's main population concentration—an urbanized area having at least 50,000 inhabitants. The SMSA will also include outlying and adjacent counties that have close economic and social relationships with the central city. To qualify as having a close economic or social relationship, specific criteria must be met: The outlying counties must have a specified level of commuting to the central city. In addition they must also evidence "metropolitan character" on such criteria as population density, urban population, and population growth.[27]

In some parts of the country, urban areas have grown together to the extent that adjoining SMSAs are themselves socially and economically well integrated. Such areas are designated as SCSAs provided, once again, that they meet specified requirements. There were seventeen such areas in the 1980 Census, including, for example, Boston–Lawrence–Lowell in Masschusetts and New Hampshire and Los Angeles–Long Beach–Anaheim in California.

This operational definition, like all such efforts, has its serious critics. Most telling is, of course, that SMSAs are defined in terms of entire counties. As a result, considerable territory that is not suburban may be included. The Bureau of Census frankly acknowledges that it proceeds to use counties less for reasons of definitional purity than "because of the wide range of statistical data that can be obtained by county but not for subcounty areas."[28]

In sum, although it is not possible to define and delimit perfectly what we mean by the city, we can come satisfactorily close. Certainly no definitional problems appear that are so insurmountable as to justify the view that we cannot

---

[27]This description is practically verbatim from U.S. Department of Commerce, Bureau of the Census, *1980 Census of Population,* "Standard Metropolitan Statistical Areas and Standard Consolidated Statistical Areas: 1980," PC80-S1-5 (Washington, D.C.: Government Printing Office, 1980), p. 4.

[28]Ibid.

designate cities sufficiently well to study them. After all, it is difficult to define the boundary between childhood and adulthood, but few of us doubt that both can be examined with clarity and profit.

SUMMARY

The city is a fact of life, although many of us would prefer to have it otherwise. Cities have been the locus of what many Americans consider to be our most severe problems—from crime to air pollution. Yet it is equally clear that our cities reveal the best in us. Politics is that grand process by which we face our differences and problems and seek the means to solve them. Contrary to so much loose popular discussion, my view is that politics is an important part of any set of solutions to our problems, not the problem itself.

In this chapter we have begun to lay the conceptual and semantic groundwork for careful analysis of American city politics. The essential perspective is that contemporary urban politics is most accurately conceived as systematic conflict among competing visions of political economy. In an important sense the conflict is ideological in its structure, and I propose that we face that squarely.

The central concepts have been defined as follows:

1. Politics is the most inclusive process by which social conflicts are managed.
2. Ideologies are clusters of beliefs that are elaborate, integrated, and relatively coherent and that connect thought with a program of action.
3. Political economy is the study of the relationship between the political and economic institutions of a culture.
4. A city is a relatively dense human population concentration on the land, the members exhibiting heterogeneity.

CHAPTER 2

*Three Approaches
to Systematic
Political Economy:
Neoconservative,
Liberal, and Radical*

When the economy gets a cold, individual cities may get pneumonia. During the 1970s, the nation's economy showed some clear symptoms: reduction in productivity gains throughout the decade and absolute productivity decline beginning in 1979, continuing deterioration in the balance of trade, declining international competitiveness of some U.S. products, and a falling off of sales and employment in the nation's major manufacturing industries, particularly automobiles and steel.[1]

By 1975, New York City had a case of "fiscal crisis." Having exceeded its budget for several years, the city faced some hard choices. Its leaders could reduce public services and cut back on city payroll and jobs, or they could declare bankruptcy. The political conflicts that were generated as each public figure and each political interest put forward its analysis of the problem gave us a whole new formulation of the public agenda for cities. In retrospect, the agenda prior to the New York City fiscal crisis was dominated by the concern for social, political, and economic justice for the relatively deprived. After the crisis, the new agenda read: Protect the economic base, trim the fat from the public budget, manage public

[1] J. W. Kendrick, "Productivity Trends and the Recent Slowdown," in William Fellner, ed., *Contemporary Economic Problems* (Washington, D.C.: American Enterprise Institute, 1979), pp. 17–70.

resources carefully. Far from being simply a unique event in a unique city, the New York City fiscal crisis was both a concrete and symbolic shock wave sent out across the urbanscape—the pivotal event in redefining the very nature of our cities in light of economic downturn.

Right from the beginning the debate over causes of the problem and proposed solutions took the form of well-established lines of political-economic dispute. Behind the usual finger-pointing and scapegoating, the serious ideological differences began to surface. That point could scarcely be better made than by quoting the pithy commentaries printed in the *New York Times*, July 30, 1975 (Copyright © 1975 by The New York Times Company. Reprinted by permission):

> Milton Friedman, professor of economics, University of Chicago (whose perspective we will define later in this chapter as neoconservative): "—Go bankrupt. That will make it impossible for New York City in the future to borrow any money and force New York to live within its budget. The only other alternative is the obvious one—tighten its belt, pay off its debt, live within its means and become an honest city again. That's a much better solution from the long run point of view, but whether it's a politically feasible solution I don't know, whereas the first one is."
>
> John Kenneth Galbraith, professor of economics, Harvard University (whose views will be associated with liberalism): "I think it's fair to say that no problem associated with New York City could not be solved by providing more money. The remarkable thing is not that this city's government costs so much, but that so many people of wealth have left. It's outrageous that the development of the metropolitan community has been organized with escape hatches that allow people to enjoy the proximity of the city while not paying their share of taxes. It's outrageous that a person can avoid city income tax by moving to New Jersey or Connecticut. Fiscal foxholes are what the suburbs are."
>
> Michael Harrington, chairman of the Democratic Socialist Organizing Committee (whose views will be associated with radical political economy): "By the passage of three laws in Washington you could end the crisis immediately—the federalization of welfare, the Kennedy-Corman health-security bill and the Hawkins-Humphrey full-employment bill. Taking off the back of New York City the costs of the failures of George Wallace and others to handle the problem of poverty (by federalizing welfare), catching up with all the other advanced industrial democracies (through a national system of health care) and achieving full-employment (through the kind of planning that Hawkins and Humphrey are talking about) would leave plenty still to do in New York, but the fiscal crisis would be over."

Unintentionally, the press leaves the impression, when it publishes conflicting viewpoints such as these, that the differences are simply ad hoc matters of personal opinion. They are, of course, the tips of intellectual icebergs. The commentators were chosen because they have well-deserved reputations for elaborate, careful, systematic thought. The task of this chapter is to trace the contours of what lies below the usual surface conflicts and to describe the basic assumptions of the ideologies of political economy operating with increasing clarity in contemporary urban politics.

These ideological orientations to political economy operate at such a fundamental level for us that we are not always conscious of them. We raise them to consciousness to examine them, to make it easier for us to recognize and evaluate the logic by which each ideology operates—each taking the same facts but interpreting them differently. Contrary to the common perception, then, we must realize that the facts never speak for themselves. The ordering framework into which they are placed determines their meaning.[2]

Three principal analytic perspectives are typically applied to understand the political economy of urban problems: radical, liberal, and neoconservative.[3]

NEOCONSERVATIVE POLITICAL ECONOMY

Each of the three versions of political economy is manifest in a variety of formats: (1) They are often stated in terms of a personal ethic; (2) at other times they are stated as a relatively systematic body of fundamental precepts that combines description and prescription; and (3) at still other times they are imbedded in research methods. The relationship of ideology to research method is complex and variable, but the usual pattern is one in which the assumptions of the ideology are taken as basic assumptions (as the economists posit an "economic person" who acts like a neoconservative). Or the elements of ideology may be taken as hypotheses in a program of scientific inquiry. Such is the stance of academics and other systematic analysts. But when the effort is both to explain and convince others of the correctness of the ideology, it is presented as a body of fundamental precepts. This second embodiment of ideology is the usual formulation for public discourse by citizens, commentators, and politicians. In still another guise, ideology is expressed by individuals as a personal belief system, as justification of their actions and recommendations of proper rules of conduct to others. It is as a personal ethic that each of these ideologies will be most easily recognized. Let us begin there.

---

[2]For a more complete discussion, see Steven Rosen and Walter Jones, *The Logic of International Relations* (Cambridge, Mass.: Winthrop Publishers, 1980), Chap. 6.

[3]David M. Gordon, *Problems in Political Economy: An Urban Perspective,* 2nd ed. (Lexington, Mass.: D. C. Heath, 1977), pp. 1–64.

Neoconservatism as a Personal Ethic

Neoconservatism is essentially updated and applied capitalism. When it is internalized as a personal ethic, its lessons are generalized to a large number of concerns not conventionally classified as economic.

In 1956 Francis X. Sutton and some of his colleagues at the Harvard Business School analyzed the content of a number of leading business journals, looking for, among other things, the "values of the business ideology."[4] What they found then is much the same ethic more recently popularized by writers such as Ayn Rand, Robert Ringer, and George Gilder. Those "values," taken together, describe capitalism as a personal ethic. They include:

1. *Individualism.* The leading tenet of the ethic is an injunction for each person to be self-reliant. It urges the centrality of private, self-interested decisions. Dependence on any collectivity is to be strictly avoided, most especially dependence upon the state.

2. *Materialism and productivity.* Individuals are expected to define their self-interests primarily in material terms. Their contributions are to be measured in terms of their material productivity. When a neoconservative asks "What is old John worth?" he is not likely to be looking for an assessment of John's abstract moral virtue. Worth and value equal material accumulation.

3. *Universal competition.* The competitive "instinct" is the mainspring in the economic watch. Individual, materialistic self-seeking is not seen as a base activity but as a realistic acceptance of "human nature." When we all compete, we get the best from ourselves and, albeit unintentionally, produce the most for others. It is wise, we are enjoined, to assume that other people should be seen more as potential competitors than as motivated by altruism.

4. *A qualified endorsement of democracy.* The ethic is strong in its defense of economic equality of opportunity. That means that all products and all individuals are free to enter the market; there should be no "artificial" barriers. It also endorses political equality in that each vote should count the same. Beyond such basics, however, the ethic is critical of efforts to equalize. In fact, there is a strong defense of inequality of wealth and income. Economic inequality reflects differences in "natural abilities" of individual entrepreneurs and is the motivating force of individual effort.

The personal character traits of the neoconservative are expected to include activism and optimism. To be active, continuously moving toward one's objectives, is evidence of clarity of purpose and a harbinger of success. All inactivity

---

[4]Francis X. Sutton et al., *The American Business Creed* (Cambridge, Mass.: Harvard University Press, 1956). Copyright © 1956 by Harvard University Press and reprinted by permission.

tends to be lumped into the "unproductive" whether laziness or "idle dreaming" is the cause. Optimism is justified, the ethic insists. If the individual calculates "rationally" and acts "prudently," it must be assumed that the universe will not gratuitously throw up obstacles to his or her success.

Neoconservatism as Systematic Thought

The socioeconomic "realities" as conceived by neoconservatives were also explicated by Sutton and his colleagues. As they put it, the prudent person assumes that the relevant universe is operating in accordance with knowable rules. To understand and act on such rules is simply to exercise "practical realism." In other words, these laws of the universe are not a part of the everyday experience of most of us, but we should take it as a matter of faith that they are there. The chief expression of this external ordering principle is, of course, the Invisible Hand of the Marketplace.

The central function of the Invisible Hand is to "aggregate" individual actions. There is always the possibility that, because of the competitive motivations of individuals, universal, destructive conflict might result. Socioeconomic life is kept from resembling domestic war by the Invisible Hand, which produces stable, harmonious equilibria. This general theory of equilibrium is simply assumed by everyday actors and is fundamental to orthodox economics as well.[5] This basic postulate carries three important implications. First, it assumes that social equilibrium exists and is self-maintaining. That is movements and actions that depart from the equilibrium will produce countermovements that re-establish it. Second, the notion of equilibrium implies that society is relatively free of conflicts: "that individuals acting privately and independently are capable of . . . produc-[ing] 'harmonious' social situations with which few are basically discontented, from which few would like to move."[6] But, third, this does not imply a static society. Changes come gradually, if at all, moving slowly from one harmonious equilibrium to the next. To be explicit, then, the theory of general equilibrium leaves politics—which we have defined as social conflict—a rather marginal role. Often politics will be pursued in ways that are "disfunctional," that is, by people and interests seeking to unbalance the forces of equilibrium. When politics succeeds, it may upset the natural forces of equilibrium, thereby producing distortions in the market.

The law of supply and demand is an implication of the theory of equilibrium.

[5]It is also worth our noting that equilibrium assumptions are also used in the structural-functionalist approaches in sociology and political science and in systems analysis in political science.

[6]D. M. Gordon, *Problems in Political Economy*, p. 12.

It tells us that the market comes to equilibrium at the lowest possible price for a commodity as a result of the competition among a number of producers each seeking to capture a larger share of the market for themselves.

These "laws" are conceived to be created and affirmed by nature. Dissent from them is treated as simply foolish—like ignoring the law of gravity and walking off a cliff. So the connection between the rules of natural order and religious commitment is easily made, as did the president of the American Farm Bureau Federation, John Schuman, when he addressed that organization's convention: "Economic laws are closely related to moral and natural laws." He affirmed, "They are as surely God-given as are the great truths that have been recorded and demonstrated in the Bible. There is a law of supply and demand which constitutes an 'economic' truth as well as a basic moral law."[7]

Neoconservatism as Method

When most political actors are confronted with the assumptions that underlie their political positions, they defend them as "truth." Such discussions characteristically degenerate into affirmative hosannahs from the believers and hostile name-calling from the opposition. The impulse of positivistic social science has been to provide some additional grounds upon which to discuss such divisive matters. A first premise of scientific method is that "fact" must be made separate from "value." This is again not the proper forum in which to review the reams of material published in support or denial of that fact-value dichotomy. Let us simply recognize that neoconservatives in recent American history have been strongly attracted to the view that such a separation is necessary and possible. Neoconservative social science researchers then seek to suspend their personal values but conduct research with those values translated into "models" or hypotheses to be tested.

Let us further recognize that the academic discipline of economics, to which political scientists concerned with matters of political economy rightfully turn, has long been perceived as more advanced in its use of scientific method and at the same time more conservative in its social and political orientations than the other social sciences. Whether, and why, that is so is a matter of continuing controversy. There are those economists, such as Gunnar Myrdal, who insist that there is no such thing as a value-neutral social science: "Research is always and by logical necessity based on moral and political valuations, and the researcher should be obliged to account for them explicitly."[8]

Economists then, either knowingly or naïvely, keep a mask of scientific

---

[7]Quoted in Ross Talbot and Don Hadwiger, *The Policy Process in American Agriculture* (San Francisco: Chandler, 1968), p. 30.

[8]Gunnar Myrdal, *Objectivity in Social Research* (New York: Pantheon, 1969), p. 74.

objectivity over their conservatism. George Stigler, a self-avowed conservative of the Chicago School and Nobel Prize winner, argues that the careful study of economics simply makes one conservative.[9] Others deny that economists are necessarily conservative. They argue that economists may get that reputation simply because they seek to narrow their concerns to some very specific factual questions. "It is a little hard to see how ideology sneaks into an attempt to discover how purchases of frozen orange juice respond to changes in price," observes Robert Solow. And he concludes: "Neither does it seem in principle very ideological to study the working of a capitalist economy, if that is the kind of economy we have."[10]

The relationship between ideology and political economy presents a kind of "tarbaby" problem in which the more we seek to throw off values, the more sticky they become. Fritz Machlup, a widely respected proponent of positivist economics, sums it up with an ironic twist: "To stay away from metaphysics one has to know a good bit about it."[11]

In short, scientific method utilizing the fundamental assumptions of capitalism as "givens" is the preferred method of neoconservatives. Not that all who use scientific method are neoconservatives. Many liberals and occasional radical political economists do as well.[12] To understand more fully what method neoconservatives prefer and to indicate the connections of their work to the study of cities, we must be more specific about the work of particular political economists.

PUBLIC CHOICE THEORY AS NEOCONSERVATISM

There is some diversity within neoconservatism as regards method and approach. Here we will review the basic orientations of two scientific research programs (SRPs) within the neoconservative frame of reference: public choice theory and the "institutional" economic variation associated with Vincent and Elinor Ostrom.

Still in its formative stages, public choice theory exhibits internal variations and a diverse research agenda. It has thus far contributed minimally to urban

[9]George Stigler, "The Politics of Political Economists," *Quarterly Journal of Economics,* November 1959.

[10]Robert Solow, "Science and Ideology in Economics," in Ryan C. Amacher, Robert D. Tollison, and Thomas D. Willett, eds., *The Economic Approach to Public Policy* (Ithaca, N.Y.: Cornell University Press, 1976), p. 72.

[11]Fritz Machlup, *Methodology of Economics and Other Social Sciences* (New York: Academic Press, 1978), p. 138.

[12]For a useful, brief orientation to some of this diversity, see Bruno Frey, *Modern Political Economy* (New York: John Wiley & Sons, 1978), Chap. 5.

research, but the enthusiasm of adherents and the rigor of its methods make it an attractive approach with a growing following among political scientists. Its contributions to an understanding of politics in general are already substantial. These findings will be used where applicable in the remainder of the book.

Essentially, public choice is, as Frey defines it, "the application of the methods of modern economics to the study of political processes."[13] William Mitchell, a political scientist prominently associated with public choice, writing in the journal *Public Choice,* finds three variations within it: axiomatic theory, game theory, and public finance.[14] The effort in all three is to reduce human motivation to a simple model that can be used as the basis of mathematical-logical reasoning, that is, as the attempt to set out the logical consequences of "a set of psychological assumptions in a rigorous fashion."[15]

Those assumptions, which constitute a severely reduced model of human nature, consist of the following:

1. *Scarcity.* There is an inadequate supply of goods (public or private) for all individuals to have as much of them as they want.
2. *Individualism.* Social outcomes are the result of individual choice and behavior. Individuals rank their preferences; that is, they are "transitive." Social decision-making mechanisms (like voting) are procedures for "aggregating" individual "preferences."
3. *Self-interest.* The primary, though not necessarily exclusive, basis for individual preference is what they want for themselves.
4. *Rationality.* Individuals have specified and ordered preferences. They know their most preferred outcome in any choice situation and will seek to "maximize" or "optimize" their gains.[16]

The simplicity and clarity of this formulation is a necessary prerequisite to algebraic expression. To illustrate, the simplest expression of the desire of an individual to "maximize net benefits" would be

$$NB = TB - TC$$

[13]Ibid., p. 66. As a young subdiscipline, it has been called by a variety of names (e.g., often it is jus referred to as "political economy"). Political scientists will recognize the term "mathematical political science" or "positive political theory." In Europe, the designation "Economic theory of politics" is more common.

[14]William Mitchell, "Textbook Public Choice: A Review Essay," *Public Choice,* Vol. 38 (1982), pp. 97–112.

[15]Norman Froelich and Joe Oppenheimer, *Modern Political Economy* (Englewood Cliffs, N.J.: Prentice-Hall, 1978), p. 3.

[16]This formulation draws from Robert L. Bish, *The Public Economy of Metropolitan Areas* (Chicago: Markham, 1971), and Froehlich and Oppenheimer, ibid. The terms in quotation marks are part of the specialized language of public choice with which initiates must become familiar.

where *NB* is the net benefit, *TB* is total benefits, and *TC* equals total costs.[17]

Such formulations, of course, originate in analysis of purely economic behavior. But the public choice theorists assume that the basic relationships and problems "are so general that they are independent of particular institutions."[18] The classical "economic," man that hypothetical individual who acts in terms of the model just described, is no different from the political person. Politics understood in this context is "a procedure to come to social, i.e., collective, decisions on the basis of individual preferences."[19]

SUBSTANTIVE INTERESTS OF PUBLIC CHOICE THEORISTS

The historical roots of public choice theory are to be found in Wicksell and Schumpeter.[20] The modern refinement of the theories derive their classical formulations in the works of Black, Downs, Buchanan, and Tullock.[21] Their central concern was for aggregation (i.e., the logic of the relationship between individual preferences and collective decisions). Voting as the primal act of public choice received a great deal of attention from the early public choice theorists. But as public choice has developed, its adherents have moved into a great variety of substantive political concerns: leadership, bureaucratic behavior, and democracy, for example.

Political Leadership.   Political leadership is examined by public choice theorists as being analogous to economic entrepreneurship,[22] which is to say, the "political entrepreneur is an individual who invests his own time or other resources to coordinate and combine other factors of production to supply collective goods."[23]

"Collective goods" is a widely used concept among public choice theorists.

[17]Froehlich and Oppenheimer, ibid., p. 36.

[18]Frey, *Modern Political Economy*, p. 68.

[19]Ibid.

[20]Knut Wicksell, *Finanztheoretische Untersuchungen* (Jena: Gustav Fisher, 1896), and Joseph Schumpeter, *Capitalism, Socialism and Democracy* (New York: Harper & Row, 1942).

[21]See Duncan Black, *The Theory of Committees and Elections* (Cambridge: Cambridge Press, 1958); Anthony Downs, *An Economic Theory of Democracy* (New York: Harper & Row, 1957); and James Buchanan and Gordon Tullock, *The Calculus of Consent* (Ann Arbor: University of Michigan Press, 1962).

[22]See Norman Froelich, Joe A. Oppenheimer, and Oran Young, *Political Leadership and Collective Goods* (Princeton: N.J.: Princeton University Press, 1971); Mancur Olson, *The Logic of Collective Action: Public Goods and the Theory of Groups* (Cambridge, Mass.: Harvard University Press, 1965). Also associated with this substantive interest is the "theories of political exchange," see Robert L. Curry and L. L. Wade, *A Theory of Political Exchange: Economic Reasoning in Political Analysis* (Englewood Cliffs, N.J.: Prentice-Hall, 1968).

[23]Froelich and Oppenheimer, *Modern Political Economy*, p. 68.

Collective goods are to be distinguished from private goods. Like a park or a street, a collective good is a product or service that "cannot be withheld from any member of a specified group once it is supplied to one member of that group." Public goods are "indivisible," in other words. Public choice theorists use this concept of leadership to analyze political group formation, action, and strategies.[24]

Mancur Olson finds, for example, that the large economic associations that lobby so successfully are different from some less effective groups because they are able to maintain large memberships. They accomplish that because their leadership recognizes the need for providing other benefits to the members—"selective incentives," as he terms them. What constitutes selective incentives depends on the needs or wants of the members and the creativity of the political entrepreneur, but group rates on auto insurance and weekly social occasions are time-honored examples.

Bureaucratic Behavior.   Public choice theorists conceive of decision making within public bureaucracies as a form of entrepreneurship as well. For example, in his *Politics of Bureaucracy*, Gordon Tullock analyzes the situation in which rational, self-interested bureaucrats seek to maximize their gains in large public bureaucracies.[25] He posits that ambitious public employees seeking to advance their careers will seek to please their superiors. To look good, employees will suppress unfavorable information and package the rest to look good. Large-scale bureaucracies thus become error prone and show great difficulty in adapting to changing conditions. A more recent study finds that bureaucrats exercise disproportionate power at the polls as well.[26]

Democratic Theory.   Anthony Downs has provided considerable insight into the conditions that attend electoral choice in a democracy. For example, he has explicated the logic by which both political parties are attracted to the ideological center in their effort to be elected.[27] More broadly, public choice theory has shown an interest in democracy as an ideal. James Buchanan, one of the central figures of

[24]Olson, *The Logic of Collective Action,* and Robert Salisbury, "An Exchange Theory of Interest Groups, *Midwest Journal of Political Science,* Vol. 8 (February 1969), pp. 1–32. The work of the "game theorists" provides many of the formulations of strategic considerations under a variety of conditions; see the works of Stephen J. Brams, including *Game Theory and Politics* (New York: The Free Press, 1975). Coalition building as a political strategy is discussed along with a number of other concerns in the pioneering work of William H. Riker and Peter Ordeshook, *An Introduction to Positive Political Theory* (Englewood Cliffs, N.J.: Prentice-Hall, 1973).

[25]Gordon Tullock, *Politics of Bureaucracy* (Washington, D.C.: Public Affairs Press, 1965).

[26]Bruno Frey and Werner Pommerehne, "How Powerful Are Public Bureaucrats as Voters?" *Public Choice,* Vol. 38, no. 3 (1982), pp. 253–262.

[27]Downs, *An Economic Theory of Democracy.*

public choice, is among those formulating a philosophical reconstruction of the grounds upon which the state is founded. Like the contemporary philosophers Rawls and Nozick, he seeks to revive the conception that the state is based on contract. Buchanan's concern for a firm constitutional (contractual) basis for political order is most fully advanced in his *The Limits of Liberty*, where he is concerned with two topics—the construction of a new contractarian theory of the state and a discussion of the issue of whether there are forces that tend to make a state grow beyond its legitimate limits.[28] It is this concern that has led Buchanan to turn his attention to the need for "constitutional revolution," as he calls it.[29] "My efforts have been motivated by the observation that the American constitutional structure is in disarray. . . . The Leviathan state is a reality of our time."[30] Particularly destructive has been the undermining of the "American fiscal constitution, namely, the balanced budget rule" by the political acceptance of Keynesian economic theory. Based on this analysis, "I [Buchanan] am now engaged in an attempt to design a 'tax constitution.' We are examining ways and means through which the revenue-grabbing proclivities of governments might be disciplined by constitutional constraints imposed on tax bases and rates."[31] Although aimed at broad national political questions, it is clear that Buchanan's proposals would have important implications for American cities. President Reagan embraced a similar proposal in 1982.[32]

THE INSTITUTIONAL ALTERNATIVE

The group of scholars associated with the Workshop in Political Theory and Policy Analysis at Indiana University, codirected by Vincent and Elinor Ostrom, share the basic assumptions of the public choice theorists. They begin with adaptation of the major concepts of economics to political analysis—specifically, they take on the methodological individualism of economics with its focus on

---

[28]Scott Gordon, "The New Contractarians,"*Journal of Political Economy,* Vol. 84 (June 1976); pp. 573–590. This article compares and discusses the contract theories of Buchanan, Rawls, and Nozick. It is worth noting that Buchanan claims to be presenting a wholly "positive" theory of politics. I agree with Gordon that this is not the case. See particularly the discussion of Buchanan and the "naturalistic fallacy," p. 583.

[29]James Buchanan, "From Private Preferences to Public Philosophy: The Development of Public Choice," in *The Economics of Politics* (The Institute of Economic Affairs), no. 18 (1978), p. 16.

[30]Ibid.

[31]Ibid., pp. 16–17.

[32]Public choice theorists have dealt with a variety of other public policy questions. For example, Bruno Frey has in a variety of studies examined inflation and income distribution. For a summary of those findings and a bibliography, see his *Modern Political Economy.* Also of interest is the work of Douglas Hibbs and Heino Fassbender, *Contemporary Political Economy: Studies on the Interdependence of Politics and Economics* (Amsterdam: North-Holland, 1981).

self-interested rationality and strategies of maximization.[33] This provides an intellectual core as they undertake interdisciplinary reformulation of the traditional concerns of public administration as it relates to public policy. Many of their important contributions have been made in examining local policies. Beyond this connection with basic economic assumptions, the diversity of scholarly methods and concerns makes it difficult to consistently associate this group with neo-conservatism.[34]

In many ways the approach of the Ostroms is more like the variation of economic analysis sometimes called "institutional economics," which is viewed as unorthodox by most mainstream economists.[35] "Institutionalism" as a variation on the study of political economy gives relatively greater weight to the effect of particular institutional arrangements in determining particular behaviors than more orthodox economic theory does. This is what Vincent Ostrom has called the "law and order" assumption. Thus, while public choice formulations hypothesize a basic actor who is relatively autonomous in his choice making, the Ostroms assume that behavior is more importantly shaped by the political setting. But this does not take institutionalists far from classical economic assumptions: "Classical economic theory postulates that economic man will act within the limits of 'lawful' conduct." V. Ostrom reminds us, "In the absence of any law and order assumption, it might be necessary to assume a Hobbesian state of war as the prevailing human condition." That war is prevented in the private sector by the Invisible Hand. The "free market" of course does not exist in the public sector. It is the existence of institutional constraints that assures order in public bureaucracy.[36] Individual bureaucrats, then, may still be seen as pursuing a personal maximizing strategy, but within constraints imposed by the institutional structure.

Obviously, this formulation suggests that more of our attention should focus on the scope and character of political institutions. It also puts "politics" back into the process: "The provision of public goods and services depends upon decisions taken by diverse sets of decision-makers, and the political feasibility of each collective enterprise depends upon a favorable course of decisions in all essential

---

[33]See Vincent Ostrom, *The Intellectual Crisis in Public Administration* (University, Ala.: University of Alabama Press, 1973), esp. pp. 50–52.

[34]For a sampling of that diversity, see the collection edited by Elinor Ostrom, *Strategies of Political Inquiry* (Beverly Hills, Calif.: Sage Publications, 1982), particularly the article by Roger Benjamin, "The Historical Nature of Social-Scientific Knowledge: The Case of Comparative Political Inquiry," pp. 69–98. Also see Phillip M. Gregg, *Problems of Theory in Policy Analysis* (Lexington, Mass.: Lexington Books, 1976).

[35]For a more complete discussion of institutional economics, see Philip A. Klein, "American Institutionalism: Premature Death, Permanent Resurrection,"*Journal of Economic Issues*, Vol. 12, (June 1978), pp. 251–276; Allan Gruchy, "Institutional Economics: Its Influence and Prospects,"*American Journal of Economics and Sociology*,Vol. 37 (July 1978), pp. 271–281; and Gunnar Myrdal, "Institutional Economics," *Journal of Economic Issues*, Vol. 12 (December 1978), pp. 42–76.

[36]V. Ostrom, *The Intellectual Crisis*, pp. 50–52.

decision structures over time. Public administration lies within the domain of politics.''[37]

Bish and the Ostroms' *Understanding Urban Government*, a critique of the movement to reform urban governments by consolidating them into a more rationalized, centrally directed hierarchy, is an excellent illustration of the variation and its consequences.[38] Their method is congruent with public choice assumptions, but it is not formulated mathematically. It focuses on the consequences of rational choice makers' actions within a variety of institutional settings. But their findings contradict some of the favorite prescriptions of traditional economic organizational theory. Particularly, ''sufficient evidence exists to cast profound doubts upon reform proposals to improve urban governance by the consolidation of all units of government into a single unit of government for each metropolitan area.''[39] Instead they found solid reasons for preferring smaller units more under citizen control, even though unrationalized. ''The logic inherent in the design of the American political system is based upon a presumption that overlapping jurisdictions will give citizens access to multiple sets of officials to tend their interests. . . . authority must be fragmented if officials are to be held accountable for their actions.''[40]

Other studies conducted by members of the workshop examine service delivery in a variety of policy areas. Police behavior in particular has been carefully examined.[41] Some analytical attention has also been paid to housing, education, water, sewerage, and fire policies, among others.[42]

Critique of Neoconservatism

To repeat, this is not the place to be exhaustive. But it is necessary to suggest at least the highlights of common criticism of each ideological perspective. It is the nature of all ideologies, perhaps of all ideas, that they illuminate some of our experience extremely well but that they distort and obscure other parts of it. So my effort here is not refutation so much as it is clarification. In the case of neoconservatism, there are three basic criticisms that recur: (1) The analysis is

[37]Ibid., pp. 111–12.

[38]Robert L. Bish, Elinor Ostrom, and Vincent Ostrom, *Understanding Urban Government* (Washington, D.C.: American Enterprise Institute, 1973).

[39]They are specifically critical of the proposals of the Committee for Economic Development, an influential group representing large business interests, contained in *Modernizing Local Government* (New York: Committee for Economic Development, 1966).

[40]Bish et al., *Understanding Urban Government*, p. 93.

[41]Elinor Ostrom, Roger B. Parks, and Gordon P. Whitaker, *Patterns of Metropolitan Policing* (Cambridge, Mass.: Ballinger, 1978).

[42]Elinor Ostrom, *The Delivery of Urban Services: Outcomes of Change* (Beverly Hills, Calif.: Sage Publications, 1976).

inadequately focused on politics, (2) the assumptions of neoconservatism are "unrealistic," and (3) the logic of economic analysis as applied to public activity is faulty.

INADEQUATE CONCEPTION OF POLITICS

It could be argued that public choice is not political economy at all, if we understand that political economy involves inquiry as to the relationship between political and economic processes. Actually, public choice theorists use economic terms and concepts to study politics but say little about how the two spheres interact with one another.[43] They nonetheless advance from a tacit implication that the modes of inquiry in economics as a discipline and the modes of behavior in the private sector are superior to those used in analysis and action in the public sector. This bias may be true or false, but it may not be assumed in systematic, open-minded inquiry.

The impulse to proceed by analogy to economic analysis is understandable and even desirable so long as it illuminates rather than distorts the terrain to be examined. But economics may have purchased its rigor and clarity—so much desired by careful analysts—at the cost of oversimplification. Bruno Frey, himself a public choice theorist, recognizes this problem when he exhorts classical economists to abandon their stereotypical conception of the state and recognize that "pursuit of one's own interests, the fundamental principle of market behavior, is negated in the political arena."[44] If not "negated," it is at least considerably more complicated.

The Ostroms' variation on neoconservatism, it must be noted, is considerably more satisfactory on these grounds. It specifies both governmental institutions and politics as important components of their study.

THE "REALITY" OF THE ASSUMPTIONS

A number of critics of orthodox economics in general, and its political application specifically, contend that the most fundamental assumptions—the nature of the "economic person," the Invisible Hand of the Marketplace, equilibrium, the competitive nature of the market—are naïve oversimplifications that seriously distort the meanings of human action. Economics has maintained an extraordinary insularity from the other social sciences as it has defined itself against such criticism. For example, the fields of anthropology, sociology, and psychology all contain rich research traditions that speak volumes about the

[43]Philip L. Beardsley, *Conflicting Ideologies in Political Economy* (Beverly Hills, Calif.: Sage Publications, 1981), p. 18.
[44]Frey, *Modern Political Economy*, p. 6.

complexities of human motivation. Yet occasionally one finds such stereotypical dismissals of entire bodies of knowledge as contained in the following quotation from a leading economist: "It is like what happens if I say that Freudian theory is obvious nonsense: I am told that I only say that because of my relation with my mother. I protest that my mother had nothing to do with it. 'See!' says my Freudian friend and walks away, a sure winner."[45]

But not all critics are simple-minded Freudians. Robert Heilbroner, for example, recognizes that the "economic man" assumptions are assumptions about actual behaviors "and these assumptions, while valid enough of the time to give the scientific model its usefulness, are not valid all of the time. Behavior, in a word, contains an element of indeterminacy that [distorts] both . . . real social processes and . . . the accuracy of their representation in mathematical models."[46] Along with a number of others, Heilbroner doubts that the behavior patterns of contemporary executives correspond well to the orthodox expectations. He finds the mentality of our major corporate leaders increasingly noncapitalist.[47] The integration of firms into a world-scale "planning system," as Galbraith has called it, is the major set of forces to which modern executives are accommodating their behavior. That set of changes is also connected with the obsolescence of the orthodox assumption of a free market. Galbraith tells us that by the 1930s, the assumption that there was a competitive structure of firms was already untenable.[48] "Oligopoly" has replaced the competitive market structure:

> Even the more casual scholars had difficulty in disguising from themselves the fact that markets for steel, automobiles, rubber products, chemicals, aluminum, other nonferrous metals, electrical gear and appliances, most processed foods, soap, tobacco, intoxicants, and other basic products were shared not by many producers, each without power over its prices, but by a handful of producers with a great deal of such power.[49]

Most orthodox economists are unperturbed by such observations. Machlup would remind us that economic man and other such assumptions are not supposed to be real but "a man-made, an artificial device for use in economic theorizing."[50] Milton Friedman, in elaborating this position, has gone so far as to argue not only that it is unnecessary for assumptions in scientific research to be realistic, but that it

[45]Solow, "Science and Ideology in Economics," p. 69.

[46]Robert Heilbroner, "On the Limited 'Relevance' of Economics," in Amacher, Tollison, and Willett, eds., *The Economic Approach to Public Policy*, p. 61.

[47]See Robert Heilbroner, *Business Civilization in Decline* (London: Marion Boyars, 1976).

[48]John Kenneth Galbraith, *Economics and the Public Purpose* (New York: New American Library, 1973), p. 15.

[49]Ibid.

[50]Machlup, *Methodology of Economics*, p. 298.

is a positive advantage if they are not: ''to be important . . . a hypothesis must be descriptively false in its assumptions.''[51]

LOGICAL INADEQUACIES

Two logical problems have been commonly noted by those dealing with public choice theories. The first is generally labeled Arrow's impossibility theorem and the second popularly discussed as the ''tragedy of the commons.''

Arrow's Impossibility Theorem.   Recall that public choice founded its claim to broad applicability on the assumption that individual preference patterns can be aggregated. Kenneth Arrow, a Nobel Prize winner in economics, has found that this claim is not logically sound.[52] In other words, it is not possible for decision makers in a democratic society to meet the conditions of any theory based on a logic of comprehensive rationality. A more specific application of this finding is often called the ''voter's paradox.'' It holds that individual choices cannot be aggregated through a majority voting procedure that will produce a single best proximation of individual preferences for all parties.

To illustrate the voter's paradox more concretely, suppose that there was formed a committee of three to consider whether your city should assume control over the gas and electric company. As the discussion develops, three proposals emerge: A = public ownership, B = private operation within broad public policy guidelines supervised by a public utilities commission, and C = private ownership. Red, a committee member whose ideology approximates what we will later in this chapter define as radical political economy, prefers A (public ownership) to B (mixed) and B to C (private ownership). Red's choice is termed ''transitive'' as it conforms to the rule ''If A is preferred to B and B is preferred to C, then A is preferred to C.'' We asked Red and he agreed that this logic accords with his preferences. Gray is a liberal and prefers B to C and C to A, reasoning that public ownership produces more problems than private. White, a neoconservative, prefers C to A and A to B (he argues that he could not really tolerate either option but if forced to choose would prefer the possibility of rational control of a governmental bureaucracy to the random distortions of the market in a mixed system) and C to B. (See Figure 2.1.)

---

[51]Milton Friedman, *Essays in Positive Economics* (Chicago: University of Chicago Press, 1953), p. 14. The liberal economist Samuelson has attacked this premise, calling it ''the extreme version of the F-twist.'' See *The Collected Scientific Papers of Paul A. Samuelson* (Cambridge, Mass.: MIT Press, 1966), Vol. 2 p. 1774. For a critique of the ''realism'' of the general equilibrium assumption, see Janos Kornai, *Anti-Equilibrium* (Amsterdam: North Holland, 1971).

[52]Kenneth Arrow, *Social Choice and Individual Values* (New York: John Wiley & Sons, 1963).

Committee Member	Preference Pattern
Red	A > B B > C A > C
Gray	B > C C > A B > A
White	C > A A > B C > B
Majority	A > B B > C C > A

FIGURE 2.1 Schematic of voter's paradox

Viewed from the perspective of each individual committee member, then, their choices are rational and "transitive." But when the committee votes on each pair of alternatives using the majority rule principle of democracy, a paradox results. Here is how that works. When we ask the committee to choose between public ownership and mixed control, public ownership is favored by 2 to 1 (Red and White versus Gray). When we ask the committee to choose between mixed control and private ownership, mixed control is preferred, also by 2 to 1 (Red and Gray versus White). Logic (the transitivity rule) would lead to the expectation that collective preferences should produce the result that if A is preferred to B (public ownership to mixed) and B is preferred to C (mixed to private), then A should be preferred to C (public to private) by the committee. But this is not the collective result. Two members, Gray and White have expressly argued that they prefer C to A (private to public). Here exactly is the paradox: Individual preferences are transitive but the collective preference is not.

The impossibility theorem has scarcely been ignored by public choice theorists. They have sought to minimize its impact on their mode of analysis in a variety of ways, but few have accepted the finding as an Achilles heel.[53]

---

[53]This literature is far too full and technical to reflect here. The interested reader will find Bruno Frey's discussion in *Modern Political Economy*, pp. 70–77, a good overview. The idea of "peakedness" is the best known statement of restriction on individual preference orderings; see, particularly, Black, *The Theory of Committees and Elections*.

The Tragedy of the Commons.

Traditional political science showed greater concern for the idea of a public interest, that is, the idea that there is an identifiable collective good that is somehow different from just the sum of what is good for the individual members of the society. In the heyday of behavioralism, the concept was critiqued and largely dismissed as an epiphenomenon—a phantom.[54] The alternative emerged that the whole was simply the sum of its parts. No need to worry about protecting or promoting the public interest; if we take care of our private interests, that is sufficient.

Such a formulation is, of course, a close approximation of the fundamental precepts of neoconservatism. Public choice theorists have translated the notion of the public interest into their terms as "collective goods." As we discussed earlier, the most important difference between collective and private goods in the public choice literature is that private goods are divisible and public goods are not. That is, private goods like bread can be cut up and sold by the piece. Those who don't pay, don't get any. Collective goods like clean air, public safety, public libraries, and parks benefit all, whether they have paid for them or not.

The logical problem for public choice theorists has been most compellingly stated in terms of an analogy by Garret Hardin, which he calls the "tragedy of the commons."[55] He intends to demonstrate that when individuals pursue rational self-interest in the use of certain collective goods, those goods are destroyed. In other words, rational self-interest can generate collective bads.[56]

Hardin dramatizes the tragedy of the commons with analogy, although it derives from a mathematical formulation. The tragedy develops in this way. There is a pasture that is open to all—a public good. It is expected that each herdperson will keep as many cattle as possible on the commons. This is fine until the commons begins to crowd. At this point, Hardin tells us, the inherent logic of the commons begets tragedy. That is because, as an economically rational being, each herdsperson seeks to maximize his or her gain. More or less consciously, the herdsperson asks "What is the utility to me of adding one more animal to my herd?" The choice has the familiar "trade-off" characteristics, that is, both positive and negative consequences that must be balanced against one another.

The positive side of the trade-off is the farmer's gaining all the revenue from the sale of the additional animal, a positive utility of $+ 1$. The negative side of the trade-off results from the effects of overgrazing. But those costs are shared by all the herdspeople equally. If there are 50 farmers, say, then the negative utility to the

[54]Walter Lippman, *The Phantom Public* (New York: Harcourt Brace, 1925).

[55]Garrett Hardin, "The Tragedy of the Commons," *Science*, Vol. 162 (December 13, 1968), pp. 1243–1248.

[56]James Buchanan, "Public Goods and Public Bads," in John Crecine, ed. *Financing the Metropolis* (Beverly Hills, Calif.: Sage Publications, 1970), Chap. 1.

individual farmer of adding the additional animal is only $-.02$ (1/50). Balancing costs and benefits the rational conclusion is clear. Add the cow. And another. . . . Eventually the commons becomes less a pasture than a feeder lot. "Ruin is the destination toward which all men rush, each pursuing his own best interest in a society that believes in the freedom of the commons. Freedom in a commons brings ruin to all."[57]

Reactions among public choice theorists to this critique vary. Charles Rowley, a British economist, suggests, for example, that "Society might be far better off if the 'problem' of social cost had not been discovered."[58] That is, he thinks that it would be better if we ignored that certain consequences of unintended effects (sometimes called spillovers, externalities, or neighborhood effects) are damaging to the society as a whole. The logic of that argument appears to rest upon the presumption that the problem is created by there being common goods at all. As Burton says, "The really serious environmental problems all arise where there are common and not private property rights."[59]

The Ostroms, on the other hand, take the problems of the commons quite seriously. They would recognize a category of problems, which they prefer to call "common pool problems." that are subject to the tragic consequences Hardin suggests. Such common pool resources as wildlife, fish, oil, groundwater, lakes, streams, and air are examples. To prevent the tragedy, in their view, will require the development of creative rules and institutional arrangements that are specific to the particular pool resource. General rules or centralized bureaucratic arrangements will probably not solve the problem.[60] They further accept Hardin's formulation that there are no "technical" solutions that superior science or mathematics can provide. But they argue, nonetheless, that solutions do exist.[61] Those solutions will be problem specific and politically created. Elinor Ostrom insists that we can "devise social arrangements (user charges, prices, taxing arrangements, or other forms of regulation) that will induce individuals to take into account the social costs of their . . . action."[62]

[57]Hardin, "The Tragedy of the Commons." The mathematical formulation is to be found originally in William Foster Lloyd, *Two Lectures on the Checks to Population* (Oxford: Oxford University Press, 1833). More contemporary discussion is H. V. Muhsam, "An Algebraic Theory of the Commons," an appendix to his "A World Population Policy for the World Population Year," *Journal of Peace Research,* Vol. 1–2 (1973), pp. 97–99.

[58]From the prologue to *The Myth of Social Cost,* Steven S. Cheung, ec. (London: The Institute of Economic Affairs, 1978), p. 13.

[59]Ibid.

[60]Vincent and Elinor Ostrom, "A Theory for Institutional Analysis of Common Pool Problems," in Garrett Hardin and John Baden, eds., *Managing the Commons* (San Francisco: W. H. Freeman, 1977).

[61]Elinor Ostrom, "Collective Action and the Tragedy of the Commons," in ibid., pp. 173–181.

[62]Ibid., p. 180.

LIBERAL POLITICAL ECONOMY

Liberalism shares many of the assumptions of conservatism. In fact, as regards political economy particularly, there are those who argue that there are no important differences in the basic principles. Liberalism is committed to capitalism, much as neoconservatism is. This has long been the argument of the political left; "scratch a liberal and you find a conservative," one of my students in the 1960s told me. And sure enough as I read one of my colleague's most recent work, *The Unheavenly City*, it became clear to me that Edward Banfield's apparent liberalism had given way in the wake of the urban riots of the 1960s to neoconservatism. But liberals have long been attacked by the political right as well. Muddled, knee-jerk, bleeding hearts is the sort of kindness with which liberalism was often described during the 1970s as neoconservatism was making substantial political gains.

Liberalism is vulnerable to these criticisms because it is less a clearly formulated set of philosophical precepts than we will find on either the left or right. As Gordon says, "Its underlying logical structure has not so often been formulated logically and coherently as it has been suggested or evoked in its specific applications."[63] Rather than a complete system of thought, liberalism has more been an ethos with a history. In America that history is most visible as it affects the policy struggles that have dominated our public life since the Great Depression and New Deal.

Liberalism as a Personal Ethic

As you might expect of a pragmatic mode of thinking, there is less a set of principles to announce than there is a stance toward the world. The philosopher Morris R. Cohen once summed up that stance as a personal commitment to "free inquiry, free discussion and accommodation."[64] To be more complete, liberalism assumes:

Belief in a "Free Market of Ideas."   Oliver Wendell Holmes stated a cornerstone of liberal commitment when he argued that a good society maintained processes by which all ideas, no matter how seemingly deviant, might be expressed. The validity of all ideas is a matter for debate, discussion, and experimentation.

Faith in Popular Judgment.   There is a strong populist strain in liberalism. There could be no free market of ideas if people were not to be ultimately trusted to choose the right alternative. There are forces that can distort

---

[63]Gordon, *Problems in Political Economy*, p. 11.
[64]Morris R. Cohen, *The Faith of a Liberal* (New York: Holt, 1946), p. 117.

the vision of the average citizen, liberals recognize. Franklin Roosevelt argued that people who were hungry were not free.

Impulse to Equality.   Growing out of the experience of the Great Depression, liberals tend to the view that benign public policies can overcome the extremes of inequality. Cooperativeness and generosity are required of those who have much to see to it that those ''less fortunate'' are allowed to participate in the culture.

Willingness to Compromise.   While the idealist thinks of compromise as inevitably a dilution of the good, the liberal makes compromise a virtue. If society is to prosper, we must be willing to accommodate to ideas that may be unfamiliar at first or do not maximize our personal self-interest. The ability to make workable compromises is both an act of personal generosity and an important ingredient of statesmanship.

Avoidance of Doctrine.   Liberals seek to avoid embracing any particular ideology, tending to the view that truth is more to be found ''somewhere in between'' competing values and interests. This is of course why they are willing to compromise.

Liberalism as Systematic Thought

But liberalism is not nearly so devoid of content as its harshest critics suggest. Nor is liberalism without its own intellectual history: John Locke, John Stuart Mill, Roger Williams, especially Thomas Jefferson in the American tradition, Henry Thoreau, Abraham Lincoln, Oliver Wendell Holmes, Louis Brandeis, Ezra Pound, John Dewey, and, of course, Franklin D. Roosevelt are all taken to be the intellectual forebears of modern American liberalism.[65] The main tenets of contemporary liberal thought are as follows:

Individualism.   Not in fundamental contrast to neoconservatism on this issue, liberalism displays important variations nonetheless. Liberalism has not been historically content to allow individual interest to be reduced to economic individualism. Human nature is more complex, including a healthy need for

[65]Walter E. Volkomer, ed., *The Liberal Tradition in American Thought* (New York: Capricorn Books, 1969). For an important interpretation of the liberal tradition, see Louis Hartz, *The Liberal Tradition in America* (New York: Harcourt Brace and World, 1955).

nonmaterial satisfactions—like the solitude of Walden Pond. That nature is also depicted as less rational than the neoconservatives envision. Liberals have been more influenced by the complex findings of social science. Although far from making Freudianism a house orthodoxy, liberalism was importantly influenced by the view that irrational elements loom large in their impact on both individual and social behavior.[66]

This particular form of individualism explains liberalism's shifting position on the proper role of government. While the country was predominantly agricultural, liberals like Jefferson embraced a relatively pure form of laissez-faire, believing that it would allow for fullest development of both the economic and personal needs of the individual. But by the early nineteenth century, the economic structure had shifted. Industrial capitalism gave rise to large urban centers that spawned conditions of life that served economic needs of individuals, to be sure, but at great costs to their personal needs. In the industrial economy, liberals felt that only positive action by government could assure individual fulfillment. With the economic reverses of the 1970s and 1980s, many liberals have reverted to their capitalist roots.

Capitalism.   Liberals are capitalists. Their prior concern for individual welfare leads them to the conclusion that only under some specific circumstances does the Invisible Hand malfunction or misappropriate, and the job of government is to correct those failures.

Positive Government.   Which specific policy areas require governmental attention may vary with particular historical circumstances. But liberals have been relatively consistent and clear in the principle upon which they base their view of government's proper role (viz., government will have to act from time to time to protect individual freedom). In terms of political economy, then, the liberal stance is that, in the relationship between public and private sectors, the public sector is rightly dominant.

The relationship between private property rights and other public rights makes a good illustration of the liberal position. American liberals have not opposed property rights, contrary to the often iterated neoconservative criticism. Quite the contrary, they have historically advocated measures to create a wider distribution of property in the society. Yet, when the rights of property are in conflict with other rights—for example, the right to a safe and healthful environment for a large number of citizens—liberals are willing to resolve that conflict by

---

[66]See, especially, Sigmund Freud, *Civilization and Its Discontents* (New York: W. W. Norton, 1962).

recourse to the principle that property is less important than the individual. Abraham Lincoln summarized the liberal view when he wrote: "Republicans . . . are both for the man and the dollar; but in cases of conflict, the man before the dollar."[67] That view was often echoed in the speeches of Franklin Delano Roosevelt. In his view, the depression and the march of fascism should have taught us that genuine individual freedom cannot exist without economic security and independence: "People who are hungry and out of a job are the stuff of which dictatorships are made."[68]

Applying this general set of precepts, liberals have tended to the following applications in the modern era.

Intervention in the Operation of the Economy.
That intervention has taken a great variety of forms and rationales, but again, on a central principle: Regulate to keep the free market functioning. If concentrated economic power in the form of monopoly or oligopoly inhibits a fair, competitive market structure, then liberals advocate regulation. If the economic system fluctuates erratically, then government may seek to stabilize the business cycle.

Encourage Greater Economic Equality.
As liberalism adapted its principles to the problems of the Great Depression, it came to the analysis that the economy had faltered, by contrast to neoconservative analysts like Milton Friedman, who contend that the depression was caused by government intervention. If the economy faltered, liberals reasoned (relying broadly on the economic theories of John Maynard Keynes), it will be stimulated back to health if more people have more money to spend. Policies designed to redistribute income, create employment in both the private and governmental sectors, and support small entrepreneurs became part of what was sometimes derisively called a "share the wealth" approach.

Encourage Greater Political Equality.
The great importance of government in the liberal formulation necessarily requires that government be made accessible and responsive. Liberals are strong advocates of civil liberties, reasoning that free speech is the cornerstone of individual liberty and the best guarantee that government will remain responsive. When substantive guarantees are also protected by consistent and fair procedures, liberals assume that political democracy is reasonably assured.

[67]Quoted in Volkomer, *The Liberal Tradition in American Thought*, p. 12.
[68]Quoted in Edward McNall Burns, *Ideas in Conflict* (New York: W. W. Norton, 1960), p. 70.

Enable the State to Protect the Interests of All.   Liberals are optimistic that if their precepts are carefully observed, the state will serve in everyone's interests. As Gordon nicely summarizes the contrast, "In neither the liberal nor the conservative perspective does the State serve the interests of only one class, as radicals argue. To conservatives, it can barely serve anyone's interest, and to liberals it can effectively serve the interests of all."[69]

Finally, contemporary liberals are notable for a number of other dispositions: secularism, support of a strong central government and a strong executive branch, particularly, praise for the Supreme Court for its role as protector of individual liberties, skepticism that states' rights are often a cover for discriminatory policies, and internationalism in foreign affairs. But such orientations appear more pragmatic adaptions, pegged to a particular time period rather than the core concerns of liberals. They may be bartered with the next turn of the historical wheel.

Liberalism as Method

It would be a distortion to suggest that liberalism has a single method. Liberals accept, even value, diversity in methods of research. As the behavioral tradition of research matured, however, it emerged that the claim of "positivistic," "scientific," political science to "value neutrality" was cast in severe doubt. The patterns of interpretation of the myriad isolated research findings soon settled into familiar ideological terms that bore a strong family resemblance to liberalism. Perhaps the clearest single illustration of this tendency occurred in the academic debate that was the most formative of contemporary urban politics—the "community power" controversy. Much more will be said of this matter in Chapter 6. But, briefly, for our current purposes, let me sketch the debate.

Floyd Hunter, a sociologist, had in 1953 studied the concentration of political and economic power in Atlanta, Georgia, and had made the kind of findings congenial to radical political economists of the day. That is, he found an elite, composed largely of the economic leadership who did not hold office but who manipulated political outcomes in the city in their own interests. A large number of follow-up studies made substantially the same findings in other cities.

By the late 1950s, a reaction had formed. A group of political scientists at Yale University, notably, Robert Dahl, Raymond Wolfinger, and Nelson Polsby, undertook research that they contended directly refuted Hunter's findings. They found no single structure of power in the cities they examined but, instead, what they called "pluralism." Pluralism meant shifting coalitions of groups and individuals, varying from issue to issue, economic leadership being relatively unim-

---

[69]D. M. Gordon, *Problems in Political Economy*, p. 13.

portant but connected to the overt political process when it participated at all. Pluralism had a great impact on political science of the 1960s, not just urban politics but studies of American politics, political theory, and even comparative politics. It enjoyed but a brief reign of confidence, however, being attacked both by critics from the left who sought to vindicate Hunter's conclusions and from the right by those who wanted to acknowledge the power of an economic leadership, but to declare it benign. In sum, pluralism was reconstituted liberalism.

The pluralist theory was an outstanding intellectual achievement. As David Ricci has written of it, ''Its conceptualization was brilliant, conceding the obvious discrepancies between reality and original Liberal beliefs about the nature of man and politics. Its net result was to construct a new rationale for Liberalism, to fashion a neo-liberalism.''[70]

The broad precepts of liberalism were reformulated by the pluralists as a theory of democracy. Recall that behavioralism, the scientific tradition in postwar political science, was making a number of findings that appeared to contradict the view that America was democratic at all. Low levels of citizen awareness and knowledge of politics, for example, appeared to undermine the basis of faith in liberal democracy.

The pluralists utilized and extended the methods of behavioral social science. Like the public choice theorists, the pluralists' methods are analytical and reductionist, though their basic assumptions are less rigorously formulated and applied.[71] The basic assumptions of pluralist method are that

1. Democratic politics may be reduced to process. A classic work of political science, written before the pluralist formulation, defined democracy as both a way of deciding who governs and also broadly to what ends.[72] That is, democracy is both a process and a cluster of shared values. Pluralists tended to reduce democracy one step farther and assume that democracy was simply a process. ''The democratic method is that institutional arrangement for arriving at political decisions in which individuals acquire the power to decide by means of a competitive struggle for the people's vote.''[73]

2. Economics is distinguishable from politics. Scientific method, of course, requires analytical distinctions. Pluralists were particularly anxious to establish the separateness of political processes from economics, arguing that

[70]David Ricci, *Community Power and Democratic Theory* (New York: Random House, 1971), p. 158.

[71]The most basic formulations of pluralism are to be found in Robert Dahl and Charles Lindblom, *Politics, Economics, and Welfare* (New York: Harper Torchbooks, 1965), and in Dahl's *Who Governs?*

[72]Robert MacIver, *The Web of Government* (New York: The Free Press, 1965).

[73]Joseph Schumpeter, *Capitalism, Socialism and Democracy* (New York: Harper & Row, 1962; original edition, 1942), p. 269.

political forms (democratic, authoritarian, etc.) do not as a matter of necessity connect with any particular economic system (capitalism, socialism).

3. Political power is widely dispersed. Pluralists assume that, "Instead of a single center of sovereign power, there must be multiple centers of power, none of which is, or can be, wholly sovereign."[74] The political landscape is composed of groups and activists, each having some capacity to gain their will, even against opposition. How much power each political actor has depends upon his or her ability to create and mobilize his or her "political resources." Political resources are simply an available means of realizing potential power. Money, of course, would head a list of examples of political resources. But a complete list would include many more—control over information, knowledge, leadership skill, numbers of followers, and the like. Dahl found in his study of New Haven that political resources were "noncumulative, i.e., knowledge, wealth, social position, access to officials and other resources are unequally distributed."[75] Among the several important implications of this pluralist assumption is that no one group or static coalition of groups has all the resources. That is essentially why pluralist research has consistently found that there is no "power structure" in the cities they have studied—if we understand by power structure that we mean a small group of people not necessarily accountable to the general population, who meet with one another to make policy decisions, that the primary criterion for their policy decisions is their own self-interest, and that the elected public officials are generally subordinated to this small group.

An additional implication of this assumption of dispersed power is that the only way in which to understand what might be called the "public interest" whether of a city or a nation is by summing up the wide variety of individual and group interests. In other words, the public interest is nothing more than the policy that is acceptable as a compromise among all the contending groups and activists.

Finally, note that the pluralist assumption is that not all individuals have an impact on the political process. Individual voters are less important as basic actors than are groups and certain self-selected activists. The electoral process is less important than are the group activities traditionally called "lobbying" in determining the decisions of office holders and the content of policy.

4. Business interests are but one of many groups contending for power. Pluralist research led to the recurrent finding that business groups, while often powerful, more often were not. Business groups tended to be divided among themselves and/or self-limited to only those public issues that most directly affected them. In the New Haven study, for example, Nelson Polsby insisted

---

[74]Dahl, *Pluralist Democracy*, p. 24.
[75]Dahl, *Who Governs?*, p. 228.

that the business leadership specialized in the urban renewal issue, leaving the other political issues to nonbusiness interests.[76]

5. Public policy changes occur incrementally rather than comprehensively. Because public officials act largely out of the motive to compromise the competing demands of groups and interests, they do not seek broad, comprehensive changes. Broad proposals for change attract large numbers of opponents. Instead, public decision makers do as much as or as little as they think they have to in the face of pressure. Policies are adapted bit by bit—that is, incrementally.[77]

CRITICAL LIBERALISM: A VARIATION

Criticism of pluralism comes from other liberals as well as from neoconservatives and radicals. More traditional liberals argue that pluralism is too accommodated to the methods of science and the economic assumptions of capitalism. Politically active liberals have generally ignored pluralism. But a number of other liberals have substantially different views of the nature of the political process in America than those portrayed by the pluralists. I will call this variation critical liberalism. Critical liberals are less accepting of the overt character of American politics that the pluralists describe.[78]

The most important difference between critical liberals and pluralists occurs in connection with their perspective on our central topic of concern—political economy. Critical liberals insist that the economic sector has disproportionate power and receives more benefits from government than is appropriate. A variety of studies of particular sectors of the American and world economies reach such conclusions. Barnet and Melman, for example, describe the long-standing and continuing refinement of the "military-industrial complex." Similar patterns of corporate domination of the public sector have been described in connection with the automobile industry, the energy companies, and the agribusiness complex.[79]

[76]Nelson Polsky, *Community Power and Democratic Theory* (New Haven, Conn.: Yale University Press, 1963).

[77]Aaron Wildavsky, *The Politics of the Budgetary Process*, 2nd ed. (Boston: Little, Brown, 1974).

[78]The term "critical liberal" is from Philip Beardsley, *Conflicting Ideologies in Political Economy*. For a more complete discussion and bibliography, see his Chapter 2. The writing of John Kenneth Galbraith is the best known and most complete statement of this perspective; see especially his *Economics and the Public Purpose*. Here I will use as an illustration of the perspective the work of Walter Karp, especially his *Indispensible Enemies* (New York: Saturday Review Press, 1973).

[79]Richard J. Barnet, *The Economy of Death* (New York: Athenaeum, 1970); Seymour Melman, *The Permanent War Economy* (New York: Simon & Schuster, 1974); E. Rothschild, *Paradise Lost: The Decline of the Auto-Industrial Age* (New York: Random House, 1974); J. Ridgeway, *The Last Play: The Struggle to Monopolize the World's Energy Resources* (New York: New

The specific implications of these developments for urban areas are not fully developed in this literature, but they are strongly suggested by David Morris in his *Self-Reliant Cities*. There he traces the loss of local self-governance to regional and national energy companies.[80]

Many critical liberals are not content with this populist view of corporate power. Walter Karp, for example, agrees that the corporate sector exercises disproportionate power but adds that political power has also been usurped by "party oligarchs," those leaders of the political parties who have a long-standing and profound impact on the electoral and governing process. This political elite steals power that rightfully belongs to citizens too. Karp argues that party oligarchs are even more interested in maintaining their own control than in winning elections.[81]

Critique of Liberalism

Liberalism Puts a Pretty Face on Harsh Realities.   Liberals, and particularly pluralists, are often accused of rationalizing the contemporary distribution of power and privilege. Because they reduce American democracy to a set of mechanistic processes, some critics urge that liberals have lost their vision of a better, more humane society—a vision that attended the birth of liberalism but that it lacks in its contemporary incarnation.

Conservative political thinkers find the poverty of liberalism to be that it is simply a muddled version of conservative political philosophy. Liberals, they say, make good intentions into bad policy. The effort to help people is misguided; people can only help themselves. Liberal efforts to regulate the economy and provide greater equality of income and opportunity only mask the harsh realities of human nature and the competitive struggle.

To the radical, the failure of liberalism is that it obscures the real character of elite domination of the economic and political order. By ameliorating the worst consequences of capitalist institutions, it diverts Americans from understanding that they are being manipulated and exploited.

Liberalism Lacks Principles.   Not a philosophical system based on a firm set of stable ideals, liberalism is vulnerable to the criticism that it is muddled, "wishy-washy," unable to provide a stable base of ideals upon which to build a stable present or to project a more ideal future.

American Library, 1973); Jim Hightower, *Eat Your Heart Out* (New York: Random House, 1975). Theodore Lowi, in his *End of Liberalism* (New York: Norton, 1979), has called this pattern "interest group liberalism."

[80]David Morris, *Self-reliant Cities* (San Francisco: Sierra Club Books, 1982).

[81]Karp, *Indispensible Enemies*, Chaps. 1 and 2.

Pluralism Is Excessively Simplified. The effort to reduce complex phenomena to their basic assumptions is a necessary effort in any scientific endeavor. Pluralists pursuing behavioral methods of analysis have been criticized for their excessive reductionism. Jack Walker, for example, says that by reducing democracy to group process, pluralists "stripped democracy of much of its radical élan and diluted its utopian vision."[82] This is so because pluralists tend to accept the assumption that Americans must "rely on the wisdom, loyalty and skill of their political leaders, not on the population at large."[83] Political leaders are themselves treated by the critical liberals as a large part of the antidemocratic tendency of our politics. To many critics, the political power holders, like the economic power holders, have accumulated enough resources to become a threat to the democratic process. This, they contend, is inadequately appreciated by the pluralists.

The Separation of Economics from Politics Is Unrealistic. It is not possible to understand the operation of the political process without recognizing the effects of economic actors. A capitalist culture will introduce different systematic biases into its institutions and processes than will a socialist culture. The effort to make analytical distinctions between these two spheres of activity leads to misunderstanding and distortion. Liberals, particularly the pluralists, have failed to appreciate this reality, say their critics.

RADICAL POLITICAL ECONOMY

When teenagers in the 1970s used the term "radical," it contained all the ambiguities that most Americans feel about that idea—prohibited, strange, wild, innovative, crazy, risky, improper, fun. But, to many Americans, there is none of the positive in political radicalism; it is simply a "threat to our way of life." Scholars also show some ambiguity in their treatment of political radicalism. One tradition of research consistently associates radicals with the sickness of "authoritarian personality," a cluster of traits that are fixated, ethnocentric, fascistic, intolerant, fanatically devoted to leaders, and oppressively demanding of followers.[84] Political extremists of the right and left have been found to exhibit such pathologies. This section does not deal with extremist politics. By radical political economy, I mean systematic, serious alternatives for creating a political-economic order, even though those alternatives are based on fundamentally (radical means

---

[82]Jack Walker, "A Critique of the Elitist Theory of Democracy," *American Political Science Review*, Vol. 60 (June 1966), pp. 285–295.

[83]Ibid.

[84]This huge literature is summarized and advanced in Milton Rokeach, *The Open and the Closed Mind* (New York: Basic Books, 1960).

going to the root) different assumptions than most Americans are accustomed to discuss. Extremists of the right do not discredit neoconservatism nor do extremists of the left necessarily discredit radical political economy.

Radicalism as a Personal Ethic

There are those who describe the "radical person" as being in better psychological and social health than his or her fellow citizens.[85] Charles Hampden-Turner, for example, argues that radical people grow and fulfill their potentials by recognizing that they exist freely, whereas conservative persons are stunted, anomic, and despite their self-proclamation, not at all free. Radicals come in many forms, but the principles most common to their personal ethic are the following:

An Existentialist World View.   Along with European thinkers as diverse as the theologian Soren Kierkegaard and philosophers Edmund Husserl, Martin Heidegger, and Jean-Paul Sartre, contemporary radicals share an existential world view. As Sartre put it, "existence comes before essence,"[86] which is to say, the most undoubtable and irreducible fact of life is that we exist. All meaning, interpretation, intellectualization, and so on are after and subordinate to that fact. This doctrine is meant to focus our attention on the importance of subjectivity, to make it clear that human consciousness creates reality. The existentialists, born out of the despair of war-torn Europe, asserted such a perspective because they were deeply disturbed by the depersonalization of humans that attended the advances of science and technology, of industrial organization, and of mechanistic and rationalist philosophies.

As do existentialists, radicals propose to rescue humans from the status of puppets of fate to which the modern world threatens to condemn them. Human nature is not something fixed; rather, it is what we make it by the pattern of our choices. Few claim that such freedom and responsibility will make us happy, but it will give us dignity.

Among the many implications of this existentialist orientation, two appear most important. First, the radical tends to a standard of secular humanism, believing that humans are the measure of all things.[87] This is not to deny something

---

[85]Charles Hampden-Turner, *Radical Man* (Garden City, N.Y.: Anchor Books, 1971).

[86]Cited in Jean-Paul Sartre, "Existentialism: Jean-Paul Sartre," in Morton White, ed., *The Age of Analysis* (Boston: Houghton Mifflin, 1955), p. 122.

[87]Of course, many radicals connect themselves to religious doctrines as the source of their attitudes. When acting in the world, however, they too appear to formulate themselves as secular humanists. It should also be recognized that a number of religious groups reject the secular humanist perspective and yet engage in social and political action. Like the Moral

like "the fatherhood of God" but to emphasize the brother- and sisterhood of all. A second important implication of the radical world view is the notion that we become fully human only in the act of rebellion. Because we have the capacity to synthesize, symbolize, and explore, we are able to perceive and rebel against "the absurdity of atrophying cultures, empty forms, and the repressive banality of physical coercion."[88]

The Possibility of Progressive Change.   Radicals believe that if humans engage in the assertion of their capacities to choose and rebel, the human condition is able to be improved.

Emphasis on Action.   Progressive change will not result from contemplation alone, but from action. The radical recognizes that social change and personal learning occur simultaneously in the process of experience. One must risk failure—and that is precisely why it is necessary to improve the quality of our thought and our condition.

Strong Sense of Personal Competence.   To adopt the radical ethic requires one with unusually strong faith in themselves, short of narcissism. One must trust one's own perceptions and make conscious moral decisions to choose unpopular directions. A basic radical stance lies in the personal decision "to be stronger than his condition and if his condition is unjust, he has only one way to overcome it, which is to be just himself."[89]

Totalism.   Radicals tend to the view that one of the snares of the modern condition is its overspecialization with a resultant loss of perspective and value oversimplification. The antidote to these tendencies lies in a conscious choice to seek to understand the interdependence of the world in all its complexity—not to screen out complexity, but to invite it into the world view.

However useful this summary of the personal ethic of radicals, it leaves us a good distance from understanding the substance of radical political economy. A formulation this general applies to a wide range of radical programs. And it should be obvious that radical commitment is to an experimental rather than to a dogmatic

---

Majority, these religious groups are often called radical, although radical right. My classification does not include such groups among the radical but as an extreme element within neoconservatism.

[88]Hampden-Turner, *Radical Man,* p. 41.

[89]Richard Peterson, "The Student Left in American Higher Education," *Daedalus,* Vol. 97 (Winter 1968), p. 311.

approach. So I have no intention of oversimplifying the range of ideals and commitments of radicals as I now choose to portray radical political economy primarily with an explication of neo-Marxism. That discussion will be followed by some of the variety of radical thought and action present in America.

One additional aside is necessary. There are those who are skeptical of the association of radical personality as we have just described it and Marxism. Their argument would be that Marxists are dogmatists, more true believers and authoritarian personalities than the radicals just described. Such a view is likely to be held by those who have not read much of a more pragmatic and nondoctrinaire Marxism that has emerged in recent years. This contemporary Marxist interpretation continues to trace the roots of urban development to the capitalist mode of production but retains a healthy respect for the complexity of adaptations that occur within American culture. In these writings, Marx more represents a broad guideline to long-term development than a gospel that anticipates every detail and unique configuration of contemporary political economy.[90]

Radicalism as Systematic Thought: Marxism

Radical political economy is often mystifying for introductory students. There is ample reason for this. Partly, Marxism is seldom done at all, and it is practically never done fairly, in high school classrooms. Its treatment is much like that of the early courses in comparative religions, which was to teach the ideal version of Christianity and compare it with the harsh realities, contradictions, and failures of each other religious system. The aim of that kind of education is affirmation of the order, not understanding. Another reason Marx is difficult for

[90]For a brief discussion of this use, see Richard Rich, *The Politics of Urban Public Services* (Lexington, Mass.: Lexington Books, 1982). The body of general works from a neo-Marxist perspective is quite substantial and focuses to a notable degree upon the urban setting. See, besides the Fainstein volume, William Tabb and Larry Sawyers, *Marxism and the Metropolis* (New York: Oxford Press, 1978); James O'Connor, *The Fiscal Crisis of the State* (New York: St. Martins Press, 1973); Ben Fine, *Economic Theory and Ideology* (New York: Holmes and Meier, 1981); R. Alcalay and D. Mermelstein, *The Fiscal Crisis of American Cities* (New York: Vintage, 1978); Michael Harloe, *Captive Cities* (London: John Wiley, 1977); Manuel Castells, *The Urban Question* (Cambridge, Mass.: MIT Press, 1977); and also by Castells, *Economic Crisis and American Society* (Princeton, N.J.: Princeton University Press, 1980); André Gorz, *Ecology as Politics* (Boston: South End Press, 1980); Barry Bluestone and B. Harrison, *Capital and Communities: The Causes and Consequences of Private Disinvestment* (Washington, D.C.: Progressive Alliance, 1980); Bluestone and Harrison, *The Deindustrialization of America* (New York: Basic Books, 1982); S. Amin, *Accumulation on a World Scale: A Critique of the Theory of Underdevelopment* (New York: Monthly Review Press, 1974); Robert J. Gordon, "The Demand for and Supply of Inflation," *Journal of Law and Economics,* Vol. 18 (December 1975), pp. 807–836; Pierre Clavel et al., *Urban and Regional Planning in an Age of Austerity* (New York: Pergamon, 1980); D. M. Gordon, *Problems in Political Economy,* Ira Katznelson, *City Trenches* (New York: Pantheon, 1981); Samuel Bowles, Robert Gordon, and Robert Weisskopf, *Beyond the Wasteland* (forthcoming).

beginners is because Marx's mode of thought is more like Eastern philosophy, in that it is circular and holistic, unlike the Western mode of thought, which is linear and analytic. It should finally be recognized that most Marxist scholars probably underestimate the difficulty that this poses for introductory students. So the first encounter with Marxist writings is likely to produce discouragement, especially since aversion is so easily rationalized in a culture that popularly treats Marxism as evil. My effort here is to state in extremely simplified form some of the fundamental principles of Marxism first.

Historical Materialism. For Marx, economics causes the shape of politics in society. There can be no meaningful separation of economics from politics. Indeed, not just politics, but philosophy, law, ethics and even religion are determined by the distribution and control of wealth in the particular society at the particular stage in its history. For this reason, the state must be understood in each historical stage to be the executive committee of the dominant economic class. No matter how cleverly concealed, the real purpose of the state is to promote and protect the power of those who control the forces of production. Understood in this way, the state is not fundamentally a welfare agency or an instrument for promoting social justice. It exists to provide the basically coercive instruments of social control—the armies, courts, police, and jails that enable the owning classes to exploit those who must work to obtain material subsistence (the proletariat).[91]

Dialectical Materialism. Marx is not just discussing one state at one point in time. His is a theory of historical development. States change when the forces of production change, as, for example, when production becomes industrialized, leaving agriculture less central. Understood in the broadest terms, this process of historical change proceeds dialectically, that is, as a struggle of opposites. The dominating cluster of productive forces in a society organizes itself, creates rules and instruments of control; this order Marx calls the "thesis." As those who are being exploited come to recognize this (i.e., develop "class consciousness"), they propose the terms of a new order—an "antithesis" or opposite. The struggle between these opposites results eventually in not the triumph of one over the other, but a "synthesis." Each synthesis in turn becomes a new thesis and will soon be confronted by its antithesis. This historical process produces distinctive periods of history—tribal, feudal, capitalistic, socialistic—until the highest synthesis, a "perfect state," is reached. That state is what Marx called communistic. To emphasize an important implication, it appears that no contemporary nation would qualify as communistic in Marx's meaning.

---

[91]This summary owes much to Edward McNall Burns, *Ideas in Conflict* (New York: W. W. Norton, 1960), Chap. 5.

The Theories of Class Struggle and Revolution.   The distribution of wealth results in a division between have's and have not's. Who comprises each group varies; in ancient times the struggle was between masters and slaves or patricians and plebians. During the Middle Ages, the classes coincided with the guild masters and journeymen, and lords and cerfs. In the modern epoch, it has come to a struggle between capitalists and workers.

Revolution is necessary. No old order easily gives up its privileges, even when it is clear it has no just claims on them. "Force," Marx contends, "is the midwife of every old society pregnant with a new one."[92] But while force attends revolution, it does not lead it. A revolution, he insisted, cannot be created by any party or band of people, no matter how zealous. Instead, revolution is the product of a revolutionary situation, which can only result from many causes—chronic discontent, dissension among the members of the ruling class, the recurrence of crises and depressions with increasing frequency, strikes, riots, and mass demonstrations. Revolution cannot occur or succeed until the masses become convinced that they do not want the old regime and it is clear that it cannot govern. It is a long, slow, but inevitable process, he insisted, that might take "15, 20, 50 years of civil war and national struggles" not only to change conditions but to change ourselves.[93]

The Doctrine of Surplus Value.   Physical work creates value, according to Marx. That is, all exchange value is the result of some humans expending their energy upon nature. The wood in a tree is, of course, created by nature, but it is given exchange value only when a worker cuts it down and shapes it into a salable product. So the value of any product is determined by the quantity of labor required to produce it. Capital creates nothing. It is instead created by labor. But the capitalist takes the excess value, beyond that necessary for the worker's subsistence, for himself. This excess over the costs of production—interest, rent, and profits—is surplus value. As the capitalist does not create the surplus, the confiscation of the surplus values is theft from the laborer.

The Theory of the State.   Marx saw the state as performing differing functions at each stage of historical development. In the capitalist epoch, the role of government is essentially to enforce the rules of the game of capitalism. More specifically, this means the rules protecting private property, preventing worker combinations (i.e., unionization), regulating access to and control of land, and limiting poor relief (i.e., welfare) to forms acceptable to capitalists.

Modern Marxists differ as to whether this remains an accurate formulation.

---

[92]Karl Marx, *Capital* (New York: Modern Library, 1906), p. 824.
[93]Burns, *Ideas in Conflict*, p. 150.

Samuel Bowles and Herbert Gintis, for example, contend that the Marxist formulation applies to the early stages of capitalist development but that the role of the state changes in "advanced capitalism."[94] Precisely how the state functions in advanced capitalism is the point at which modern thinkers diverge. Some contend that the primary role of the state becomes to facilitate accumulation and that the power of a mass electorate ultimately conforms to the needs of capital.[95] Others argue that the economic elite has enough influence simply to nullify the power of the electorate.[96] Both those views hold the state relatively outside the structural development of capitalism. A number of other Marxists see the state as substantially intertwined in the contradictions of advanced capitalism. James O'Connor, for example, believes that the state must try to fulfill two basic and contradictory functions—accumulation and legitimation.[97] The actions of the state to make policy appear legitimate to the electorate may substantially contribute to the disruption of the continued accumulation.

Modern Marxism and the City: Method and Central Issues

Contemporary radical political economists believe that both neoconservative and liberal analysis miss central issues. Their conception of the city is inadequate, and therefore their prescriptions for urban problems will fail. This is primarily because these approaches seek more to treat symptoms of the problems than the basic causes. By contrast the Marxist analyst "believes that it will be virtually impossible to remedy urban ills without a fundamental alteration of the political economic system."[98]

METHOD

In general, Marxist analysis is less concerned with method than with content. Marxists are specifically critical of the preoccupation with method and technique that characterizes so much contemporary social science. "Rigor" is important but can easily become an excuse for rigidity, oversimplification, and avoidance of uncomfortable issues, they argue. More fundamentally, the mode of rationalistic, scientific inquiry currently the norm among social scientists leads

[94]Samuel Bowles and Herbert Gintis, "The Crisis of Liberal Democratic Capitalism: The Case of the United States," *Politics and Society*, Vol. 11, no. 1 (1982), pp. 51–94.

[95]See Fred Block, "The Ruling Class Does Not Rule," *Socialist Review*, Vol. 3 (May 1977), pp. 4–12.

[96]See Ralph Miliband, *The State in Capitalist Society* (London: Weindenfeld Nicolson, 1969).

[97]O'Connor, *The Fiscal Crisis of the State*.

[98]Tabb and Sawyers, *Marxism and the Metropolis*, p. 6.

them to take the current organizing principles of the civilization as "given" rather than a proper object of discussion. "Mainstream social scientists assume in their explanatory models that capitalism is a permanent system; their analysis fails to explain how it changes over time."[99]

Nonetheless, modern Marxist analysis is methodologically self-conscious. Marx's assumptions are taken as the starting point of their inquiry, against which they seek to compare the greater complexity of modern life. What we can describe are some methodological dispositions—not rigorous rules of inquiry—but guidelines. The methodological presumptions of contemporary Marxist analysis include the following:

1. *Holism*. Societies, nations, and cities are a part of an integrated, interdependent set of processes. They cannot be adequately understood through the static analytic methods of modern social science.

2. *Multidisciplinary*. "Fundamental to (the approach) is a rejection of disciplinary boundaries and isolated levels of analysis."[100] What is occurring in the city is not understandable in terms of the familiar dichotomies of economics and politics, social and personal, rural and urban, even local and world. They are all part of a set of constantly changing processes, led by changes in the mode and control of material production.

3. *Historical*. The fundamental organization of civilization is dynamic and evolving. Its development must be grasped as a whole to be understood. This necessarily means carefully reconstructing the past in its fullness.

4. *Comparative*. The effort to identify outcomes of historical forces leads to comparative studies. This is because "only this [comparative] mode can identify what phenomena are unique to particular social formations and what are general trends in modern capitalism."[101]

5. *Engaged*. To Marxists, theory and practice is another dichotomy that must be abandoned. To truly understand, one must participate. The stance of scholarly "objectivity" is a mask or a delusion. The basis of all knowledge, Marxists assume, is in participating in change. As Mao Tse-tung expressed it, "If you want knowledge, you must take part in the practice of changing reality. If you want to know the taste of a pear, you must change the pear by eating it yourself. . . . If you want to know the theory and methods of revolution, you must take part in revolution. All genuine knowledge originates in direct experience."[102]

---

[99]Ibid., p. 7.

[100]Fainstein and Fainstein, *Urban Policy Under Capitalism*, p. 16.

[101]Ibid., p. 17.

[102]Mao Tse Tung, "On Practice," in *Selected Works* (Peking: Foreign Languages Press, 1964), Vol. 1, p. 399.

CONTEMPORARY CENTRAL ISSUES

In the Marxist formulation we are in the period of decaying capitalism. The forces of transformation that attend this historical period are the ones shaping and changing our cities. In general, the issues that most define the period are the following.

Crisis.   As the contradictions within the capitalist order grow, periodic crises result. The social disruptions that we experience in the modern world are not caused by simple, isolated economic problems; rather "we are living in an economic crisis caused by a general process of social disruption in most advanced capitalist societies, which has called into question the structure of social relationships underlying the pattern of capital accumulation."[103]

There are four types of crisis that occur in this stage, each reflecting the interaction of such forces as evolving objective conditions, mass consciousness, and political action, according to Jurgen Habermas:

1. *Direct class conflict within the realm of production.*[104] An example of such conflict would be a strike of workers, say, city employees, against management.

2. *Accumulation crisis.* Symptoms are lagging productivity, obsolescence of plant and organizational infrastructure, governmental insolvency, and savings being diverted into unproductive speculation. Examples of the conflicts attending the accumulation crisis are fiscal crises such as the New York City fiscal crisis and breakdowns in the provision of city services.

3. *Realization crisis.* Manifestations are insufficient aggregate demand for the products of the economy and declining profitability. The realization crisis results in high levels of unemployment, declining tax bases in the cities, and high rates of bankruptcy of retail establishments.

4. *Legitimation crisis.* There is a withdrawal of voluntary compliance with dominant norms by large segments of the public. Riots and urban political movements illustrate the legitimation crisis. The recurrence and increasing intensity of these crises mark the pace of decay of the capitalist order.

Imperialism.   A basic principle of capitalist enterprise is that it must be expanding its profitability or it will inevitably decline. So the principle dynamic of

---

[103]Castells, *The Economic Crisis and American Society*, p. 5.

[104]My summary of Habermas is based on his *Legitimation Crisis* (Boston: Beacon Press, 1973), as refined and applied by Fainstein and Fainstein, *Urban Policy*, p. 179.

the order is that the owners must increase their stocks of wealth. Few barriers exist to this process in the early stages of capitalism. There are ample resources, available labor, and many opportunities to amass sufficient capital to enter a market. But in the latter stages of capitalist development, capitalism must become imperialistic to find and control the means necessary for continuing profitability. When domestic energy sources become more scarce, for example, our businesses require a foreign policy that will assure the cooperation of the governments of the oil-rich nations.

This principle operates domestically as well as internationally. Cheap labor power is also required for profitable production. Central-city governments must keep a flexible labor force in place and quiescent. As William Tabb has formulated it, the black ghetto is the object of imperial city government policy, an internal colony.[105]

The Current Form of the Class Struggle.   In summary, "the physical and social structure of the city is seen by Marxists as the evolving product of the social forces of production and the class relations they engender."[106] The focus of their inquiry is less upon the specifics of land use in the city than on the role of class struggle in forming the physical structure of the modern metropolis. David Gordon, for example, argues that manufacturers originally located their factories in the cities because that setting isolated workers from each other. This gave owners the power advantage to keep workers' wages down. But by the end of the nineteenth century, the labor movement had substantially overcome this isolation, and unions were putting considerable pressure on management. The manufacturers then began to build their plants on the outskirts of the cities to escape growing worker power, and thus the process of suburbanization was set in motion.

Among the many topics discussed by the Union for Radical Political Economics, in their conference on Marx and the Metropolis held in New York City in 1975, many raised the question of class. The research agenda proposed and discussed there dealt with such general questions as "How do class relations manifest themselves in the city?" "Do we view the city as a part of the super-structure of the society of which it is a part?" "How can we tie urban form and function to the mode of production?" "How, from a class perspective, do we view local taxation, housing markets, and urban transportation?" "How do regional differences in class structure affect the process of urbanization?" and, "What are the experiences of urban development in socialist countries?" Such questions are a fair summary of the contemporary Marxist research agenda.

---

[105]William Tabb, *Politican Economy of the Black Ghetto* (New York: W. W. Norton, 1963).
[106]Tabb and Sawyers, *Marxism and the Metropolis,* p. 8.

Variations on Radical Political Economy

There is great variety among radicals. Far from the stereotype that the political right seeks to perpetuate of conformity and herd instinct on the left, its perennial problem has been to find common ground upon which to organize. Just to suggest some of that variety, there is "cultural radicalism" and nondoctrinal "economic democracy."

Cultural radicalism is itself a diverse collection of ideas. But most cultural radicals agree that Marx is either wrong or irrelevant. Particularly, they refuse to subordinate their chief concerns to analyses of economic questions. Certain cultural radicals recognize the importance of material accumulation as a shaping force and important determinant of the capitalist order, but they reject the Marxist emphasis on the working class.

Among the chief concerns of cultural radicals are (1) some varieties of feminism, namely, those who view the struggle for sexual liberation as the critical terrain of concern and ideological struggle;[107] (2) ecology, namely, environmental degradation; (3) the problems of youth, that is, the economic, political, and cultural position of the young in the context of capitalism; and (4) racism, seen by some as the most central ideological apparatus for political demobilization and social paralysis.[108]

Nondoctrinaire radicalism is also various. California's Campaign for Economic Democracy (CED), ACORN, and the Massachusetts Fair Share, as well as a number of groups called Citizens Action were outgrowths of the civil rights and student movements. They specifically deny that they are ideologically committed to socialism, which they feel is for practical political reasons not feasible in American politics. Many of the activists in these movements attach themselves to the "progressive" wing of the Democratic party, but most have deliberately sought to establish themselves in local politics. Following the kinds of strategies cultivated by Saul Alinsky, they avoid intellectualization and instead seek action on specific issues.[109] CED, for example, came to exercise considerable influence in the city of Santa Monica, California, during the 1970s beginning with a successful campaign for a rent control ordinance. Health and environmental issues have also provided a vehicle for organizing. Tom Hayden and his colleagues in CED are strongly interested in changes that open up the political processes. Like the populists, they focus much attention on reforms that enable greater citizen

---

[107]For a focus of feminist concerns specifically on urban life, see Catherine Stimpson, Elsa Dixler, Martha Nelson, and Kathryn Yatrakis, *Women and the American City* (Chicago: University of Chicago Press, 1981).

[108]This summary owes much to Stanley Aronowitz, "Remaking the American Left," *Socialist Review*, Vol. 67 (January–February 1983), pp. 9–54.

[109]Saul Alinsky, *Rules for Radicals* (New York: Harper & Row, 1968).

participation, for example, abandonment of the at-large method of local election. This apparent issue-oriented pragmatism is not without its intellectual component, however. Hayden's writing makes his reasoning rather clear; and writings like Martin Carnoy and Derek Shearer's *Economic Democracy* provide an explanation of their action that moves very close to what we could call democratic socialism.[110]

Critique of Radical Political Economy

Most of the criticism of radical economy contained in popular, and even some more thoughtful, discourse is simply stereotypical. It is the kind of criticism that avoids issues and seeks to dismiss even the necessity of serious discussion. Irving Kristol, for example, indulges in such an effort in the concluding essay of an issue of his neoconservative magazine, *The Public Interest:* "The vision of radical economics today," he summarizes,

> . . . is that of a democratic equalitarian community in which individual self-interest would be rendered a negligible force through education, peer group pressure, community festivals, and a constant flow of elevating rhetoric. It is a romantic-utopian vision in its substance, though scrupulously secular-rationalist in its articulation. It is, in truth, utopian socialism in modern academic dress. That it should find expression within the economic profession itself, instead of inciting a mass exodus from that profession, is but one more testimonial to the intellectual confusion of our age.[111]

Nonetheless, all belief systems have their weaknesses, inconsistencies, and anomalies, and radical political economy certainly provides no exception. The most obvious observation is that the great variety within the radical perspective means that it is inherently inconsistent and likely to be ineffective as a basis for political movement. More central and to the point, contemporary critics of Marxism make the following arguments:

1. *Marxism has proved an inaccurate guide to actual historical development.* Although a favorite critique of non-Marxists, this is a recognized problem

---

[110]*Economic Democracy* (White Plains, N.Y.: M. E. Sharp, 1980). A number of academic writers have made analyses and critiques of contemporary capitalism that also fit the general idea of pragmatic adaptation toward a nondogmatic, democratic socialism. See, particularly, the works of Robert Heilbroner, especially *Business Civilization in Decline* and *Between Capitalism and Socialism* (New York: Random House, 1970). Also see many of the works of Michael Harrington, although he is more connected to Marxism than these others; see his *Socialism* (New York: Saturday Review Press, 1970). And, finally, see one of the originators of pluralist theory in more recent formulation: Charles Lindblom, *Politics and Markets* (New York: Basic Books, 1977).

[111]Irving Kristol, "Rationalism in Economics, *"Public Interest* (special issue), "The Crisis in Economic Theory" (1980), p. 217.

among many Marxists. For example, the Swedish Marxist Goran Therborn acknowledges that "Fundamental aspects of Marxist theory have been called into question both by its historic defeats, so far, in North America and Western Europe, and by the aftermath of its successes—Stalinism, the Sino-Soviet split, the present social and political condition of that third of the world claiming to be governed by Marxist theory."[112] The Marxist George Lukacs, explains "our analysis stood still, but capitalism continued to evolve. We stopped with Lenin. After him there has been no Marxism."[113] Of course, contemporary Marxists consider themselves engaged in required updating.

More specifically, the critics argue that capitalism has had considerably more staying power than the Marxists imagined. Capitalism appeared to be in transition in the United States and England in the 1930s, but it did not collapse. Wherever capitalism underwent violent change, as in Germany and Italy, the direction of movement was to the right, not to the left. And when the fascists were defeated in those countries, capitalism re-emerged in excellent health.

Searching for the elements of Marxist theory that have not been borne out, Robert Heilbroner—himself predicting the passing of "business civilization"—makes the widely shared judgment: Contrary to Marxist expectations, "the present day industrial working class is not revolutionary in its temper."[114] For an extended period of time, industrial workers have benefited from the general post-World War II economic expansion. As a result, the political temper and social outlook of the American working class became progressively less proletarian and more bourgeois, serving to destroy the unity and discipline necessary to a revolutionary class.

Technological change during that same period also failed to add to the ranks of the revolutionary workers, but instead opened the way for expansion of the white-collar middle class. The result was no strong class consciousness among the working class and no revolutionary movement. A number of contemporary Marxists insist that the postwar period is an historical aberration. They suggest that America in the recessionary 1980s was just beginning to witness the economic changes that will push industrial workers back into the class consciousness from which they have escaped. Marx was right, they contend, but the timetable is more extended than some had expected—stay the course, a popular neoconservative slogan of the Reagan presidency, found its radical echo.

2. *Marxism has important internal contradictions.* Several critics of Marxism

---

[112]Goran Therborn, *Science, Class and Society* (London: New Left Books, 1976), p. 38. Also, see Louis Althusser, *Essays in Self-Criticism* (London: New Left Books, 1976).

[113]George Lukacs, "A Final Rethinking: George Lukacs Talks with Franco Ferrarotti," *Social Policy* (July–August 1972), p. 57.

[114]Heilbroner, *Business Civilization in Decline,* pp. 42–43.

have pointed out problems in the construction of Marx's primary theory. Alvin Gouldner is fairly representative of those critics when he argues that Marx has a nuclear contradiction that runs through all his thought.[115] This contradiction consists primarily of a tension between determinist and voluntarist tendencies. The determinist tendency in Marxism consists in the idea that what he is describing as an historical process is objective and inevitable. The voluntarist tendency consists in that portion of Marx that urges people to engage in revolutionary practices.[116] In other words, Marxism lays claim to being both a social science and also "a doctrine of violent revolution."[117]

The consequences of this "contradiction" are many and complex. Most important, it leaves it unclear as to whether we are creatures of free will or simply transmitters of historical inevitabilities.

According to Gouldner, the consequence of this contradiction goes beyond mere classification. He uses that distinction to uncover problems in primary Marxist analysis. "He demonstrates how voluntarist and determinist elements sneak in and out of Marxian analysis, without their relationships to one another ever being clearly resolved."[118]

3. *Marxism really has no method.* The argument of the critics on this point is that there are no efforts of Marxists to utilize accepted canons of proof. Although they use the term "science," the scientific Marxists are not really following such modes of analysis. To illustrate more specifically, the logic of accepted scientific method requires "falsifiability"; that is, there must be built into the process of inquiry the possibility that the propositions being examined can be found false. Critics claim that Marxists are not so bound. The result is that the neoconservative research method can discover the "truth" of Marxist assumptions as well as its own. But Marxist scholars, it is claimed, can never find that their assumptions are false. If the assumption is not borne out in any given inquiry, Marxists simply fall back on the assumption that "eventually," "inevitably" it will. It is for this reason that many critics of Marxism insist that it is more properly understood to be a religious system than a mode of social scientific inquiry.

4. *The key concept of "class" lacks clarity.* A final criticism of Marxism is advanced by those who would use scientific method in the study of political economy. These critics insist that key concepts in any explanation—Marxist or otherwise—must be stated in terms precise enough to enable measure-

[115]Alvin Gouldner, *The Two Marxisms: Contradictions and Anomalies in the Development of Theory* (New York: The Seabury Press, 1980).

[116]The term "praxis" is used by Marx and his followers as a synonym for the term "practice" contained in the text. Gouldner points out that in the Marxist use of that concept can be found this primal contradiction, which he illuminates; see pp. 33–34.

[117]Ibid., p. 32.

[118]Michael D. Kennedy, review of Gouldner's "The Two Marxisms," in *The Review of Radical Political Economics,* Vol. 13 (Winter 1982), p. 67.

ment. A number of the key concepts of Marxism, they argue, are not that clear. The important concept "class" in Marxism, for example, they say, is used in such a variety of ways that it is not certain what is meant. A large number of American unionists, for example, think of themselves as capitalists. Are they part of the ruling class? Or are they self-deceived and given their actual class placement by objective conditions? Which objective conditions? The critics do not believe that Marxists have made, or perhaps can make, adequate response. Meantime, many of those same critics say that American society appears not to be characterized by class conflict of the type Marx anticipated.

SUMMARY

This chapter has established the terms of systematic conflict over the urban political economy. The remainder of the book will demonstrate how commitment to one or another of these perspectives forms the basis of our most profound disagreements on policy and on the proper role of politics and the very form of our institutions of urban governance.

More specifically, we have clarified the meaning of neoconservative, liberal, and radical political economies by describing each first as a personal ethic, then as an explanatory system, and finally as a method of studying and describing the political economies of cities. The essential features of each is as follows:

Neoconservative

1. As a personal ethic, neoconservatism consists of a cluster of personal value commitments to individualism, materialism and productivity, universal competition, and a qualified endorsement of democracy, among others.

2. As systematic thought, neoconservatism adds certain socioeconomic "realities" that must be assumed. The existence of certain "natural laws" of the universe is assumed to include (among others) the Invisible Hand of the Marketplace, which serves to maintain a "general equilibrium" rather than allowing the chaos that universal competition might produce.

3. We have identified public choice theory as a rather good illustration of neoconservatism when it is being formulated as a method for studying political economy. But, as with each of the three basic perspectives we have identified, there are important variations on the same theme. Perhaps the most important variation is the institutional alternative of Vincent and Elinor Ostrom.

4. Finally, as with each version of political economy, we have reiterated the

most common criticisms of neoconservatism. The critics commonly accuse public choice theories of having an inadequate conception of politics, although most acknowledge that the Ostroms' formulation is better. Second, critics argue that the assumptions of the neoconservatives are unrealistic oversimplifications. And, last, a number of criticisms are aimed specifically at the logical consistency of neoconservatism.

Liberal

1. Liberals are committed to a personal ethic that emphasizes fair procedures more than substantive outcomes. Free political speech and association are central to a "free market of ideas." Beyond that, liberals tend to equate a willingness to compromise with statesmanship and to expect generosity in dealing with those who have been "less fortunate." But, in general, liberalism is more an ethos with an history than a coherent philosophy.

2. As systematic thought, liberalism is more concrete. Historical examination reveals liberals' attraction to individualism and capitalism, but with a vision of positive government that calls for occasional government intervention into the economy. The role of the state is to encourage greater economic and political equality. Liberals assume that proper procedures can assure that the state can protect the interests of all.

3. In recent history, the method of liberals has been called pluralism. In pluralism as method and findings, democratic politics may be reduced to process, economics may be analytically distinguished from politics, political power is widely dispersed, and business interests are but one of many groups contending for power. Changes in the content of public policy occur incrementally rather than comprehensively.

4. The critics of liberalism argue that liberalism puts a pretty face on some harsh realities; that is, liberalism lacks principles and clarity, and particularly when expressed as pluralism, it is excessively simplified.

Radical

1. Radicals in a modern setting are generally characterized by a roughly existentialist world view. Among other things, this leads to a formulation that progressive change is possible, though far from easy or assured. Action is emphasized both as a vehicle of change and a source of knowledge. Radicals tend to a strong sense of their personal competence and an affinity for totalistic understandings rather than resting content with the present patterns of specialization.

2. As systematic thought, radicalism is strongly associated with Marxism. Viewed as a system of thought, Marx's leading tenets are historical materialism, the dialectic, theories of class struggle and revolutionary change, the doctrine of surplus value, and a theory of the role of the state in capitalist societies.

3. Radicals are less concerned with method than with content; nonetheless, modern Marxists are methodologically self-conscious. Their stance emphasizes holistic, multidisciplinary, comparative research, which is historically developed. In contrast to the social scientific stance of detached objectivity, the Marxist insists that real knowledge comes from being engaged in action for change.

4. The major criticisms made of Marxism are that it has proved to be an inaccurate guide to actual historical development, it has a number of central internal contradictions, it is lacking a clear method and thus is not able to be "falsified" as required by scientific methods, and many of its central concepts—"class," for example—are defined too imprecisely to be the basis of careful analysis.

Each of these ideologies has strengths and weaknesses. Each also sees a different set of facts, problems, and solutions. How profound these differences are will be illustrated as we turn to what might seem to the uninitiated a simple and straight forward task of defining the environment of the American city.

CHAPTER 3

*The Economic,
Physical, and Social
Environment
of the City*

WHY STUDY THE URBAN ENVIRONMENT?

Politics is crucially shaped by the environment in which it is set. Hence, knowledge of the environment is necessary to a full understanding of how politics works. Knowing the environment enlightens us in three important ways.

First, it heightens our sense of ordinary politics, as distinct from the more dramatic and visible events that many think of as the central concerns of politics. By packaging political news, the media provide the service of concise summary, but at the cost of making events often appear unconnected with the broader social, economic, and political processes. By contrast with the dramatic and newsworthy, ordinary politics has to do with the thousands of established patterns of thought and behavior, sometimes considered to be so unimportant that they were not really even seen: Environments tend to be invisible. A large number of actual and potential conflicts are handled by the established pattern of reflex responses. This is because human skills are consciously learned, but later, through repetition, they become reflexive in nature.[1]

---

[1]Arthur Koestler, *The Act of Creation* (New York: Macmillan, 1964), p. 38.

It is true that what most of us regard as most important and interesting in our lives are the novel and nonrepetitive activities; however, most social scientists understand that even the novel cannot be understood except in the context of the ordinary.

Second, the environment imposes constraints. Many of us, imbued as we are with that can-do attitude that is so prevalent in American society, seem to think that any new direction can be taken at any time. If a faucet leaks, fix it; if cars cause smog, ban them. However, such easy alternatives often have a hard time in the political system because the broader environment is not that pliant. Edward Banfield has put the position in extraordinarily bold form. In discussing the "logic" of metropolitan growth, he discerns three environmental factors that he chooses to call "imperatives": demographic, technological, and economic. "The word 'imperatives' is used to emphasize the inexorable, constraining character of the three factors that together comprise the logic of metropolitan growth. . . . Given a rate of population growth, a transportation technology, and a distribution of income, certain consequences must inevitably follow; that the city and its hinterland must develop according to a predictable pattern. . . . The argument is not that nothing can be done to improve matters. Rather, it is that only those things can be done which lie within the boundaries—rather narrow ones to be sure—fixed by the logic of the growth process."[2]

Without accepting the strong determinacy of Banfield's formulation, we must still understand that we are not given the luxury of absolute free choice; the particular environment of the city already exists and its growth follows a kind of logic of its own.

Finally, by examining the setting of urban politics, we learn something of the sources of political change. To fail to examine the environment of politics is to leave the impression that the political process is disembodied and autonomous, which is a distortion of the relationship it bears to other processes of the culture. As David Easton has put it, without examining the environment, we could not proceed to suggest a kind of analysis designed to shed light on the way in which political systems are able to persist and change or cope with the stresses to which they are constantly exposed.[3]

In this chapter we will scan the urban environment, selecting materials from the disciplines of history, economics, urban ecology and geography, sociology, and psychology. Here we will find the deepest roots of the ideological conflicts sketched in the previous chapter. In particular, we will pursue the interpretation that American cities are primarily the creations of capitalism.

---

[2]Edward Banfield, *The Unheavenly City* (Boston: Little, Brown, 1970), p. 24.
[3]David Easton, *A Framework for Political Analysis* (Englewood Cliffs, N.J.: Prentice-Hall, 1965), p. 71.

THE URBAN ECONOMIC BASE

American cities are best understood as the creations of economic forces. This is not to argue that every important function of our cities is economically determined but that cities are fundamentally constructs that have formed to make exchange of goods and services easier and less costly. As one prominent urbanist has put it, "it is only a modest oversimplification to equate the interests of cities with the interests of their export industries."[4]

One of the most widely used analytical frameworks for examining the urban economy is the export-base construct.[5] Export-base theory assumes that it is the basic economic activities that build cities. A basic activity is one that brings income into the city from outside, whereas nonbasic activities supply goods and services within the local area but do not bring money from outside. Thus the urban area is depicted as a wide-open economy that is heavily dependent on external trade, very much like a small industrially advanced nation in the world market. Both Switzerland and Wichita, it is assumed, must export or die. The best examples of basic activities are, of course, factories that sell their products outside the city.

Economic geographers have undertaken a number of studies of the basic/nonbasic ratios of American cities.[6] For example, a study of the economic base of Oshkosh, Wisconsin, found six nonbasic employees for every ten basic ones; Madison, Wisconsin, has eight nonbasic for every ten basic.[7] Relatively higher employment in basic industries has been found in most of the studies of small- or medium-sized cities, which implies the necessity of large basic industry employment in the early stages of urban growth. As cities become larger and, economically speaking, more mature, it has been found that the basic-to-nonbasic employment ratios tend to approach equality. "With greater urban size comes the tendency toward greater local self-sufficiency."[8]

While export-base theory is by no means universally accepted by urban economists,[9] it has come to be accepted in its most immediate implication; that is,

[4]Paul Peterson, *City Limits* (Chicago: University of Chicago Press, 1981), p. 23.

[5]Wilbur R. Thompson, *A Preface to Urban Economics* (Baltimore: Johns Hopkins University Press, 1965), pp. 27–60.

[6]See Richard Hartshorne, "Twin City District: A Unique Form of Urban Landscape," *Geographical Review*, Vol. 22 (July 1932), pp. 431–442.

[7]John W. Alexander, "The Basic–Non-Basic Concept of Urban Economic Functions," *Economic Geography*, Vol. 30 (July 1954), pp. 246– 61.

[8]Wilbur Thompson, "Internal and External Factors in the Development of Urban Economics," in Harvey Perloff and Lowden Wingo, Jr., eds., *Issues in Urban Economics* (Baltimore: John Hopkins University Press, 1968), p. 45.

[9]Harvey Perloff et al., *Regions, Resources, and Economic Growth* (Baltimore: Johns Hopkins University Press for Resources for the Future, 1960).

"export industries clearly generate a net flow of income into the local economy from which the necessary imports can be financed. In this most immediate sense of current money flow, the export sector is basic and the local service sector is derivative in origin."[10] But export-base assumptions have been subjected to many challenges. For example, the export industries that formed a given urban center become less important as the city ages. To continue to thrive, a city must be an attractive place for new firms to locate. This means that it must cultivate a full array of nonbasic functions (services and educational and recreational facilities) to offer these prospective newcomers. For these reasons, the nonbasic activities can become as important in the vitality of the economic base as are the exporting industries.[11]

Further, and perhaps more important, the changes in the structure of the American economy that were occurring during the late 1970s and 1980s may render export-base industries less important as determinants of the growth of the local economy. A study of twelve growing cities in the South and Midwest gathered some evidence that growth in the export base may not be accompanied by a corresponding growth in the local economy.[12] Philadelphia, for example, showed an increase in exports of 49.91 percent in the time period studied, but the expected multiplier does not occur, as its total economy increased at only 33.48 percent. The study also found that some of the cities that did grow rapidly may well have done so for reasons other than expansion of their economic base. Denver, for example, experienced a 5.93 percent growth in its export sector and a 55.04 percent growth in its overall economy. But in analyzing the reasons for that impressive overall growth, the authors suggest that "import substitution may be a more powerful strategy" for cities looking to improve their local economies.[13] So, while export base is a clearly important determinant of the health of local economies, it may be becoming less so.

CAPITALISM AND THE CITY

Capitalism is but one mode of economic organization, but it is difficult to deny that it has been by far the most significant pattern of economic organization that has given our cities their physical form and thereby shaped the social and political orders as well. However, to recognize the role of capitalism in the creation and

[10]Thompson, "Internal and External Factors," p. 43.

[11]For a more complete elaboration of this insight, see Charles Tiebout, "Exports and Regional Economic Growth," *Journal of Political Economy,* Vol. 64, no. 2 (1956), pp. 160–164.

[12]Norton Long and Jeffrey Wittmaier, "The Export Base and the Performance of the Local Economy," in F. Stevens Redburn and Terry Buss, eds., *Public Policies for Distressed Communities* (Lexington, Mass.: Lexington Books, 1982), pp. 119–127.

[13]Ibid., p. 122.

transformation of the American city is not to assume that urbanization and capitalism are the same thing. Perhaps the best way to understand their separability is historically. When we take even a cursory overview of urban development, we get both a strong sense of the important effects of capitalism in shaping our cities and a sense of how city growth has some independence from capitalism.

Economic historians vary considerably in their designation of the stages through which American cities have passed. But for our relatively simple purposes here, we will assume that there are five major developmental stages: precapitalist, agrarian capitalist, industrial capitalist, New Deal capitalist, and multinational capitalist.[14]

Precapitalism (Colonization to 1789)

The earliest cities in America were founded within the basic economic pattern of mercantilism, not capitalism. That pattern allowed trading companies and individuals favored by the government of a "mother country" to colonize and exploit the resources of distant territories. Those resources were to be imported back to the home country for processing and/or distribution. There were, of course, a great variety of reasons for the creation of colonial towns and cities in addition to the matter of economic exploitation. It was religious fervor that brought the Puritans to found Boston, for instance. And the early settlements on the tip of Manhattan Island banded together for defense behind the wall that only later became Wall Street. But mercantilist policies were the most important single factor in precapitalist city growth. New York and Boston were port cities. Philadelphia and Williamsburg, Virginia—known as the "Tobacco Planters' Capital"—were also well on the way to city status before the writing of the federal Constitution.

Agrarian Capitalism (1789 to the Civil War)

The new Constitution proved hospitable to a nascent capitalism. Especially the efforts of Alexander Hamilton, as first Secretary of the Treasury, laid a firm foundation for what was to be the urban-industrial capitalism of the post-Civil War period. But in the meantime the efforts of Thomas Jefferson, antiurbanite, had produced a set of policies that made the agricultural development of the Western lands the first order of business for the new nation. The Ordinances of 1784, 1785,

---

[14]For a good overview and relevant literature on the controversies related to urban periodization, see Alfred Watkins, *The Practice of Urban Economics* (Beverly Hills, Calif.: Sage Publications, 1980), especially Chap. 6 and 7.

and 1787 together provided for sale of public lands in the undeveloped territories. The Northwest region was divided into six mile-square townships, cut up into thirty-six lots of a mile square (640 acres) each. The minimum price per acre was originally $1.

The cities that rose to prominence in this period were the ones responsive to the economic needs of agricultural marketing. The needs of farmers are not all in the fields. Marketing centers are required for processing, distribution, and transportation of agricultural goods. A number of cities flowered as they met the needs of an agriculturally dominated economy. Lexington, Kentucky, by the 1790s had already emerged as the steamboat trade on the Ohio River flourished. To its proud residents it was "The Philadelphia of Kentucky."[15]

But Lexington soon felt the competitive pressures of Cincinnati, Ohio. Cincinnati was the first city of industry of the New West; its initial economic functions were as an agricultural marketing center, and particularly as a slaughterhouse. By the 1830s Cincinnati's boosters proclaimed it "Porkopolis" to the chagrin of the famous and aristocratic Mrs. Trollope. The cities of Chicago and St. Louis, however, come to dominance late in this period. In the 1870s, Chicago became pre-eminent over Cincinnati in the same functions—especially meat packing. St. Louis and New Orleans peaked in the 1850–1860 period as agricultural shipping and distribution centers along the Mississippi.

Industrial Capitalism (Civil War to the New Deal)

The Industrial Revolution transformed the American economy from one dominated by a large number of small-scale agriculturally related producers to an economy of more centralized economic forms. Concentration of wealth began to make possible centralization of productive enterprises and require large available pools of labor. Between 1860 and 1920, then, the urban population rose from 6.2 million to 54.2 million. This explosion of cities gives us our most profound urban experience. It was an experience that made us ambivalent. On the one hand, this urban industrialization had given us what is widely regarded as the most productive and efficient economic form yet devised by humankind. The economic structure fundamentally formed at that time has provided more people with more material goods than has any other system in the world. On the other hand, industrial cities are nightmarish, filled with filth, turmoil, human degradation, and unconscionable disparities of wealth and power. And while it must be reiterated that industrialism need not be coupled with capitalism, it surely was in America at this time. As one urbanist summarizes the results of that connection, "Municipalities handed over

[15]Wilson Smith, ed., *Cities of Our Past and Present* (New York: John Wiley & Sons, 1964), p. 37.

their land and resources to private profit, and our cities became the abused by-product of national industrial development.''[16]

Certain of the established cities of the agrarian capitalist period extended themselves, others declined. New York and Chicago gained regional ascendancy. Atlanta was quickly rebuilt following the Civil War and became the most Northern of Southern cities in the process of industrial development. Certain cities became the distinctive creations of industrial capitalism. Pittsburgh, for example, emerged from the economic stimulation of the Civil War, manufacturing half the steel and one-third the glass produced in the country. Pittsburgh attracted the full array of laborers. Before the war, it was freed blacks from Virginia and Maryland, and in the 1880s, it absorbed immigrants from Italy, Poland, Russia, and Central Europe. By 1890 Pittsburgh held a quarter-million people. But the thriving economy of the city made it the classic industrial city: A traveler in the 1880s wrote, ''In truth, Pittsburgh is a smoky, dismal city at her best. At her worst, nothing darker, dingier or more dispiriting can be imagined.''[17]

Detroit illustrates a city that flowered later in the period. By 1930 it was one of only five American cities with populations of a million or more—New York, Chicago, Philadelphia, and Los Angeles being the others. Built on automobile production, it was a showcase of American capitalistic attainment. The boom of the 1920s led many to believe that Detroit had demonstrated that industrial capitalism could produce a city with the productivity of a Pittsburgh without the squalor. French Strother, journalist and administrative assistant to Herbert Hoover, wrote of Detroit in 1926, ''There are no tenements in Detroit. . . . The schools of Detroit are not merely good, they are among the best in the world.''[18]

New Deal Capitalism (1932 to World War II)

The Great Depression ended the long expansive infancy of industrial capitalism. Counterforces had been at work throughout the period. The labor movement developed rapidly in cities such as Pittsburgh and Detroit. Farmers had long agitated against the ''trusts'' that they felt deprived them of their profitability, keeping them in constant economic marginality. The New Deal of Franklin D. Roosevelt subjected the free market to the regulation of the government but showed no propensity to eliminate it. The New Deal period, then, remains fundamentally capitalitic, although government and the private sector become increasingly intertwined in what is often called a ''mixed economy.''

[16]Jane R. Lowe, *Cities in a Race with Time* (New York: Random House, 1967), p. 10.

[17]Willard Glazier, *Peculiarities of American Cities* (New York: R. H. Ferguson & Co., 1885), p. 334.

[18]French Strother, ''What Kind of a Pittsburgh Is Detroit,'' *The World's Work*, Vol. 52 (October 1926), pp. 635–636.

The conflict among neoconservative, liberal, and radical versions of political economy would emphasize very different interpretations of the effects of the New Deal upon the entire economic system and, particularly, the economies of our cities. I will make no effort to reconcile those differences in this brief historical summary. But let us recognize that this period provides the experience upon which the contemporary debate rests. In addition, some few patterns emerged during that time period that, most will agree, were important and relatively indisputable. First, few new cities emerged, and the ones created in the age of industrial capitalism continued to dominate the economic functions of the previous period. Because radical redistribution of private capital ceased during this time period, the New Deal laid the policy groundwork for the consolidation of previously created urban forms. The policies that were to have the most far-reaching impacts in this process were those promoting dedensification, undercutting local autonomy, and stunting local political organization.

1. *Dedensification.* Suburbanization had been in evidence since the beginning of the century, but the framework for its rapid extension was created in this period. Dedensification is the result of economic changes, like increasingly cheap automobiles and gasoline and greater investment in highways. That effect is largely postwar. But it is also the result of active policy choices. Then Governor Franklin Roosevelt of New York announced his perspective in 1931: "Farsighted men and women are at last aware of the fact that our population is overbalanced—too many people live in very large cities and too few in the smaller communities."[19]

2. *Loss of local autonomy.* American cities have never had much independence of action. But the policies of the New Deal once again had the effect of extending a pattern already in place. A variety of policies understandably aimed at providing the federal government with the power to pull the country out of the depression undermined local control. It was a conscious choice to create what Paul Peterson has called "the limited city."[20]

3. *Undermining of urban political organization.* The New Deal undermined the political "machines," as reformers called them, and the often "boss"-dominated form of political organization that was so prominent a feature of the city at the turn of the century. Already in decline, the machines were severely undercut by the institutionalized welfare and employment programs of the New Deal. A bureaucracy that was not locally accountable replaced the local ward captain as the source of public benefits.

In all, the New Deal period, so often characterized as anticapitalist in popular discussion, should more accurately be described as enshrining the central-

---

[19] Quoted in David Morris, *Self-Reliant Cities* (San Francisco: Sierra Club Books, 1982), p. 24.
[20] Peterson, *City Limits.* This point is in contradistinction to the more often discussed, and intended, effect of the New Deal to strengthen the city in its relationship to its state government.

ity of the economic system. The effect on our cities was to shape urban development in a way that accelerated the forces of dedensification and that made local political control and responsibility increasingly difficult.

Multinationalism (1945 to Present)

The emergence of large-scale nationally and internationally integrated economic enterprises after World War II provides the setting of contemporary urban political economy. The capitalist imperative of growth, technological advance in transportation and communication, the need for resources, cheaper labor, and new markets all provide the incentives for firms to move all or parts of their operations to other countries. Just as steel production imperatives drew firms to Pittsburgh in the era of industrial capitalism, in the recent epoch, firms are drawn to copper in Chile, oil in the Middle East, inexpensive labor in Taiwan or Mexico, and rising consumer demand in Europe.

This economic development has its effect on the shape of the American cityscape as well. The regional shifts in economic growth, job opportunities, and population from the industrial northeast to the south, southwest and, to some degree, northwest regions of the country are but the domestic parallel of the multinational development. The rise of the Sunbelt cities is, of course, partly a matter of getting warm, but it is mostly a matter of making money. Markets, cheaper labor, and resources also may be found in the Sunbelt. As Watkins and Perry note, "While [the northeastern cities] were saddled with an old, slowly growing industrial foundation, the Sunbelt cities, because they had previously been blocked from adopting these same activities, were in a more flexible position to shift with the changing needs of the economy."[21] The postwar boom of Los Angeles was just the beginning. Miami, Atlanta, Houston, Denver, Albuquerque, Phoenix, San Diego, and Seattle are the cities that have flowered in the era of multinationalism.

THE POLITICS OF THE CURRENT ERA

Change generates conflict. And as we are always somehow changing, we are always fighting. But the struggles are not to be trivialized. Not all politics is petty. And certainly the politics generated by the emergence of multinationalism is

[21]A. J. Watkins and D. C. Perry, "Regional Change and the Impact of Uneven Urban Development," in D. C. Perry and A. J. Watkins, eds., *The Rise of the Sunbelt Cities* (Beverly Hills, Calif.: Sage Publications, 1977). For a careful statistical presentation that forms the basis of the generalizations in this section, see Scott South and Dudley Poston, Jr., "The U.S. Metropolitan System: Regional Change 1950–1970," *Urban Affairs Quarterly*, Vol. 18 (December 1982), pp. 187–206.

profoundly important. Upon its outcome will depend the direction not merely of urban growth but the quality of our lives.

The most basic grounds for disagreement about what is the proper interpretation of the nature, meaning, direction, and correct response to the multinational era of urban development were anticipated in Chapter 2. Neoconservatives have very different formulations from either liberals or radicals on these questions.

The Neoconservative Formulation: Convergence

In general, neoconservatives argue that the northeastern cities are not severely threatened. Their problems arise from the fact that the cities of the Sunbelt temporarily offer a more favorable climate for economic development. In the longer run, a state of equilibrium will be re-established between the two regions. As that happens, the extreme disparities can be expected to level off, and all cities will grow in a more harmonious and uniform fashion. This process is called "convergence" by urban economists.[22]

The process of convergence is not painless—the wealthy, more developed region will be made slightly poorer as the less developed region gains. So there will be disruption and a sense of problem, but the present conditions in the Northeast are not harbingers of crisis. "Rather they only reaffirm the existence of a self-regulating market mechanism."[23] On a more theoretical level, convergence theory rests on two assumptions: (1) There exists a persistent tendency for the economies of two regions to conform to the conditions assumed by the general theory of equilibrium; and (2) factors that in the short run upset the equilibrium will be offset by equal and opposite counteracting pressures.

Within this general pattern, a number of neoconservatives argue that the economic health of cities is directly tied to the country's overall effectiveness in competing in a world economic market. And, as John Kasarda has observed, "In many traditional industrial sectors, such as the production of electrical components, heavy machinery, textiles, and steel, the competitive position of the United States has been severely weakened by more cost-effective production elsewhere in the world."[24]

Consequently, the optimism implied in convergence assumptions must be tempered by the realization that convergence in the multinational era is on a

---

[22]See Jeffrey Williamson, "Regional Inequality and the Process of National Development," *Economic Development and Cultural Change,* Vol. 13 (1965), pp. 3–45. Also George Borts and Jerome Stein, *Economic Growth in a Free Market* (New York: Columbia University Press, 1964).

[23]Watkins, *The Practice of Urban Economics,* p. 16.

[24]John Kasarda, "Symposium: The State of the Nation's Cities," *Urban Affairs Quarterly,* Vol. 18 (December 1982), p. 183.

worldwide scale. As a result, cities that are disproportionately built upon these older industries "will remain at a high level of economic distress. Further declines in their total population sizes and employment bases are inevitable."[25]

Given these circumstances, the economic forces dictate a minor, but facilitative, role for government and politics. Effective policies for reviving the economies of particular cities, it is argued, must be based upon the law of comparative advantage. Rather than "squandering public dollars in futile attempts to rebuild inexorably declining urban industries, revised policies should help cities to adapt to new economic realities and exploit their emerging competitive strengths."[26] It is generally agreed that these strengths lie primarily in the business service sectors, particularly administrative, financial, and professional services; in the cultural, recreational, and tourist industries; and in certain "high-technology" industries. This rather clearly means that the Sunbelt cities are expected to enjoy the competitive edge for the immediate future.

The convergence formulation also underlies the neoconservative attack on government. During the New Deal, and especially as a result of the liberal War on Poverty, government expanded its role through exercise of its taxing and spending powers. The regulatory effect of those "well-meaning but wrong-headed" efforts was to put government in opposition to the operation of the free market. For convergence to occur, government will have to be cut back.

The Liberal Alternative: Neoconservative Politics Is the Explanation

In keeping with a more pragmatic, political, and less theoretical orientation, the liberal explanation of the contemporary era is a complex of ideas. First, there is little direct confrontation of the neoconservative explanation of convergence just described. The liberal tendency is to grant that large capital movement is necessary and healthy. Critical liberals like Charles Lindblom have, however, begun to take on the view that "the market" can be a "prison" as well as a liberator.[27] More often the liberal explanation of the economic successes of the Sunbelt is that it is the result of consciously pursued neoconservative political strategies. Neoconservatives have been selling the idealization of a free market for years, they say. The neoconservatives launched a propaganda campaign during the Nixon-Agnew years to discredit liberal social programs. It began in the 1970 congressional election campaign, according to Richard Morris, in which President

[25]Ibid.
[26]Ibid.
[27]Charles Lindblom, "The Market as Prison," *Journal of Politics*, Vol. 44 (May 1982), pp. 234–236.

Nixon ordered Spiro Agnew to "hammer away at the permissiveness theme without letup."[28]

Liberal policies were to be blamed for everything from campus protest, drugs, and pornography to the breakdown of the family. This was known at the time as "The Social Issue." Increasingly, conservatives tied this social theme to the deterioration of cities. "Permissiveness had led to a wave of moral deterioration that was carrying cities to their doom."[29] The final link in the neoconservative strategic chain was to connect increasing costs of social services in the cities with the flight of business. It was such policies as high taxes, pro-consumer laws, high-salaried city civil servants, and liberal welfare benefits, exploited by "cheats," that made the Northeast unable to compete with the Sunbelt.

Needless to say, liberals find the neoconservative "social issue" more a political ploy than an accurate formulation. Herbert Gans, a prominent urban sociologist at Columbia University, puts the liberal response succinctly: "The currently popular notion that federal policies sapped urban moral fibers and bred dependency patterns that prevented cities and their inhabitants from solving their problems themselves is ideological balderdash to rationalize Republican policies for the rich."[30] They argue that the market forces celebrated by neoconservatives have never worked adequately for those who lack the money to enter the market. Gans continues, "In the old days, before the federal government developed urban policies and the free market ruled the cities, poor urban residents suffered from joblessness and disease; overcrowded housing turned into slums; low income areas were wracked by crime; and most other contemporary 'urban' problems existed as well. In fact, they were worse. . . ."[31]

Liberal explanation for the prosperity of the Sunbelt is again political and complex. In general, they note that a great many federal and private sector policy decisions unfairly discriminated against the older cities and favored the Sunbelt. For example, Richard Morris, in detailing a number of these policy biases, discusses the role of the banks in precipitating the New York City "fiscal crisis." The neoconservative formulation is that the banks decided to withdraw from lending to the city in 1975 because they were horrified at the imbalance of the city's budget. But the liberal Morris says, "the banks withdrew from the cities in 1973, well before there was any sound financial basis for concluding that the city was in trouble. The data indicates that banks more precipitated the urban fiscal crisis by driving up debt service costs than reacted to it once it was in full swing."[32]

[28]Richard Morris, *Bum Rap on America's Cities* (Englewood Cliffs, N.J.: Prentice-Hall, 1980), p. 4.
[29]Ibid.
[30]Kasarda, "Symposium," p. 169.
[31]Ibid.
[32]Morris, *Bum Rap on America's Cities*, p. 12.

The Radical Formulation: Uneven
Peripheral Development

Joining the debate at a more theoretical level, radicals would directly dispute the convergence theory. The economic system does not necessarily move toward equilibrium, the noted Swedish economist Gunnar Myrdal, theorized in the mid-1950s. Instead, the process of overall economic growth is a process of "uneven development and deviation amplifying feedback cycles." He explained, "the system is by itself not moving toward any sort of balance but is constantly on the move away from such a situation. In the normal case, a change does not call forth countervailing changes but, instead, supporting changes, which move the system in the same direction as the first change but much further."[33]

Applied to the contemporary period, Myrdal's formulation suggests that we will see a continued state of slow growth and accelerating decline among many of the industrial cities, and those Sunbelt cities that have gained a headstart will expand their economic advantages. In sum, on quite different theoretical bases, radicals and neoconservatives seem to agree in the broad outline of the American urban future.

But this superficial agreement masks crucial differences. Most important, the neoconservative formulation suggests that the "market forces" and "convergence" processes are somehow natural laws—that they have an inevitable constraining character that is not subject to our individual or collective wills; Harvey Molotch, a Marxist political economist, to the contrary: "I believe that urban growth occurs through the mobilization of organized interests."[34] This means that patterns of growth are deliberately created and may be modified by self-consciously undertaken social intervention. Put a bit more concretely, the radical perspective holds a position more like that of the liberal on this particular subject: that the dominant capitalist leadership has deliberately fashioned policies to exploit the resources and other economic advantages of the Sunbelt.

Once having seduced and exploited, the dominant class will abandon when continued growth demands. The individual firms will simply refuse to recognize the public contributions to their success and leave the social costs they have created behind, assuming no responsibility for them. It is that formulation that leads radicals to contradict the neoconservative implication that a region benefits from being "developed." In fact, it may suffer more than it gains. The early evidence is mixed, but it appears that "from all evidence . . . the underclass model has validity in the Sunbelt. If you are poor, in the future you may get something, but

---

[33]Gunnar Myrdal, *Economic Theory and Underdeveloped Regions* (New York: Harper & Row, 1957), p. 13.
[34]Kasarda, "Symposium," p. 172.

you will not get much.''[35] As Molotch sees it, the quality of life in American cities has not at all correlated with the country's international stature or overall economic growth rate. "Indeed some very severe problems for poor people are made possible by the great post war riches that prosperity brought into the public coffers, resulting in the destructive extravagance of urban renewal, as one example.''[36]

Based on this analysis, radicals argue, the accelerating pattern of capitalism in this period will be to allow less and less wealth to trickle down to the working classes in American cities. This is especially so as an international economic order is created. In the new conditions, American cities and workers will have decreasing bargaining power and a smaller share of the wealth when an economic function can easily relocate anywhere in the world it chooses.

The most visible manifestation of uneven peripheral development is the movement of capital—more specifically, the decision of a corporation to close down all or a part of its operations in a particular city. "Corporate flight," or capital mobility, is at the base of much economic dislocation, according to radical analysis. As Bluestone and Harrison point out, "[T]he shocking fact is that between 1969 and 1976 at least 15 million jobs were destroyed in the United States as a result of plant closings and shut downs.''[37] But radicals do not argue for a national policy to prevent capital mobility. "The real problem is the accelerating velocity of capital movement, and the fact the very real social and economic devastation which this . . . causes is rarely considered in the decisions of corporate managers.'' The basic proposal is not to stop capital movement. It is instead to "assure that this transfer of capital from one use or location to another will meet real human needs without disregarding the full impact of such decisions on people and their communities.''[38]

In summary, in the radical analysis, uneven development at the periphery (in the current era, the periphery is in the Sunbelt and in the Third World) is simply the march of capitalism as it accumulates contradictions and exacerbates class conflicts.[39] So while the neoconservative urges that we allow the "natural market forces" to work, the radical presses for national economic policies that recognize capital mobility as both a necessity and a problem.

[35]Peter Lupsha and William Siembieda, "The Poverty of Urban Services in the Land of Plenty: An Analysis and Interpretation," in Perry and Watkins, eds., *The Rise of the Sunbelt Cities*, p. 188.

[36]Kasarda, "Symposium," p. 184. For a more detailed elaboration of this point in historical perspective, see John Mollenkopf, "The Postwar Politics of Urban Development," in William K. Tabb and Larry Sawyers, eds., *Marxism and the Metropolis* (New York: Oxford University Press, 1978), pp. 117–152.

[37]Barry Bluestone, Bennett Harrison, and Lawrence Baker, *Corporate Flight* (Washington, D.C.: A Progressive Alliance Book, 1981), p. 13. Also see Bennett Harrison and Barry Bluestone, The *Deindustrialization of America* (New York: Basic Books, 1982).

[38]Ibid., p. 21.

[39]For a fuller treatment of this perspective in an international context see John Walton, "The International Economy and Peripheral Urbanization," in Fainstein and Fainstein, eds., *Urban Policy under Capitalism*, pp. 119–135.

THE CITY AS SOCIAL ENVIRONMENT

American cities have always generated what we called the "social issue" in the preceding section. The Republican strategy of the 1970s to associate cities with "permissiveness," crime, and general social disorganization is simply the current chapter of a story as old as the country itself. Thomas Jefferson, for example, warned against urbanization: "I view great cities as pestilential to the morals, the health and the liberties of man."[40] We may assume that women were not immune either. In fact, the overwhelming chorus of political and intellectual voices throughout our history has been antiurban.[41] This provides us with an important paradox: Cities are loved as machines of economic production, but despised as social environments.

But the long, careful, and systematic studies of the social environment of the cities does not support the most bold assertion of the antiurbanists. The academic work accomplished in the fields of urban sociology, ecology, and criminology suggests that the presumed association between social "problems" and urbanization is, at the least, too facile. What we will find in this literature is, once again, that it reproduces the scholarly controversies we have been tracing—competing interpretations between neoconservative, liberal, and radical political economies. To make the basis of this controversy clear, we must first understand the ecological perspective.

The Ecology of Cities

As we have just seen, the location and physical character of American cities is primarily determined by economic forces. Urban change is the result of new technologies of production, shifting needs for resources, labor costs, and the like. Urban ecologists have long studied the social effects of city growth. A brief review of that tradition will give us a strong sense of the connections between the economic and social spheres.

Ecology is the study of organisms "at home," in interaction with their living and nonliving environments. Systematic ecological reasoning was first applied to the study of plants in the late nineteenth century,[42] to animal life early in the twentieth century, and to human beings beginning in the 1920s. The earliest and most influential development in the field of human ecology is found in the work of

---

[40]Paul Ford, ed., *The Works of Thomas Jefferson* (New York: G. P. Putnam, 1904), Vol. 9, pp. 146–147.

[41]Morton White and Lucia White, *The Intellectual versus the City* (New York: New American Library, 1962).

[42]Ernst H. Haeckel, *The History of Creation*, (New York: Appleton, 1884), Vol. II. This work, by the biologist Haeckel, appears to be the earliest statement from the ecological perspective.

two Chicago sociologists, Robert E. Park and Earnest W. Burgess.[43] Through the study of ecology—plant, animal, and human—we have come to realize how intricate and carefully balanced is that web of relationships that make up the ecosystem.

Robert Park put the fundamental postulate of human ecology succinctly when he said, "Most, if not all, cultural changes in society will be correlated with changes in territorial organization, and every change in the territorial and occupational distribution of the population will effect changes in the existing culture."[44] In adopting the ecological frame of reference in this chapter, we shall assume that there is an intimate congruity between the social order and physical space, between social and physical distance, and between social differentiation and residential proximity.[45] As a result, a map of a contemporary American city can be understood as "a dramatic example of a geographical division of labor."[46] That map is separated into component parts that are located at different points; yet the components are coordinated. As a result of this spatial differentiation, Scott Greer notes, "Where you live tells those persons with information about a city such things as your general income level, the kind of people you live among, your probable prestige or social honor, and any number of less basic matters."[47] Of course, that's a long way from knowing you intimately, but it's a beginning.

What has all this to say to the study of politics? Most simply, I am assuming that the physical layout of the city affects social relationships, leading to social tensions, which create urban conflict, which necessitates the creation of public policy. We examine that proposition (and don't forget that propositions are less binding than proposals) by reviewing selectively certain of the theories and findings of the field of ecology.

The best-known ecological construct is the formulation of the classical ecologists Park and Burgess. The concentric zone hypothesis is based on the presumption of economic causation, that is, the expectation of potential urban land buyers that the city's economy will expand is what causes the social differentiation they describe.

While it has been decisively criticized in many of its particulars, it still provides useful introductory insight into the urban shaping forces. The hypothesis states that the pattern of growth of cities can best be understood as producing five concentric zones, each zone defining an area of distinctive land use (see Figure 3.1):

[43]See, particularly, Robert E. Park, Ernest W. Burgess, and Roderick D. McKenzie, eds., *The City* (Chicago: University of Chicago Press, 1925).

[44]Robert Park, *Human Communities* (New York: The Free Press, 1952), p. 14.

[45]Ralph Tomlinson, *Urban Structure* (New York: Random House, 1969), p. 9.

[46]Scott Greer, *Governing the Metropolis* (New York: John Wiley & Sons, 1962), p. 31.

[47]Ibid.

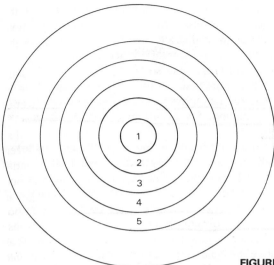

FIGURE 3.1   Concentric Zone Theory

1. *The central business district.* The physical center of the city, this zone is the site of the focal activities of urban life. It is the retail district with its department stores, shops, office buildings, banks, hotels, theaters.

2. *The zone in transition.* Encircling the downtown area is a zone of mixed uses: some business and light manufacturing, but primarily deteriorating residences and rooming houses—slums, to put it indelicately. Here are the regions of poverty and of organized and unorganized crime and vice. In many American cities, the zone in transition has been inhabited primarily by colonies of recent immigrants who must have low-cost housing and close proximity to work.

3. *The zone of independent workers' homes.* This area is inhabited by industrial workers who have escaped from the zone in transition but who desire to live within easy access of their work. In American cities, the second generations of immigrant families have lived here.

4. *The zone of better residences.* Here are more expensive, usually single-family dwellings, upper-income apartment buildings, and occasionally exclusive restricted neighborhoods.

5. *The commuter's zone.* In this zone are located spotty developments of satellite cities connected to the central city by lines of rapid transit. Park and Burgess assumed that these satellite cities would be populated largely by upper-income residents who could afford the relatively high cost of commuting.

These physical divisions of the city were obviously also social areas: as the classical ecologists noted, the central business district, for example, is predominantly a homeless area, the rooming house district is the habitat of the working-class family, the area in which the first immigrants settled is the locus of the patriarchal family transplanted from Europe, and so on.[48]

The concentric zone model is a particularly useful formulation of urban growth patterns because it emphasizes the intimate connections between physical differentiation and social differentiation. Social differentiation, by its nature, creates basic political cleavages.

The classical ecologist formulation is also of interest to students of urban politics because it links social differences in the city with growth itself. Growth creates the five zones of the model. Economic and technical advances permit mobility, that is, "change of residence, change of employment, or change of location of any utility or service."[49] Growth creates the tendency for each zone in the model to extend its area by invading the next outer zone. So as more working-class people move out of the zone in transition into the workers' residential zone, that zone becomes larger, creating the conditions that led earlier residents of that area to relocate in the next outward zone. In this way the forces of growth may be said to have a logic of their own. A number of social conflicts are generated in this process. When minority group residents begin to invade a previously homogeneous area, for example, the conflict can be violent.

The zone in transition is a particularly fascinating element of the concentric circle model. Here are the "problem" groups, the vice and crime subcultures, the poor, the black, the Bohemian subcultures. When we speak of the "urban problem," most of us are thinking primarily of this area. Many proposed solutions aim at eliminating or rehabilitating slums. Such solutions, however, tend to ignore the insight of the classical ecologists—that the slum is an unintended consequence of urban growth forces. In the Burgess formulation, the zone in transition results when economic persons do what comes naturally. Slums develop because the land that is immediately adjacent to the central business district is increasing in value while the buildings on the land are decreasing in value. This happens because the land may be a potential site for high-income-producing uses, but the building on the land will probably have to be torn down to accommodate the new function.

Let us illustrate the process with a hypothetical lot near a central business district: Currently on the lot is a large rambling old home, built 100 years ago by a wealthy resident at a time when the city was smaller and the site was on its periphery. The growth of the central business district has made this lot closer and closer to the center of the city. At some point, a local real estate speculator, anticipating that the lot would some day be a possible business site, purchases it,

[48]Robert Park, "Urban Areas," in T. V. Smith and L. D. White, eds., *Chicago: An Experiment in Social Science Research* (Chicago: University of Chicago Press, 1929), pp. 114–123.

[49]R. D. McKenzie, "The Scope of Human Ecology," *Publications of the American Sociological Society,* Vol. 20 (1926); pp. 141–154.

hoping that its value will continue to increase. The best strategy is to hold onto the property until the purchaser can obtain the highest possible price for it. In the meantime the owner must minimize any losses by making some use of the house. It is reasonably inexpensive to divide the house into small apartments or rooms to rent. Improvements seem out of the question since our speculator knows that money put into the building comes out of the eventual profit margin when he or she sells the site for the land. The owner's rational economic strategy is simply to minimize costs while the land increases in value. Thus is born the rat-infested, badly kept-up, inadequately heated tenement so characteristic of slum areas in America. The "heavy" in this drama—the slumlord of popular rhetoric—turns out to be not a hard-hearted Simon Legree but, rather, the hero from the urban growth drama: a Mr. or Ms. America doing business as usual. Small wonder one of the slogans of the ecology movement has become, "We have met the enemy and he is us."

We should not take the tenets of classical ecology too literally. They imply unnecessary determinism of economic and biological forces.[50] No area of the city can be assumed to be "natural" in the sense that its location is inevitable.[51] It has been shown that many portions of the city are not put to their highest economic use at all. Some are deliberately kept as they are for more symbolic reasons: The scenic old Beacon Hill area of Boston, an upper middle-income residential area, is an example of symbolic land use. So, too, is Central Park on Manhattan Island. Moreover, the classical ecological viewpoint does not help us to understand contemporary midcity blight.[52]

Certain criticisms of the classical model have led to a variety of alternative generalizations. Descriptions of patterned urban differentiation by economic and social function have included sector, radial, and multiple nuclei.[53] The existence of differing spatial distributions of these functions does not detract from our simple, central observation, namely, that economic forces importantly structure the social relations of a city.

That social relations are correlated with spatial relations simply means that persons sharing similar values, interests, or needs tend to cluster together and to

[50]Milla Alihan, *Social Ecology: A Critical Analysis* (New York: Columbia University Press, 1938). An excellent collection of articles defining and critiquing the classical, neo-orthodox, social-area analysis and sociocultural approaches is found in George Theodorson, *Studies in Human Ecology* (New York: Harper & Rowe, 1961). See also Warner E. Gettys, "Human Ecology and Social Theory," *Social Forces,* Vol. 18 (May 1940), pp. 469–476.

[51]See Milla Aliham, "The Concept of Natural Area," *The American Sociological Review,* Vol. 11 (August 1946), pp. 423–427, and Eshrey Shevky and Wendell Bell, *Social Area Analysis* (Palo Alto, Calif.: Stanford University Press, 1955). These two works describe a technique for designating social areas using census information to determine "social rank," "urbanization," and "segregation" of census tracts within a city.

[52]Nan Sigel, "The Unchanging Area in Transition," *Land Economics,* Vol. 43 (August 1967), p. 392.

[53]For a simple review of these descriptions and additional bibliography, see Ralph Tomlinson, *Urban Structure.*

separate themselves from unlike groups. There are three distinctive bases of urban social segregation: ethnicity, social rank, and life-style.[54] First, we note that the larger American cities are mosaics, composed of elements of cultures from other parts of the world. New York City, for example, contains settlements of immigrants from virtually every nationality of any size—Irish, Italian, German, Japanese, and so on. This kind of social differentiation is called "ethnicity."

Second, people tend to distinguish among themselves on the basis of their jobs. People in similar occupations receive much the same share of goods and services and of the social advantages. They may attain similar educational levels. Furthermore, when people become accustomed to, or immersed in, the world of their jobs, they come to share "a way of looking at things, of conceptualizing and evaluating, which is unique to [their] kind of job and no other. In other words . . . [they] develop little cultural worlds of their own."[55] Sub-cultures emerge, based on differences in occupation, income, and education. The term applied to this basis of social differentiation is "social rank."

The third ground of social groupings we call "life-style." There are some who, regardless of their ethnic origins or social rank, prefer a particular mode of living. They may be prepared to pay the costs of living near the beach, for example, to permit a life-style oriented to swimming, surfing, or voyeurism. And in most major cities there is an area like Park Avenue in New York where the wealthy bear extraordinarily high rents to have the advantages of easy access to restaurants, theaters, and museums. It is the life-style of urban wealth that determines their location. Such social segregation by ethnicity, social rank, and life-style means that people develop differing expectations as to what goals the city ought to serve.

In addition to these patterns of social segregation that we are accustomed to think of as "normal," we also associate urbanization with social pathologies. A brief review of several social manifestations of urban life will serve to heighten our sense of the connection between the social environment and politics as well as to foreshadow some of the political issues that cities face. In general, this section deals with some of the highlights of the vast literature dealing with social disorganization.

Theories of Social Disorganization

We are all familiar with the view that cities are sick—that they are, as Thomas Jefferson described them, "hotbeds of vice and crime." Cities, from this perspective, incubate vast and deadly personal and social pathologies, ranging from personal psychoses to organized crime. A whole tradition of sociological study has grown up around the assumption that urban sickness is the result of the

[54]This formulation is based on the Shevky-Bell typology of social area analysis.

[55]Scott Greer, *Governing the Metropolis* (New York: John Wiley & Sons, 1962), p. 25.

social disorganization that has resulted from the breaking apart of society on the reefs of change. Social disorganization generally means "the disruption of relations between the functioning parts of a social system so as to jeopardize the attainment of common goals."[56] Marshall Clinard, among others, specifically traces social disorganization to urbanization: "Urbanism, with its mobility, impersonality, individualism, materialism, norm and role conflicts, and rapid social change appears to be associated with higher incidence of deviant behavior."[57] Others, like Winslow, prefer to think of certain forms of deviant behavior as primarily a result of social transition. As change renders old modes questionable, new modes may emerge. Some individuals may withdraw, still others may engage in violence or politics, in an effort to adapt.[58] Whatever the best explanation—disorganization or transition—deviancy correlates well with the rise of urbanism. The classical ecologists made those associations explicit; Walter Reckless summarized their conclusions:

> Conventional crime, delinquency, mental illness in general and schizophrenia in particular, suicide, prostitution, vagrancy, dependency, illegitimacy, infant mortality, as well as associated problems such as high death and disease rates, have been found to vary with the areas of the city. The highest rates are in Zones I and II [of the concentric zone model] and become successively lower out of this area. The evidence on alcoholism and the manic-depressive psychoses does not show quite this pronounced pattern for, although there are probably higher rates in Zones I and II, the differences are not as marked from one part of the city to another.[59]

The simple formulation was that cities create social disorganization and social disorganization causes deviancy. This assumption of the classical formulation has been dismissed by subsequent research on deviant behavior; the concept "social disorganization" itself has not even stood up.[60]

William F. Whyte's criticism is typical.[61] Based on his 3½-year observation of an Italian slum district, he concluded that immigrant slums were not disorganized at all. Whyte, along with subsequent students, found subdivisions of informal associations and relationships among those associations in the slum. As he found it, the problem of slum life was not lack of organization but "failure of the

[56]Robert Winslow, *Society in Transition: A Social Approach to Democracy* (New York: The Free Press, 1970), p. 66.

[57]Marshall Clinard, *Sociology of Deviant Behavior* (New York: Holt, Rinehart and Winston, 1968), p. 96.

[58]See Winslow, *Society in Transition*, Chap. 2.

[59]Walter C. Reckless, *Vice in Chicago* (Chicago: University of Chicago Press, 1933).

[60]See Ernest Mourer, "Methodological Problems in Social Disorganization," *American Sociological Review*, Vol. 6 (December 1941), pp. 839–852.

[61]William F. Whyte, *Street Corner Society* (Chicago: University of Chicago Press, 1942).

slum's own social organization to mesh with the structure—the middle-class structure—of society around it.''[62] Eliot Liebow has drawn much the same conclusions about the streetcorner society surrounding his subjects, the poor black residents of Washington, D.C.[63] These findings press upon us the realization that the city is not disorganized so much as it is the locus of a variety of people with differing goals and interests and differing abilities to accomplish them.

In sum, the view that cities cause urban social problems is inadequate. Capitalism's transformations change cities and that creates changing personal and social environments. So the more intelligent questions are: (1) what is the nature of those changes; (2) what is the differential ability of individuals and socially differentiated groups to benefit from those changes; and (3) which individuals and groups will be substantially impaired in adapting to these changes? What we mean by urban social problems, then, are simply those difficulties that result from the urban growth dynamic. These problems have familiar designations: individual deviancy, family instability, anomie, poverty, welfare dependency, and urban and suburban segregation, for example. Instead of describing these problems each in turn, let us understand them once again as having different origins, manifestations, and solutions, depending upon the political-economic ideology of the analyst. That point can best be made by briefly sketching the underlying assumptions of the liberal-inspired War on Poverty, the neoconservative critique of such a perspective found in the writing of Edward Banfield, and the contrasting perspective of a variety of radicals.

Liberal Analysis of the Social Environment: The War on Poverty

Standing in the White House rose garden, Lyndon Johnson signed the Economic Opportunity Act of 1964. In expansive language, he declared his and the nation's intent to ''eradicate poverty among its people.'' The beginnings of the War on Poverty were in the Kennedy administration. Chairman of the Council of Economic Advisers, Walter Heller, was given in June 1963 responsibility for planning a coordinated antipoverty program. The program was already substantially underway when Johnson became president, but Johnson embraced it without much reservation: ''That's my kind of program. It will help people,'' he told Heller.[64]

---

[62]Whyte as paraphrased by Winslow, *Society in Transition,* p. 60.

[63]Eliot Liebow, *Tally's Corner* (Boston: Little, Brown, 1967).

[64]There are a number of discussions in the history of the program; see, particularly, Sar Leviten, *The Great Society's Poor Law* (Baltimore: Johns Hopkins University Press, 1969); John C. Donovon, *The Politics of Poverty* (New York: Pegasus, 1967); Daniel P. Moynihan, *Maximum Feasible Misunderstanding* (New York: The Free Press, 1969); and J. David Greenstone and Paul Peterson, *Race and Authority in Urban Politics* (New York: Russell Sage, 1973).

The assumptions that underlay the antipoverty effort appear relatively clear in retrospect. They were an extension and application of the liberal approach. There was no critique of capitalism implicit or explicit in the program as formulated. It was assumed that the root cause of most urban social problems was lack of access to the rewards of the economic system as then constituted. The other crucial assumptions were (1) poverty is not so much the result of the failure of individuals as it is the failure of the system. This meant that we all had some collective responsibility to aid the "less fortunate." There was, however, some departure from the traditional welfare pattern among the antipoverty planners. Some of the inner circle of planners felt that public welfare bureaucracies actually impeded the process of aiding the needy. For this reason, many of the programs initially sought to bypass welfare and local political structures. This led to (2) a decentralized program of community-based organization and action that sought to promote what proved to be one of the most controversial goals of the legislation—"maximum feasible participation" of the poor. Community action agencies (CAAs) were the organizational cornerstone of the War on Poverty. They were composed of governing boards drawn from the neighborhoods to be served. As it turned out, these agencies proved the lightning rod of criticism of the War on Poverty. There was considerable local political turmoil that resulted when the CAAs began to operate and mobilize the poor. As one commentator summarized the experience in San Francisco, "the fight for maximum feasible participation evolved from a contest between the mayor and minority group spokesmen for control of the program into a succession of power struggles within the target areas, and between them and the central administration."[65]

In pursuit of implementation of these basic assumptions, the local area was given the power to decide which of a number of programs authorized by the Economic Opportunity Act it would implement. A brief description of each makes the liberal prescription for solving the social problems of our cities clearer.

1. The Job Corps was to provide vocational education and job training for young people.

2. The Volunteers in Service to America (VISTA) was to be the domestic version of the Peace Corps. It was to provide an opportunity to volunteers to work in public projects or with community action groups.

3. The Head Start Program, the least controversial of the programs, was to provide preschool training for disadvantaged youth.

4. Neighborhood Youth Corps was to provide work experience and vocational training for youth living at home.

[65]Richard Kraemer, *Participation of the Poor* (Englewood Cliffs, N.J.: Prentice-Hall, 1969), p. 66.

This infusion of money and legitimacy into the poor communities of our cities generated considerable turmoil. War on Poverty activists made good press. A community organizer paid by the federal government shown picketing, sitting in, or leading protests against local governments provided a dramatic image of the consequences of the War on Poverty. But the press coverage was less crucial in bringing down the Office of Economic Opportunity than was the political response and effectiveness of the local political process—especially the mayor. A careful study of community action agencies in five large cities concluded that the political influence and ideology of the mayor was the major factor determining the effect of the poverty program.[66] New York Mayor John Lindsay was sympathetic to the program and is widely regarded as having engineered a highly participative program in that city. But Mayor Richard Daley of Chicago saw considerable threat to his political organization and undermined the participatory element.

Scholarly evaluation of the War on Poverty suggests that its impact varied from city to city but that it was most effective in mobilizing the poor when the local agency was relatively free from local political officials. James Vaneco studied 50 local antipoverty programs and found that the most effective ones had emphasized community organization and mobilization of the poor.[67]

These assessments of the War on Poverty rely on the assumption that those programs were "effective" when they drew more of the poor into participation. Theodore Lowi, in his criticism of what he has called "interest group liberalism," argues that more participation by the poor was not really intended to eliminate poverty.[68] Instead, he says, liberals were simply pursuing the pluralist preference for "dealing only with organized claims. . . . To the interest-group liberal, poverty is becoming just another status around which power ought to organize. . . . In so organizing it, poverty is not eliminated, but inconsistency in the manner of governments relation to society is reduced."[69]

Although a success for some urban poor, the most important evaluation of the program came from Richard Nixon. After his second inaugural, he set out to discredit and dismantle the effort. He appointed Howard Phillips to head the Office of Economic Opportunity. Phillips promptly announced that it had been a "failure."

[66]J. David Greenstone and Paul Peterson, *Race and Authority in Urban Politics* (New York: Russell Sage, 1973).

[67]James Vaneco, "Community Mobilization and Institutional Change: The Influence of the Community Action Program in Large Cities," *Social Science Quarterly*, Vol. 50 (December 1969), pp. 609–630. For corroborative findings, see Kenneth Clark and Jeanette Hopkins, *A Relevant War on Poverty* (New York: Harper & Row, 1968), Chap. 5.

[68]Theodor Lowi, *The End of Liberalism* (New York: W. W. Norton, 1969), pp. 79–85.

[69]Ibid., p. 83.

The Neoconservative Critique: Edward Banfield and the "Lower Class"

The riots in the ghettos of Newark, Detroit, and a number of other cities in the summer of 1967 proved another turning point in the contemporary history of urban conflict. Even though the Presidential Commission on Civil Disorders (the Kerner Report, as it was popularly known) blamed a long history of racial discrimination for these violent outbursts, a large number of Americans began to reformulate their positions. What was predicted to be "white backlash" did not materialize immediately. No quick turn of public opinion occurred, although in certain areas "law and order" mayors and officials were elected (Frank Rizzo in Philadelphia is a notable example). But political shifts toward the neoconservative position came slowly and steadily from this point.

The influential book by Edward Banfield, *The Unheavenly City*, marked an important turning point for scholarly formulation of urban politics as well. Along with James Q. Wilson, both of Harvard at the time they wrote, Banfield could be credited as co-founder of the subdiscipline of urban politics. Their book, *City Politics*, set the research agenda for urban research for many years. It did so in a formulation that fits with what I have earlier identified as "pluralism," the method of liberalism. But Banfield was discomforted by what he thought to be the failures of the Great Society program, and in *The Unheavenly City*, he moves to embrace neoconservative assumptions. At first, Banfield was popularly ignored, although his work was immediately influential among academics. But in 1971, when he moved from Harvard to the University of Pennsylvania, he suddenly found himself the center of public controversy on a national scale. Protesting students dubbed him "Public Pig Number One" and often disrupted his classes. Many found in his book a justification for racial discrimination, punitive criminal laws, and a reversal of the entire agenda of New Deal liberal efforts at achieving social equality. Richard Todd, writing in *The Atlantic Monthly* magazine, probably puts the reason for the public response more accurately when he suggests that Banfield concludes that one of our most serious national problems "is the growth of an unreasonable ethic of hope and charity."[70]

In any case, Banfield's formulation, when examined carefully, presents a strikingly different analysis of the nature of the social problems that we confront in the American city. Banfield contends that "certain styles of life that are learned in childhood and passed on as a kind of collective heritage operate (within the limits set by the logic of growth) to give the city its characteristic form and most of its

---

[70]Richard Todd, "Theory of the Lower Class: Edward Banfield, the Maverick of Urbanology," *The Atlantic Monthly*, Vol. 226 (September 1970), p. 55.

problems.''⁷¹ These life-styles Banfield associates not with race so much as with "class," which he defines in a unique way. He avoids the usual sociological meaning of class as relative social standing measured by attributes like income, education, or occupation; instead, he defines class in terms of the individual's "psychological orientation toward providing for a more or less distant future.''⁷² The upper classes are able, according to Banfield, to imagine a future and to discipline themselves to sacrifice present for future satisfactions; the lower class is not. As a result, the lower class becomes a "problem" population. Banfield's description of "lower"-class behavior is worth quoting at length:

> The Lower Class. At the present-oriented end of the scale, the lower-class individual lives from moment to moment. If he has any awareness of a future, it is of something fixed, fated, beyond his control: things happen to him, he does not make them happen. Impulse governs his behavior, either because he cannot discipline himself to sacrifice a present for a future satisfaction or because he has no sense of the future. He is therefore radically improvident: whatever he cannot consume immediately he considers value-less. His bodily needs (especially for sex) and his taste for "action" take precedence over everything else—and certainly over any work routine. He works only as he must to stay alive, and drifts from one unskilled job to another, taking no interest in the work.
>
> The lower-class individual has a feeble, attenuated sense of self; he suffers from feelings of self-contempt and inadequacy, and is often apathetic or dejected. . . . In his relations with others he is suspicious and hostile, aggressive yet dependent. He is unable to maintain a stable relationship with a mate; commonly he does not marry. He feels no attachment to community, neighbors, or friends (he has companions, not friends), resents all authority (for example, that of policemen, social workers, teachers, landlords, employers), and is apt to think that he has been "railroaded" and to want to "get even." He is a nonparticipant: he belongs to no voluntary organizations, has no political interests, and does not vote unless paid to do so.⁷³

Banfield's analysis of class as an urban "given" brings him to the brink of contending that nothing substantial can be done about the problems of the lower class; at one point he reports that "strong correlations have been shown to exist between IQ scores and socioeconomic status, and some investigators have claimed that the correlations are largely attributable to genetic factors.''⁷⁴ Then, he backs away somewhat, saying that he assumes that time horizon (the ability to anticipate the future) is a trait passed on to an individual early in childhood—still implying

---

⁷¹Edward Banfield, *The Unheavenly City,* p. 46.
⁷²Ibid.
⁷³Ibid., p. 53.
⁷⁴Ibid., p. 48.

strong determinism. The policy implications of Banfield's interpretation obviously call for measures designed to control the worst behaviors of the problem groups, since the prospects for changing them are remote. Some of his many recommendations are (1) paying "problem families" to send infants to day schools designed to "bring the children into normal culture," (2) permitting the police to "stop and frisk" in high-crime areas, (3) abridging the freedoms of those who are extremely likely to commit violent crimes by preventative detention, and (4) prohibiting "live television coverage of riots and/or incidents likely to provoke them."[75]

The most fundamental point of contrast between Banfield and the liberalism of the War on Poverty is that Banfield clearly embraces an individualist rather than a structuralist view of the causes of the central social problems of the city. Radical political economists, we are about to see, share the liberal assumption, but they press it further to conclude that it is the mix of capitalism with the American form of urban industrialism that gives us our social problems.

Radicals and the Social Issue: Blaming the Victim, Internal Colonialism, and Class Conflict

For most radicals the urban social environment is generated by capitalism's requirements, and "the ethos of capitalism is systematized inequality."[76] The urban social setting, as in all of American society, is given its distinctive character by the realization and necessity of economic inequality: "Very early we recognize that a satisfactory life will consist, for most of us, in fitting into some slot or other that is specifically defined as one rung on an ascending ladder of rewards and opportunities. Not to fit into that structure is to claim, literally, the status of a misfit."[77] Those who do not fit come in great variety: juvenile delinquent, thief, sex offender, suicide, prostitute, welfare recipient. Such deviancy is explained by neoconservatives largely in terms like Banfield's as wrong choices made deliberately by individuals. Radicals are inclined to call that "blaming the victim." Radicals insist that they are not denying individual free will when they argue that socioeconomic structures make it nearly impossible for some members of the society to make their way successfuly. What they are saying is that when the system is relatively closed to certain individuals, their most reasonable (even "rational"—as a public choice theorist might use the term) choice is to make use of opportunities and opportunity structures that are socially labeled "deviant." When you are hungry and cannot buy bread, you steal it, for example. When such deviancy becomes necessary on a broad scale, it is likely that the social structure is

[75]Ibid.

[76]Philip Green, *The Pursuit of Inequality* (New York: Pantheon Books, 1981), p. 1.

[77]Ibid.

more the source of the problem than is individual choice making. To blame the deviant in those circumstances is to condemn someone for making the best out of a poor situation.

Most important is the institutional structure of capitalism that requires inequalities and, in particular, a lower class. If there were no lower class, capitalists would need to create it because there is a need for a cheap and flexible labor supply. It is, therefore, "class" that is the central operating feature of the urban social environment. As Tabb and Sawyers summarize it, "the physical and social structure of the city is seen by Marxists as the evolving product of the social forces of production and the class relations they engender."[78]

It is the class struggle for space that creates what the classical ecologists were describing in the concentric zonal pattern. Segregation by economic interests produced segregation of social types, thereby generating political conflict. It is this perspective that leads neo-Marxists to the contention that the black ghetto is best understood as an "internal colony."[79] As with the colonialism against which the Founding Fathers rebelled, and the colonialism that keeps many of the Third World countries in economic subordination, the urban ghetto bears the burden of providing an inexpensive resource that capitalism requires. In the case of the black ghetto, that resource is labor. Tabb contends that the economic relations of the ghetto to the local economy closely parallel those between Third World nations and the industrially advanced countries. Specifically, he finds the following similarities: (1) The ghetto has a relatively low per capita income and a high birth rate. (2) Its residents are for the most part unskilled. (3) Businesses lack capital and managerial know-how. (4) Local markets are limited. (5) The incidence of credit default is high. (6) Little saving takes place and what is saved usually is not invested locally. (7) Goods and services tend to be "imported"; only the simplest and most labor-intensive goods and services are produced locally. (8) The one basic export is labor. (9) Aggregate demand for this export does not increase in proportion to the growth of the size of the labor force and unemployment is prevalent. (10) Consumer goods are advertised continuously on radio and television, constantly reminding ghetto residents of the availability of goods and services that they are unable to buy. (11) Welfare and other governmental transfers are needed to provide the most fundamental needs of the ghetto residents. (12) Local businesses are owned in large numbers by nonresidents, many of whom are of the dominant class. (13) Important jobs in the local economy (police, teachers, letter carriers) are held by outsiders.[80]

[78]Tabb and Sawyers, *Marxism and the Metropolis*, p. 8. It should be noted that the term "class" as it appears in the neo-Marxist usage is more in accord with traditional social science usage than is Banfield's. What Banfield means is something more like "life-style" than class. Weber's definition of class found class defined "exclusively by economic interests in the possession of goods and opportunities for income."

[79]This viewpoint is carefully argued in William Tabb, *The Political Economy of the Black Ghetto* (New York: W. W. Norton, 1970).

[80]Ibid., pp. 22–23.

It is this colonial pattern that explains the need for a welfare system. That system is as much maligned by radicals as by neoconservatives, but again for quite different reasons. To the radical, the welfare system performs a dual function: It keeps the exploited quiet and docile, and it regulates their flow into the jobs the local economy has for them. "Relief arrangements are ancillary to economic arrangements," according to Francis Fox Piven and Richard Cloward. Their basic function is to regulate labor, and they do that in two general ways: First, when mass unemployment leads to riots or other turmoil, relief programs are initiated or expanded to absorb and control enough of the unemployed to restore order. Then, as the turbulence subsides, the relief system is cut back, expelling those who are needed into the labor market. "Some of the aged, the disabled, the insane, and others who are of no use as workers are left on the relief rolls, and their treatment is so degrading and punitive as to instill in the laboring masses a fear of the fate that awaits them should they relax into beggary and pauperism."[81]

This pattern of blunting the forces of emergent class conflict is part of the radical explanation for why there has historically been so little apparent class warfare in America. Ira Katznelson, in a careful examination of Washington Heights–Inwood (a heterogeneous working-class community in Manhattan north of Harlem), provides a much fuller explanation of some of the other forces that have kept working-class consciousness from generating class warfare.[82] Particularly important, he finds, are some of the consequences of the schism between work and social life.

To summarize the radical, particularly neo-Marxist position, the economic system is the fundamental cause of the pathologies of the urban social order. Capitalism has developed a number of devices for deflecting attention from that fact and for preventing the victims from developing the class consciousness that would be a necessary prerequisite for bringing class conflict. The victims blame themselves and each other and, most important, do not challenge the power of the dominant economic class.

POLITICAL CONSEQUENCES OF THE URBAN ENVIRONMENT

Without using the term, we have thus far been examining "urban culture." Without stating the assumption, we have been proceeding in agreement with anthropologist Ruth Benedict that "the life history of the individual is first and foremost an accommodation to the patterns and standards traditionally handed

---

[81]Francis Fox Piven and Richard Cloward, *Regulating the Poor: The Functions of Public Welfare* (New York: Pantheon, 1971), p. 3.

[82]Ira Katznelson, *City Trenches: Urban Politics and the Patterning of Class in the United States* (New York: Pantheon, 1981).

down in his community."[83] So let us now define culture as the habitual ways of thinking, feeling, and behaving that characterize a society. The culture is its humanly created heredity. And let us further recognize that "socialization" is the process by which we transmit and learn about the culture. As we begin, it is also important to recognize how we come to know about political culture: "For the most part we do not first see, and then define; we define first and then see," Journalist Walter Lippman told us in the 1920s. "In the great blooming, buzzing confusion of the outer world we pick out what our culture has already defined for us, and we tend to perceive that which we have picked out in the form stereotyped for us by our culture."[84]

The proposition that we have been pursuing relative to the urban political culture can be put most simply as capitalism has given the American urban culture its fundamental shape—physically and socially. Whether that is good or bad, changeable or static, is a matter of dispute. As we shall also affirm in this section, the economic order does not simply determine everything in the urban environment. Politics provides the basis for action in accordance with a vareity of values—economic being but one.

The study of political culture and political socialization is not very old, and its findings are unevenly distributed across the range of questions that most concern students of city politics. For example, given the importance of economics in general and capitalism in particular, one would think that studies of how capitalism is culturally transmitted would have a large place in our literature. In fact, neither economists nor political scientists have made careful study of political-economic socialization. So much of what is said here will necessarily be suggestive, based as it is on a handful of studies rather than on a full research tradition. The factors most relevant to an understanding of the contemporary urban political environment are (1) the low levels of citizen trust in politics, (2) residential mobility as it affects neighborhood stability and politics, and (3) severely limited local authority. As we proceed with these topics, it will be quite clear that it is not readily possible to distinguish urban from nonurban effects. Since most of America is urban, it is probably a waste of time to try to make such a distinction. But it is also not particularly necessary to do so. What the anthropologist Clifford Geertz has said of that academic discipline might just as well be adapted to the study of urban politics: We don't study cities as much as we study politics in cities.[85]

Low Levels of Citizen Trust in Politics

Americans express declining trust in government. Research on public opinion shows some disputed findings but strong agreement that on most indicators

---

[83]Ruth Benedict, *Patterns of Culture* (New York: Mentor, 1934), p. 2.

[84]Walter Lippman, *Public Opinion* (New York: Macmillan, 1922), p. 81.

[85]Clifford Geertz, *The Interpretation of Cultures* (New York: Basic Books, 1973), p. 22.

Americans' trust of government in general reached a modern high of over 75 percent in the early 1960s. Steady erosion in that trust occurred, so that by the beginning of the decade of the 1980s, approximately 65 percent could trust the government only some of the time or hardly ever.[86] Even more Americans, 76 percent, think that governments waste a lot of their tax money, and 71 percent think that a few big interests run the government for their own benefit. As Everett Ladd concludes, "In record numbers, Americans see government as getting too powerful, as run for a few interests, as untrustworthy, as indifferent to popular needs, and as profligate."[87] Most of that reaction focuses on politics and politicians rather than on the institutions themselves, apparently. Only 25 percent of adult Americans think a big change in our form of government is needed. And when specifically asked, 67 percent say the problem is because of the individuals in office.

Such a strong trend in attitudes toward politicians may also be related to general feelings about the economy. Consumer confidence also dipped sharply in the late 1970s. In the first quarter of 1978, 50 percent of those polled expressed confidence about the short-term outlook for the economy; just one year later, that figure was 35 percent.[88]

The strong suggestion in the literature of political socialization is that declining trust is more a matter of reaction to specific contemporary conditions than it is a product of, say, parental transmission. The election of Ronald Reagan to the presidency in 1980, for example, produced a turnaround in the long-term trend of declining trust. The Center for Political Studies of the University of Michigan reported that between 1980 and 1982, political trust rose sharply among Republicans, less rapidly among Independents, and slightly among Democrats.[89] Analysis of the reasons for the turnaround suggests that confidence in government rose primarily among those attracted to the neoconservative argument that government had grown too large and powerful.[90]

This general pattern, of course, masks a great deal of variation. A number of studies have, for example, turned up important racial and subcultural differences in trust of government. It would appear that such a grouping plays a more important role in determining orientation to government than does region, state, or particular city. These studies have paid special attention to racial differences in political trust. Once again, particular situations appear to play a central role.

[86]Survey materials are from the Center for Political Studies of the Institute for Social Research, University of Michigan, Election Studies. Also see the exchange between Patrick Caddell, "Trapped in a Downward Spiral," and Warren Miller, "Misreading the Public Pulse," *Public Opinion,* Vol. 2 (October–November 1979), pp. 2–15, 60.

[87]Everett Ladd "Note to Readers," in ibid., p. 27.

[88]Caddell, "Trapped in a Downward Spiral," p. 6.

[89]Arthur Miller, "Is Confidence Rebounding?" *Public Opinion,* Vol. 6 (June–July 1983), p. 18.

[90]See M. Kent Jennings and Richard Niemi, *Generations and Politics: A Panel Study of Young and Their Parents* (Princeton N.J.: Princeton University Press, 1981).

According to Paul Abraham, the summer of 1967, which saw unprecedented rioting in the urban black ghettos, was a turning point in black trust. Reviewing the studies conducted at that time, he found that "Blacks are less trusting of whites in twenty-four of thirty-three surveys conducted during that summer."[91]

Unfortunately, there is but a handful of studies of the attitudes of other subcultures toward government. The few studies of Hispanics find few differences between the Hispanic and Anglo attitudes.[92] Several studies find that white suburban children have high levels of trust as do the Amish.[93] And studies of relatively poor white Appalachian children show that they have low levels of trust.[94]

Interestingly, women as potential office holders appear to have benefited from the general decline of trust. A 1976 Gallup Poll found that 71 percent of all Americans thought we would be governed as well or better if we had more women in politics.[95] A political consultant, working in San Diego local elections, told me in 1983 that it was worth 20 percent of the vote to be a woman candidate.

Residential Mobility and Neighborhood Instability

One of the clearer features of American urban life is that it is highly differentiated. "Unlikes" come in close contact with one another. "I live in Houston, but I don't come from Houston" one of my friends emphasizes. That statement is made in pride; it suggests "cosmopolitanism." Most Europeans find such American attitudes puzzling. Pride in, and identification with, one's locality is more the norm there. One of the most central reasons for Americans' lack of commitment to a locality is the overwhelming fact of mobility. Just as a rough indicator of the residential change pattern in the United States, in the four years between March 1975 and March 1979, 40 percent of the total population changed residence.[96] In the one year between 1975 and 1976, 17 percent of the population

[91]Paul Abramson, *Political Attitudes in America* (San Francisco: W. H. Freeman, 1983), p. 213.

[92]Chris Garcia, *Political Socialization of Chicano Children* (New York: Praeger Publishers, 1973).

[93]Dean Jaros et al., "The Malevolent Leader: Political Socialization in an American Sub-culture,"*American Political Science Review*, Vol. 62 (June 1968), pp. 564–575, and Dean Jaros and Kenneth Kolson, "The Multifarious Leader: Political Socialization of Amish, 'Yanks,' Blacks," in Richard Neimi, ed., *The Politics of Future Citizens* (San Francisco: Jossey-Bass, 1974), pp. 41–62.

[94]Jaros, "The Malevolent Leader."

[95]For a study that traces this phenomenon to "political culture" see, D. B. Hill, "Political Culture and Female Political Representation," *Journal of Politics*, Vol. 43 (February 1981), pp. 159–168.

[96]Department of Commerce, Bureau of the Census, *Current Population Reports, Geographical Mobility: March 1975 to March 1979*, Series P-20, No. 33 (Washington, D.C.: Government Printing Office, 1980), pp. 2–3.

moved. Moreover, certain people are well above that high rate. Seventy-two percent of the age group 25 to 29 years moved between 1975 and 1979. The least mobile were those 75 years and older, of whom 16 percent moved in the same four-year period. Educational attainment accelerates the rate of mobility; only 26 percent of those who had an eighth grade education or less moved, whereas 48 percent of those with at least some college education changed residences between 1976 and 1979. What such figures roughly suggest is that economic demands are an important factor in mobility. As anyone who has tried to put together grass-roots political organizations in the Sunbelt cities knows, mobility inhibits the development of political organization. There appears to be an important connection between economic change and local political vitality.

Many have examined the reasons for American mobility, but one provocative explanation has been offered by Richard Sennett. Americans would rather move than fight, he says. Middle-class families, in particular, socialize children in a pattern that produces "a guilt-over-conflict syndrome." A good life, the family life experience teaches, is a conflict-free life. Disagreement between family members is strongly suppressed, and in such a way as to suggest that no matter what the justice, the bringer of the conflict is wrong. Conflict outside the family is also to be avoided. In this way, Sennett speculates, middle-class Americans seek to insulate themselves from the diverse realities of city life. The result for families is that they become "'little islands of propriety, self-contained, intense and narrow in the outlook, self-restrictive and routine in the tenor of their family activities.'"[97]

The personal implications of Sennett's formulation are less important to us here than are the political. First, and most obviously, guilt over conflict is guilt over politics. Our very definition of politics focuses centrally on conflict. To cope with a problem, one must first confront it. Sennett's formulation suggests that we can find the roots of the strong antipolitical bias in American culture in middle-class child-raising patterns. Second, this formulation suggests that middle-class families will be uncomfortable in neighborhoods with people unlike themselves. That, of course, by no means applies solely to middle-class families. But unlike their poorer counterparts, the middle class has the economic ability to exercise choice and move. (In Chapter 4 we will discuss this as the "exit" option.)

Suburban life in many cases offers less diversity and less chance of contact and conflict with unlikes. Politics in middle-class suburbs, then, are likely to be less intense, "safer." And, finally, the guilt-over-conflict syndrome, when coupled with learned attitudes of racism, can be found to provide a cultural disposition toward a number of political phenomena—from antibusing legislation to antiblack voting behavior. Much of that connection is speculative. But a recent study suggests that it is a useful direction for further examination. Donald Kinder and David Sears have done one of the few empirical studies that seeks to determine which of two theoretical formulations best explains white reactions to racial

---

[97]Richard Sennett, *The Uses of Disorder* (New York: Alfred A. Knopf, 1970), p. 60.

political issues: a "realistic group conflict theory" or a "symbolic racism" explanation.[98] By realistic group conflict, they mean "tangible threats blacks might pose to whites' private lives"—economic competition or violence, for example. Symbolic racism is different in that it represents an attitude of "abstract, moralistic resentment of blacks," which is less the product of rational contemporary calculation than of preadult socialization. Using a Los Angeles sample, their findings, "consistently support the symbolic racism hypothesis," which is to say that stereotypical racial attitudes proved to be a major determinant of white voting even for whites who felt no immediate competition or threats from blacks. These findings are a reminder that economic causality should not be overstated. Racism may be reinforced by economic patterns, but it is to some degree an independent explanation of neighborhood instability and political behavior.

The threat of being victimized by crime is also popularly associated with antiurban attitudes and neighborhood instability. As James Q. Wilson has observed, "predatory crime does not merely victimize individuals, it impedes and, in the extreme case, prevents the formation and maintenance of community. By disrupting the delicate nexus of ties, formal and informal, by which we are linked with our neighbors, crime atomizes society and makes of its members mere individual calculators estimating their own advantage."[99] But careful studies leave us unclear as to how much it is real crime and how much it is more abstract "fear of crime" that produces the effects that Wilson so well describes.[100]

One study finds neighborhood attachment (by which they meant both greater affect for the particular neighborhood and the city) to vary among different types of residents. The older residents, the less well-educated, and women all exhibit stronger ties to the city and lower levels of fear of crime. Whatever the reality, candidates for local office became aware during the 1970s that it was mandatory to run proclaiming they were "tough on crime."

Severely Limited Local Authority

A final characteristic of the urban political environment that fundamentally determines the ability of city residents to take control of their urban environment is the lack of local autonomy. More than limited governmental power, American cities are legally powerless to manipulate some of the most central causes of the problems posed in this chapter. More than most, Americans realize what their city

[98]Donald Kinder, "Prejudice and Politics: Symbolic Racism versus Racial Threats to the Good Life," *Journal of Personality and Social Psychology*, Vol. 40 (March 1981), pp. 414–431.

[99]James Q. Wilson, *Thinking About Crime* (New York: Basic Books, 1975), p. 21.

[100]For discussion, an empirical test, and bibliography, see Thomas Hartnagel, "The Perception and Fear of Crime: Implications for Neighborhood Cohesion, Social Activity, and Community Affect," *Social Forces*, Vol. 58 (September 1979), pp. 176–193. Also, see M. Warr, "Accuracy of Public Beliefs About Crime," *Social Forces*, Vol. 59 (December 1980), pp. 456–470.

government does is controlled, mandated, or prohibited by the constitutional, legal context in which it is set. Just to highlight the most essential constraints, cities are legally subordinated to the state, the patterns of state and federal aid to cities has limited the scope of local decision making, and private business decisions can cause the urban economy to flower or die quite outside the direct control of the local government.[101]

The Missing Link: Political-Economic Socialization

What cluster of learning experiences causes some Americans to act politically as neoconservatives? as liberals? as radicals? There are a great many studies on these topics, but they tend to the polemical rather than the careful, analytical ones on which we could rely. By contrast, Kenneth Kenniston has examined political radicals carefully and at some length, but the economic dimension of their thought is severely underdeveloped in his works.[102] Neoconservatives have long complained of the "economic illiteracy" of the American public. But radicals have equally long argued that the emphasis on competitiveness, materialism, and the particular forms of individualism and privatism taught routinely in family and school is implicitly teaching capitalism. Still others might insist that orientation to political economy is less a matter of learning than of adjustment of individuals to the socioeconomic environment in which they find themselves. In the latter case, something more like small-group studies might tell us more than long-term learning processes.

SUMMARY

Scanning the city as an environment for politics, the dominating feature appears to be capitalism. American cities have historically been given their broadest shape by the forces of production and their distinctive characteristics by the particularities of the mix of their economic base. This does not make capitalism a unicausal explanation of city politics. In the first place, capitalism is a developing, not a static system—we traced it from its agrarian origins to its current multinational phase. Moreover, capitalism and urbanism are not precisely synonymous. Many of the forces that emerge within the urban environment are noneconomic.

What the current era of economic development means, offers, threatens is in strong dispute among the neoconservatives, liberals, and radicals. Essentially,

---

[101]For more elaboration of this perspective, see Peterson, *City Limits*.

[102]Kenneth Kenniston, *Young Radicals* (New York: Harcourt, Brace, 1968).

neoconservatives see natural forces of equilibrium likely to restore vital cities after the less viable ones decline. Liberals accuse the neoconservatives of engaging in a politics of discreditation of liberal policies intended to cope with the social problems created by economic and social change. Radicals find capitalism to be the source of the social problems of the city—problems that are the result of "uneven peripheral development" of capitalism in this period and that will produce additional hardships rather than solutions for most Americans.

Differing political-economic orientations also account for such strongly contrasting observations about the nature of the social problems that arise in the cities. While neoconservatives are attracted to the description of social problems as individual failures, liberals and radicals agree that much of the social deviance and crime is the result of systemic failures of capitalism. But while liberals pursue policies designed to ameliorate the effects of capitalism, radicals argue that capitalism requires internal colonies to exploit, and eventually capitalism will have to be abandoned.

Finally, looking to the specifically political dispositions created in the urban environment, it was suggested that distrust of politicians, residential mobility, and limited local control severely constrain the range of policymaking choices currently available to urban decision makers.

Chapter 4

Participants
in Urban Conflict

Just a year after investing your life savings and mortgaging at least 40 percent of your income for the next 30 years to buy your share of the American Dream—a small house—you discover that your neighbor has a zoning variance to build a 400-unit apartment complex on his adjacent property. This is the point at which most of us realize that urban politics are relevant to our personal lives. This is also the point at which we decide whether, and how, to participate in the local political process. Speaking in the more theoretical language of this book, conflict begins when someone perceives a problem. Change in the environment is likely to produce conflicts. Small wonder that cities are virtual conflict generators.

But not all conflict becomes widespread or severe enough to require government action to manage it. For a conflict to become political, it must move beyond mere personal discontent to a more organized and articulated form. That is the subject of this chapter; specifically, what are the institutional patterns by which individuals link themselves to the policymaking, policy applying, or policy adjudicating processes of government? Those "linkage" institutions as they are called by political scientists are interest groups, political parties, elections, or protests. Alternatively, the dissatisfied may choose not to participate and leave.

HOW DO WE DEFINE THE BASICS
OF POLITICAL PARTICIPATION?
IDEOLOGICAL CONFLICT AGAIN

As we think about what we can do about the proposal to build those apartments, we will discover that our perception of what are the relevant "facts"—what are the major operative forces in the situation, who are our potential allies and opponents, and the likelihood that we can do anything about it—are all conditioned by our ideological stance. Neoconservatives, liberals, and radicals have some distinctively different perspectives on the form, function, and effectiveness of the linkage institutions.

The Neoconservative Formulation:
Exit, Voice, or Loyalty

Originally, discussing the decision dilemma of a customer faced with declining quality of the product of a firm that he or she has long patronized, the economist Albert O. Hirschman provides us with a simple and useful formulation.[1] Building an apartment house in our quiet residential neighborhood will make it a less desirable place in which to live, we might think. When faced with declines in perceived product quality, Hirschman tells us, our choices are three: exit, voice, or loyalty.

The "exit" option as we saw in the preceding chapter is one that Americans take often; that is, they exercise their mobility. Exit, then, is any action by which one terminates one's status as a customer, member, or constituent. You can sell your new house and buy another somewhere else.

The "voice" option is the political one. It means bringing the problem to the attention of others and/or those responsible. Voice has all the forms that political participation may take: discussion, organizing, contacting public officials, testifying before public agencies, suing, supporting a candidate for office, running for office oneself, protesting, and sitting in, just to name a few. You can try to change the decision of the local planning commision to allow those apartments to be built. In Hirschman's formulation, the voice option gives those responsible one more chance before the exit option is exercised.

---

[1] Albert O. Hirschman, *Exit, Voice and Loyalty: Responses to Decline in Firms, Organizations and States* (Cambridge, Mass.: Harvard University Press, 1970). For an application of these ideas to local mobility, see John Orbell and Toro Uno, "A Theory of Neighborhood Problem-Solving: Political Action versus Residential Mobility," *American Political Science Review*, Vol. 66 (June 1972), pp. 471–489. Also, see Elaine B. Sharp, "Citizen Response to Urban Service Dissatisfaction: Exit, Voice and Loyalty Options Reconsidered," paper delivered at the 1982 annual meeting of the American Political Science Association, Denver, Colorado.

"Loyalty" as an option means that the citizen/customer can stay with the declining organization in the expectation that "someone will act or something will happen to improve matters."[2] You can just sit tight in your new house and hope that the apartment house will not get built for some reason or hope that you will like having 400 new neighbors.

To make Hirschman's formulation a bit more concrete, let us review a few examples. When members of the Moral Majority show up at a school board meeting to protest the teaching of evolution in the San Diego city schools, they are exercising the voice option. When they do not receive the outcome they desire, that is, when the school board says that creationism does not have the status of a scientific theory, many members of the group exercise the exit option. They take their children out of public schools and put them in their own private ones. Another illustration reminds us that it is not only we small, private citizens who are making these political choices. When U.S. Steel feels pressure to clean up the air it so pollutes the Gary, Indiana, area, its executives exercise voice and threaten exit.[3] When a firm does in fact relocate, it may leave behind a large number of former workers who say "I can't leave Industrial City. All my life has been here. All my friends and family. Everything I live for." They are exercising loyalty.

In the remainder of this chapter we will see how the linkage institutions express voice. But we will not forget that both exit and loyalty are poliltical positions as well.

The Liberal View of Participation:
The Group Theory of Politics

The basic assumption of liberal political economy, especially that version of it that we have called pluralism, is that interest groups are the primary institution that links individual goals to government. This is not to argue that groups entirely replace the individual participant in politics. But, characteristically, individuals will act collectively when they want to enhance their political effect; therefore, "when men act in consistent patterns, it is reasonable to study these patterns and designate them in collective terms."[4]

Pluralists find that groups have an even greater impact in local politics than at other governmental levels. One local councilman interviewed in a major study of city councils explained: "Pressure groups are probably more important in local government . . . because they are right here. You may see them and they see you,

[2]Hirschman, *Exit, Voice, and Loyalty*, p. 78.

[3]Matthew Crenson, *The Unpolitics of Air Pollution* (Baltimore: Johns Hopkins University Press, 1971).

[4]David B. Truman, *The Governmental Process* (New York: Alfred A. Knopf, 1955), p. 29.

and what you do affects them. It's not like in Washington, where half the time a businessman doesn't really know what the result will be for him.''[5]

As the primary institutional link between individuals and government, groups play an important role in a democratic process. The right to "petition government for a redress of grievances'' is fundamental and guaranteed along with the other First Amendment freedoms. The health of local democracy requires that groups be present, active, and to some degree effective. This observation is a necessary antidote to a widespread public view that group action is corrupt on its face, that lobbying is almost always a form of illegitimate pressuring. The legitimacy and importance of the group process has long been recognized by political scientists. Arthur Bentley pronounced the rudiments of the group theory of politics in 1908. Group theory addresses the questions of how groups are formed, what is the basis of their power, and how they affect public policy. As we proceed, we will also see that concern for the group process is not restricted to liberals.

GROUP FORMATION

Political groups form to pursue the interests or values of their members. They are the result of the processes of economic and social differentiation outlined in the previous chapter. But, as some public choice theorists have argued, political associations are not created automatically by these impersonal forces. Both Mancur Olsen and Robert Salisbury emphasize that some social changes lead to the creation of political groups whereas others do not.[6] Furthermore, some potential groups are not organized whereas some organize but stop short of taking political positions. Seeking to explain such differences in the relative development of groups, Olsen carefully examined the large economic associations that are so often politically effective. Their power, he found, resides in their ability to sustain large memberships. It is one of the functions of the group leadership to find ways in which to maintain that member support; that is, groups are formed and are made effective by political entrepreneurs. Olsen found that the most politically effective groups are the ones that "are also organized for some other purpose. . . . They perform some function in addition to lobbying for collective goods.''[7] The groups

---

[5]Betty Zisk, Heinz Eulau, and Kenneth Prewitt, "City Councilmen and the Group Struggle" *Journal of Politics,* Vol. 27 (August 1965), p. 633. Also, see Heinz Eulau, *Labyrinths of Democracy: Adaptations, Linkages, Representation, and Politics in Urban Politics* (Indianapolis: Bobbs-Merrill, 1973).

[6]Mancur Olson, *The Logic of Collective Action* (Cambridge, Mass.: Harvard University Press, 1965). Robert Salisbury, "An Exchange Theory of Interest Groups," *Midwest Journal of Political Science,* Vol. 8 (February 1969), pp. 1–32.

[7]Olson, *The Logic of Collective Action,* p. 32.

that can emerge, endure, and become politically powerful are the ones that offer "selective incentives" to their members, for example, coercion or positive inducements, such as group health programs and insurance plans.

Others, like Salisbury, focus on the leadership function in group creation and effectiveness. Translating that function into the language of public choice, Salisbury characterizes group organizers as investing capital to create a set of benefits that they offer to members at a price. "If, and as long as, enough customers buy, i.e., join, to make a viable organization, the group is in business."[8]

POLITICAL RESOURCES: THE KEY
TO GROUP POWER

All groups are not born equal. We intuitively recognize that when developers face off against the ad hoc Citizens Committee of the Neighborhood of Ferndale, the developers are likely to win. Why this is so, and why it sometimes is not so, requires explanation. The reasons are not singular and simple, but let us continue to explore the assumption that the political entrepreneurship of the group leaders accounts for relative group power.

Part of the reason for the complexity results from the fact that "power" is not a fixed attribute. Social power is relational, not a finite quality to be possessed by a leader or group. As a result, the Fire Fighters' Association will not have five hypothetical power units in every issue it joins. It may have five when pressing for fire fighters' salaries before the City Council, ten with the Mayor's Budgetary Agency (composed of some fellow city workers), but only one in appearing before the School Board to oppose building a new school in a particular area. The point is that the power of the group may vary with the particular issue, and with the body of officials being approached. Thus, we must keep in mind the relational character of power. But having power is not the product of mystical forces either. It results from the conscious creative efforts of political group leaders.

Speaking abstractly, what group leaders do is create and effectively use political resources. A political resource is an available means of realizing potential power. Just as iron in the ground is an economic resource that, when mined, processed, and shaped, becomes an automobile to be exchanged for value, so are political resources a basis of political exchange.

The coin of political exchange is a bit more complicated than it first appears. To many, political activists and novices alike, the matter is simple: Money equals power. It is not wrong to say that money is a primary political resource. Money is probably the single most important political resource; as one successful city politician once told me his rule of thumb was "[political] power runs on money.

[8]Salisbury, "An Exchange Theory of Interest Groups," p. 32.

Find where the money's flowing from and to, and you'll know how politics in this town works.'' But money is not the sole political resource and, in many cases, not the decisive resource. Leadership is another crucial one. Ample money can be squandered by an unknowing leader. There are many others:

1. Money
2. Leadership
3. Influential allies
4. Individual appeal, charisma
5. Popular ideology, values
6. Expertise
7. Organization
8. Access to decision makers
9. Access to the media, control over information
10. Control over jobs
11. Social standing
12. Ethnic solidarity
13. Votes
14. Large numbers
15. A willingness to disrupt

When you scan this list thoughtfully, you can easily imagine a number of strategies that can be built upon each resource.

Most of these resources are self-explanatory, but certain points need to be clarified. Money, for example, need not be possessed to be usable as a resource. Banks, financial institutions, and insurance companies are a few of the most influential actors on the American city. They exercise much of that influence through policies that affect the flow of money into and out of certain neighborhoods, and into and out of the city. The practice known popularly as "redlining," in which the financial institution refuses to lend money on homes in specified neighborhoods, gives the bank power based on money, even though the money does not, strictly speaking, belong to the bank.

The resources that require the most explanation are those used as the basis of unconventional or protest strategies. "Protest is one of the few ways in which a relatively powerless group can create bargaining resources.''[9] When a group finds itself without sufficient political resources, yet still feels its cause must be heard, it can use its willingness to disrupt. The effectiveness of disruption results from the intricate division of labor in urban society. Simply by inhibiting the performance

[9]Michael Lipsky, *Protest in City Politics* (Chicago: Rand McNally, 1960), p. 2.

of certain mundane, but vital, functions (garbage collection, for instance), protest-ors can bring a city to a virtual standstill. Cities, like all centralized, specialized systems, are less stable than are decentralized systems. Because of the growing centralization and interdependence of modern socioeconomic systems, Saul Alinsky envisions a kind of ultimate vulnerability:

> A while back I attended an Aspen seminar where one guy from IBM was talking about automation. All I could think of as I was listening to him was: These computers are going to put our society in a beautiful, vulnerable spot. Just equip all the people in a community with little punchers that make the same mark that Con Edison's bills have on them. Then you can say either you desegregate or we punch a hole in your cards.[10]

The aim of protest strategies is not simply destructive. These strategies seek to raise the cost of doing business as usual so as to focus attention and generate conditions of action. Such behaviors are not antisystem. In his very definition of protest, Lipsky makes that clear: Protest is "a mode of political action oriented to the objection to one or more policies or conditions, characterized by showmanship or display of an unconventional nature, and undertaken to obtain rewards from political or economic systems while working within the system."[11] Protest is Hirschman's "voice" at its most shrill.

Merely having a variety of resources available does not guarantee that a group will be powerful. Some mobilize their resources more effectively than do others. So for any set of resources, influence is a function of (1) access to the resources, (2) amount of resources, (3) skill in strategy formulation based on the resources, and (4) the rate and efficiency of exploitation of the resources.

Just this barebones discussion of resources could easily lead you to assume that each group is just as powerful as it chooses to be. Such pluralist formulations appear optimistic, implying that, if you feel intensely enough and work hard enough to mobilize, you will win. Radical political economists, in particular, find such optimism ungrounded. Political resources are distributed in a structured and persistently biased way, they would remind us. The result in any particular setting may be that no coalition of groups is powerful enough to overcome the dominance of a numerically small but resource-rich elite. Hooker Chemical Company in Niagara Falls, New York, for example, has been described as having power without much local participation, whereas those groups that seek to impose environmental regulations on that company appear to have participation without power.

---

[10]Marion K. Saunders, *The Professional Radical: Conversations with Saul Alinsky* (New York: Harper & Row, 1965).

[11]Lipsky, *Protest in City Politics.*

THE GROUP THEORY AND PUBLIC POLICY

The original group theorist, Arthur Bentley, was among the most expansive in his claims. Of political life he said "when the groups are adequately stated, everything is stated. And when I say everything, I mean everything."[12] By this he meant for us to understand that what we call public policy, or law, is actually "the equilibrium reached in the group struggle at any moment."[13] In other words, the political world consists solely of colliding groups. Once the collisions have occurred and their force registered on, say the city council, then the council declares the net impact to be law—legitimate policy. Group theorists do not assume that the council, in this example, is a "mindless balancing point" but is itself a special type of group, an official group. It has the power to make policy because of a "public understanding" that it may do so. Public decision making, as well as the content of public policy, is thus subsumed into this expansive version of group theory.

The scope of group theory has been subject to dispute. Much of the criticism of pluralism made in Chapter 2 is aimed at the broad version of group theory. Most contemporary political scientists do not believe that generalizations made about groups are sufficiently all encompassing to constitute a "general theory of politics," as Bentley claimed. Still, groups perform a variety of central political functions. As is our central claim, they are the primary links between individual and government. But, in addition, they also help individuals to orient themselves in a complex society. They help individuals to express their desires and provide the means to achieve orderly social change. More politically, groups serve the important function of bargaining agents, speaking for, protecting, and promoting particular concerns in a negotiating process.

The group phenomenon is also found to provide our politics with some of its widely recognized dysfunctions, as well. For example, the tendency to deadlock on certain issues has in recent years been traced to the intensity of "single interests" groups—groups that will not compromise and insistently veto all efforts to meet widely perceived public needs.

The Radical Formulation: Class Conflict

To the radical, the group theory of politics seriously overstates the importance of these linkage institutions. It also presents the misleading impression that

[12]Arthur Bentley, *The Process of Government* (Cambridge, Mass.: Harvard University Press, 1967, originally 1908), p. 208.
[13]Earl Latham, "The Group Basis of Politics: Notes for a Theory," *American Political Science Review*, Vol. 46 (June 1952), pp. 376–397, 392.

the political process in American cities is more open to change than it actually is. Particularly, the Marxists insist that the basic division among urban participants remains class biased, that is, the basic conflict is between those who are exploited and those who exploit. Chapter 5 addresses this concern more directly, as we seek there to determine what are the bases of coalition that bring the more particular urban interests together.

MAIN FEATURES ON THE LOCAL POLITICAL MAP: THE PLAYERS AND THEIR GAMES

Less theoretically, which are the most important groups and what are their usual strategies and goals? As we review this list of prominent participants in urban politics, let us remember that we are not just reciting a catalog of political actors. The aim is to provide you with the raw materials from which you might compose a political map of your own or any other city. No effective political actor is without a political map, although the local Exxon station seldom keeps them. A political map is a mental construct of the powerscape, a characterization of the usual political stance of the most often involved political groups in the city.

Most politically active people carry such a map with them in their heads, although they would not call it that, nor would they be generally conscious that they do. But get such people in the right circumstances and they will draw you their map, as a leading San Diego politician did for me recently. Here are the major business interests, he said, drawing a large circle in the center of the paper. Within it he added smaller circles—the Chamber of Commerce, a prominent investment banker, the owner of the local newspaper, and some others. Here are some of their chief rivals, he went on, drawing an overlapping circle with the names of a competing banking establishment, a hotel owner, and a soft drink company executive. Here are the establishment critics, some environmental groups, a small newspaper publisher . . . and so on. The point is not necessarily the accuracy of the map, for that is subject to test and change as one acts and experiences the truth of one's assumptions. What is important is that you must have such a map. Otherwise, you will get lost.

HIGHLIGHTS OF THE LOCAL POLITICAL MAP

In this section, we will consider the customary stances of several of the most important groups: businesses, unions, utilities, the media, environmental and consumer groups, civic associations, good government groups, ad hoc associations, neighborhood associations, public employees, ethnic and black groups, and new immigrant organizations.

After describing the usual position, resources, and strategies of each of these groups, we will decide whether they would likely be our allies or opponents if we should try to organize to keep that 400-unit apartment complex out of our neighborhood. This, of course, approximates the practical use political activists make of their political maps. The hope is that we will come away from this exercise with a rough prediction of our likely success. Let us begin by asking ourselves what is the likelihood of gaining that ally that is everyone's candidate for most powerful local interest.

Business

> Suit the action to the word, the word to the action, with this special observance, that you o'erstep not the modesty of nature; for anything so overdone is from the purpose of playing.
>
> *Hamlet,* Act III, Scene 2

In general, business is a quiet but powerful player of urban politics, carefully observing the need to "suit the action to the word, the word to the action." Business interests preside over the economic functions that create and shape the city, and they are its prime benefactors. If business interests were singular, agreed on, and organized, they could dominate a city's politics. Some feel that they should. However, business interests in some cities are internally divided: absentee-owned business often sees the world differently from locally owned business; retailers need different policies than do manufacturers, small businesses may often oppose the aims of large business. Even so, there are a number of goals that unite the business interests of most cities. Three are particularly important: assuring economic growth, keeping taxes and other governmental regulations at a minimum, and keeping government in support of its needs and goals.

STRIVING FOR GROWTH

Capitalistic enterprise must expand or it will contract. The imperative of the firm is growth: Business interests insist that the city should accommodate that need whenever possible. Simple population growth often serves the end of business growth. More people mean more customers and a ready labor supply. As business needs become more specialized, however, differences can readily emerge as to what type of population growth is desired—manufacturing firms want lower-income residential growth while the high-technology electronic firms of a "silicone valley" want growth in the population of professionals.

What this suggests is that businesses do not want rapid and haphazard growth but, rather, particular kinds of controlled growth. Too rapid growth is a problem; it may cause serious problems of displacement and unemployment, increase welfare costs, and raise vice and crime rates. It is this need for stable, controlled growth that has enticed business away from its early antiplanning stance; no longer is planning equated with "creeping socialism," but as intelligence required for sound management decision making.

The growth goal has been a difficult one to maximize. That is because the very process of growth creates what economists call "spillover" effects, that is, unanticipated economic and, sometimes, social consequences. Recall it is the very prospect that the central city will grow that creates what the classical ecologists call the zone in transition and less delicate folks call a slum. As these social costs of growth emerge, political pressures mount to have businesses pay higher taxes to support the public services that are required to clean up the spillovers. A dual strategy thus emerges: Allow growth in only the "desirable" elements of the population and head off the effort to shift governmental costs to business.

The first strategy involves creating policies for selective growth. Downtown department stores, for example, "want to encourage good customers to come there and discourage 'undesirable' ones, that is, people with little money to spend whose presence would make the shopping district less attractive to the good customers."[14] A variety of policies may be used to serve that end: careful police enforcement of laws against loitering, for example. More expansively, urban renewal projects have been strongly supported by business interests in pursuit of selective growth strategies, especially urban renewal projects that aim to replace low-income residents (often ethnic or black) with middle-income (often white) residents. But urban renewal has proved costly and has attracted criticism as being discriminatory. More recently, policies that encourage "gentrification" of city slum areas have found great favor with urban business interests. By gentrification is meant the return of the middle-class investor to the dilapidated neighborhood, individually buying and restoring a piece of property. Gentrification may be encouraged through government policy. For example, zoning and building codes may be reworked, tax benefits may be conferred, and historic site laws may allow additional tax breaks for people who can afford to restore an old central city dwelling.

KEEPING TAXES AND REGULATIONS MINIMAL

Business interests maintain a strong concern about tax policies. Tax reform efforts designed to increase business's contribution to local revenues will be

---

[14]Edward Banfield and James Wilson, *City Politics* (Cambridge, Mass.: Harvard-MIT Press, 1963), p. 262.

resisted. Prior to the mid-1970s, business groups had preferred a low-profile stance on tax reform, even though it was widely believed that the primary source of local revenues—the property tax—was inequitable. Businesses feared that the talk of tax reform might easily lead to efforts to get business to increase its tax burden. Proposition 13, California's tax initiative, which limited the rate of property tax increase, went a long way to reassure that state's businesses that there was little public sentiment to tax them more heavily. That became even clearer when a subsequent statewide initiative, calling for a "split-tax roll" so that business could be taxed at different rates than others, failed substantially. Fiscal reform, as it emerged in the late 1970s, had the effect of favoring the fiscal position of local business interests and, indeed, the well-to-do in general.

The political position of business, always strong in local politics, appears more secure since the mid-1970s. Fiscal conservatism makes business leaders even more attractive as candidates and consultants for local policymaking. Policies that are not conducive to maintenance of a "good business climate" are broadly under attack. More than that, business has met success in its efforts to build certain advantages for itself into local governmental structures. For example, we will later discuss in more detail the convergence of business interests and the council-manager form of government. Another example has been the slow expansion of the use of the organizational device known as the "public authority." These agencies, part governmental, part private sector, act as intermediaries by raising capital from private investors through the money and capital markets to invest in public facilities and services.[15] The Port Authority of New York and New Jersey is the oldest and best known illustration of a public authority. Since its creation in 1921, the number has grown to at least 6,000. Due to their apparent businesslike neutrality, "Public authorities have enjoyed support from all positions on the political spectrum." And while this corporate investment exerts massive influence on the development of the nation and especially the cities, it is "an influence that is largely insulated from public debate."[16]

Such arrangements go a long way in explaining how business and government have grown together in urban areas. Business interests can be quiet political actors because they are so deeply imbedded in local governmental structure.

POLITICAL DIVERSITY WITHIN BUSINESS

Powerful as business is, it would be a mistake to conclude that business interests are always and everywhere monolithic—organized, united, and engaged on every political issue that arises. They play different roles in different cities, and their interest and participation vary by issue.

[15] A full discussion of the public authority is in Annmarie Hauck Walsh, *The Public's Business: The Politics and Practices of Government Corporations* (Cambridge, Mass.: MIT Press, 1978).
[16] Ibid, pp. 4, 6.

American cities have emerged at different times and have developed their economic bases at different rates; they have exploited a variety of resources and have suffered differing setbacks. We should expect, then, that the strategies of business involvement in local politics would show considerable variation as well. Speaking most broadly, the research tradition suggests that there are four patterns of business political organization.

Business as Power Structure.   The first pattern finds business as the center of a "power structure." That is, business is in substantial control of the city, but it also accomplished that indirectly and "conspiratorially" insofar as its managers do not hold office themselves but operate from "behind the scenes" to pressure officials and to control the electoral process to assure that only those candidates favorable to business are elected. A series of controversial studies of power structure in particular cities concluded that Atlanta, Seattle, Ypsilanti, Baton Rouge, Wichita, and San Diego, for example, were governed at the time of study by a power structure.[17]

Business as Ratifier.   Other studies have concluded that business people are not so much initiators as they are "front men." Peter B. Clark finds that civic associations or staff members of governmental agencies usually generate the new ideas but that business support is necessary to get a project adopted. Quoting a member of a planning agency, "I've got a project now . . . I'm sitting on it until I can present it to the proper man to handle as his idea. . . . The man I'm going to pick has to be president of his club . . . head of his business. That's 50, 70 percent of the success of the project."[18]

The Business Veto.   Most established businesses do not need dramatic new programs to flourish. They are already central to the political economy of the city. This favored position requires a "maintaining" rather than an initiating stance toward city government. For this reason, some studies find that business executives in particular cities remain out of local politics as a general rule. They need only to mobilize when there is a threat. In its mildest form, this means simply withholding approval. In any case, it is analogous to the veto process.

Business as One Among Many Participants.   A number of studies have found that the image of business as dominant is simply not the case at all. New York, Chicago, and New Haven, for example, were researched by pluralists who

---

[17]Citations to this literature and discussion of why it is controversial are contained in Chapter 6.

[18]Peter B. Clark, *The Businessman as Civic Leader* (Glencoe, Ill.: The Free Press, 1964).

observed that business was simply one of a number of participants in city politics and often not a particularly effective one. Once again, these are still controversial findings, which, like those related to business as a power structure, will be discussed in Chapter 6.

What is the likelihood that the business interests might join our effort to keep that apartment house from being built? Not very likely. We could argue that it would cause too rapid growth, but it is only 400 units. More likely, businesses would see that rate of growth as in their interests. Moreover, the developers and financiers of such projects are themselves part of the business community.

TWO UNIQUE BUSINESS GROUPS:
THE MASS MEDIA AND PUBLIC UTILITIES

Like banks, two other businesses operate as dual actors, that is, as important economic entities in their own right but, at the same time, as prime political actors. Their dual role gives them the power to speak authoritatively about urban conflicts. They are (1) the mass media and (2) public utilities.

The mass media are primarily business interests. They have the same commitments as other businesses to growth, low taxes, and government support of the local economy, but in addition, they presume to provide a product that serves a public interest. Reporting the news, communicating the culture, and entertaining, it might be argued, constitute a collective good. By contrast to some other countries, we leave the creation and distribution of that public good in private hands. This puts the owners and operators of the media in a position in which they are constantly tempted to believe that the public interest is synonymous with their private business interests. The conservative *Chicago Tribune*, for example, fought to build McCormack Place, a convention center and exhibition hall. Editorially, it justified this position: "We fought the NRA [New Deal program for economic recovery] for the people. We fight crime and vice. . . . Why did we put so much time into [McCormack Place]? Because it is good for the city. But partly from selfish motives too. We want to build a bigger Chicago and a bigger *Tribune*. We want more circulation and more advertising. We want to keep growing and we want the city to keep growing so we can keep growing."[19]

Providing that collective good is particularly difficult to achieve when economic pressures on the newspaper business produce a noncompetitive situation. Very few cities now have genuinely competitive newspapers. Ninety-one percent of the residents of urban areas have at least two daily papers available to them, but in many cases those papers are owned by the same publishing company.

Television and radio stations operate by much the same set of political

---

[19]From an interview with W. Don Maxwell, editor of the *Tribune* with Edward Banfield, in *Political Influence* (New York: The Free Press, 1961), pp. 230–231.

economic patterns as do newspapers. Generally, there is much less radio and TV time devoted to investigative reporting of local politics, although major news items and elections are covered.

The direction of modern political campaigning puts the mass media in an even more difficult position. Even small- to medium-sized cities by the mid-1970s found that their candidates for local office had become ''media candidates''; that is, the political public relations firms had penetrated the local political process. Electioneering had become a matter of name recognition and candidate image manipulation. Access to and cooperation with reporters and technical production people within the media are a must for political success.

Finally, the impact of ostensibly nonpartisan electoral systems undercuts the effectiveness of the local political parties in certifying candidates. This, too, has the effect of magnifying the political role played by the local media. When a newspaper endorses a candidate in a California local election, that is often the only clear directive that local voters will hear.

Public utilities also occupy a dual role. By contrast to the media, they are most often publicly owned, but their political orientations are virtually identical with those of private businesses. Although their profits are usually limited by state law and many of their procedures and practices are controlled by a public utilities commission, many have proved themselves quite skilled in maximizing their political role and profitability. Particularly after the ''energy crisis'' of the early 1970s, a number of local utilities found ways in which to both induce energy conservation and raise rates. Moving into the 1980s such rate increases, coupled with the environmentalist concerns for conservation and alternative energy sources, has made utility company practices the center of some state and local controversies. It proved a crucial issue in the defeat of incumbent Texas governor in 1982. In the 1983 mayoral contest in San Diego, Maureen O'Connor based a number of her television commercials on her demand that San Diego Gas and Electric limit its rate increase requests.[20]

Labor Unions

Organized labor is generally less active and less influential in local politics than it is at the state and national levels. Locally, labor groups are surprisingly ineffective. There is a certain logic to their selectivity, however, as the governmental decisions that most directly affect the bread and butter of unions are made outside the locality: wage and hour laws, regulations affecting job benefits and tenure, and laws affecting collective bargaining and strikes. To be sure, local

[20]For a complete and comprehensive discussion of the politics of energy at the local level, see David Morris, *Self-Reliant Cities* (San Francisco: Sierra Club Books, 1982).

politics can be important in such instances as when local police decide whether they will protect strikers or harass them.[21]

Even in cities where one would expect unions to be more powerful, they achieve few victories. Kenneth Gray and David Greenstone examined the effectiveness of Detroit's Committee on Political Education (COPE), the political action arm of labor.[22] They found that "COPE has had relatively little success in [Detroit] politics."[23] Making similar findings in Houston and St. Louis, the study explained that business managers are regarded by voters and politicians alike as civic statesmen whereas unions bear the stigma of being self-interested and, therefore, not representative of the city as a whole.

This is not to discount labor as a political force, but to contrast it to the political strength of business interests. That disparity was made somewhat greater in the recession of the late 1970s and early 1980s. Nationally, union power was on the defensive. Unions were reported to be losing membership and a number of National Labor Relations elections.[24] The threat of plant closures and relocation, sometimes called the "runaway shop," enabled industries to extract wage and benefit concessions from unions "amounting to billions of dollars."[25] Politically, this put labor on the defensive as well. In the 1980 campaigns, for example, the "New Right" and corporate political action committees (PACs) outspent labor and liberal groups by a ratio of 4 to 1, $100 million to $25 million. "The ratio is closer to 10 to 1," according to Michael Parenti, a prominent radical political economist, when the money contributed to local elections, to lawmakers between elections, and to referenda campaigns and money given directly by wealthy individuals is accounted for.[26]

The local political weakness of the labor investment leaves it vulnerable in the contemporary politics of the multinational era. The efforts to protect workers against "arbitrary" or "unfair" plant closings or shifts in production once again is being pressed at the national level. For example, Senator Walter Mondale and Congressman William Ford introduced legislation in 1974, the National Employment Priorities Act (NEPA), that would have created a National Employment Relocation Administration to investigate complaints, rule on whether a plant shutdown or relocation was justified, and if not, recommend the withholding of various tax benefits from the offending industry. Whatever the merits or demerits

[21]Joel Seidman et al., *The Worker Views His Union* (Chicago: University of Chicago Press, 1958).

[22]Kenneth Gray and David Greenstone, "Organized Labor in City Politics," in Edward Banfield, ed., *Urban Government* (New York: The Free Press, 1961).

[23]Ibid., p. 372.

[24]Sidney Lens, "Disorganized Labor," *Nation*, February 24, 1979.

[25]Quoted in *The New York Times*, "Unions on the Defensive," June 13, 1982, p. 46.

[26]Michael Parenti, *Democracy for the Few*, 4th ed. (New York: St. Martins, 1983), p. 240. He bases this estimate on figures compiled from several news sources.

of the measure and, parenthetically, both radical and neoconservatives expressed basic disagreement with the initial proposal, the legislation was not reported out of committee. Nor has any other measure with similar intent been passed.[27]

Will labor be our ally in our effort to keep that apartment house from being built next door? Surely if business is not with us, labor will be. The greatest likelihood is that most of it will not. As we think about why not, we will discover that labor is—like business—often internally divided. What we would find is that most unions would be sympathetic but unlikely to commit time and scarce resources to such an issue. Other unions, like those involved in the construction industry, would oppose you because building that apartment means employment for them.

Public Employees

During the 1960s, the labor movement began to reach for new membership and expanded power by moving to new forms of affiliation with "white-collar" workers. City employees, some 4.5 million of them, are mostly represented by professional associations. But during the 1960s, those associations either became affiliated with the unions or came increasingly to function like unions in their local political activities. The American Federation of State, County and Municipal Employees (AFSCME), the International Association of Fire Fighters (AIFF), and the American Federation of Teachers (AFT) are affiliated with the AFL-CIO. Other public employees groups, though not affiliated, are quite like unions in their actions. Examples of such organizations are the National Educational Association and the Fraternal Order of Police.

Public employees have the same reasons for organizing as do other workers: to protect and promote their interests and to organize to make effective their concern for wage and salary increases, job benefits, and job security. As the public choice theorists have pointed out, they are motivated by the same need to maximize their self-interest as are humans everywhere. But as city budgets rose dramatically, and as city workers began in many cities to use strikes, or variations on strikes such as "blue flu" and other tactics of work slow down, a backlash began to develop. Critics pointed out that it is usual for three-fourths of the city budget to go for wages and salaries. Howard Jarvis, the crusty neoconservative who gave first California and then the country Proposition 13, the tax limitation amendment, bore a special hatred for public employees. Some critics blamed the New York fiscal crisis on the "excessive" wage demands of that city's employees.

---

[27]For a discussion of this legislation and a number of other efforts designed to create national policy on plant relocation and employment, see Bennett Harrison and Barry Bluestone, "The Incidence of Regulation of Plant Closings," in F. Stevens Redburn and Terry Buss, eds., *Public Policies for Distressed Communities* (Lexington, Mass.: Lexington Books, 1982), esp. pp. 154–158.

By the early 1980s, the rhetoric of the critics had such effect that one librarian wrote to a local San Diego paper: "I'm afraid to tell my daughter I'm a public employee."

City employees do have some political advantages that other groups lack. Like business groups, for different reasons, they are inside the governmental process. This makes the political resources of access, knowledge, and expertise easily theirs. City officials may find it very difficult to resist the very same people they count on to administer their policy decisions. This is, of course, the special position that public employees occupy that has led public choice theorists to be critical as well. A number of their studies either begin with assumptions of disproportionate "bureaucratic" power or verify it.[28]

The long-standing effort of the municipal reform tradition, which we will discuss more fully in Chapter 6, has aimed at providing limitations on the power of municipal employees. Limitations on the right to collective bargaining, to strike, and to engage in politics are the most common restrictions already in place in many cities. Increasingly in the 1980s, efforts were made to undermine public employee power by elimination of jobs and by opening competitive methods of providing public goods. The school voucher proposal that originated with Milton Friedman, for example, aims to "break the monopoly of the public school system" by providing a competitive private alternative to public education.

Interestingly, it is within the bureaucracy that we are likely to find our first ally in our problem with the apartment house. City planning staffs usually have a number of members who are committed to carefully planned growth. We may be able to convince them that the quality of neighborhood life is threatened by the new building. Members of the bureaucracy are particularly good allies, as they are a source of specialized knowledge about the technical requirements of such projects and also have a clear sense of what political strategies are most viable.

Environmental and Consumer Groups

For the first time in our scan of the urban political map, we turn to a group that does not believe that growth is the basic urban imperative. Environmental and consumer organizations emerged rather suddenly in the wave of ecological concern of the mid-1960s. Environmentalists formulate their political positions more out of a concern for the city as a place in which to live than as a place in which to make money. They emphasize concern for the quality of local life. San Francisco environmentalists fought to limit the height of downtown skyscrapers when

[28]See a typical discussion in Richard McKenzie and Gordon Tullock, *Modern Political Economy: An Introduction to Economics* (New York: McGraw-Hill, 1978), pp. 411–420. Also, see Perry Shapiro and Jon Sonstelie, "Representative Voter or Bureaucratic Manipulation: An Examination of Public Finances in California Before and After Proposition 13," *Public Choice*, Vol. 39, no. 1 (1982), pp. 113–142.

theTransAmerica building was being proposed. San Antonio environmentalists fought a freeway that would have come within 90 feet of the bear pits at the zoo. Environmentalists everywhere have struggled to keep freeway systems limited and aesthetic but have been most visible as opponents of nuclear power.

Environmentalists have been remarkably successful in some areas. In Seattle, for example, when the superintendent of Seattle City Light and Power Company, the fourth largest municipally owned electric utility company in the nation, proposed that the city purchase a share of two nuclear power plants, a citizens' group threatened legal action, demanding and succeeding in getting passed an alternative energy program.[29] The politics of San Diego has been importantly shaped by loosely organized, but widely shared, environmental concerns. Pete Wilson, mayor of San Diego for 12 years before he was elected to the U.S. Senate in 1983, originally ran for the mayorship strongly emphasizing a need for "controlled growth." During his tenure, one of his strongest opponents was the owner of a construction company and the explicit representative of the local construction industry. In the 1970 city elections, Wilson, again the favorite of the local environmentalists, defeated the construction industry candidate soundly. But as the local forces of growth began to press back—local construction unions burned effigies of Sierra Club types—Mayor Wilson accommodated to the pro-growth forces. By 1980 his administration was under political attack for its sponsorship of a broad program of downtown redevelopment and failure to control the growth of the northern suburbs. His proposal for a large downtown convention center was beaten by a coalition of environmentalists, consumer groups, and others who were concerned for the quality of life in San Diego.

That brief history of environmentalism in San Diego tells in microcosm much of the story of environmental groups throughout the country. Their strength lies in free-floating concerns of the residents of the particular city more than in their careful political organizing. The result has been relative inconsistency and loss of effectiveness as the scarcities of economic downturn begin to have their political effects.

Environmentalists would be sympathetic to our effort to stop the building of the apartment house, but they would probably find themselves spread too thin to offer many of their scarce resources to our cause.

Neighborhood Associations

The environmental and consumer groups are much like the more localized neighborhood groups. Neighborhood organizations also usually arise out of a concern for the quality of local life. Often it is the perception that the neighborhood

---

[29]For additional discussion, see David Morris, *Self-reliant Cities* (San Francisco: Sierra Club Books, 1982), pp. 180–82.

is in decline that precipitates the organization of a group such as the West End Neighborhood Association. Or it may be an external "threat," like the proposal we are tracing throughout this chapter to build an apartment house in our residential neighborhood. The organizational effort is a clear illustration of the voice option—rather than exiting, the neighbors band together to articulate their concerns. This associational effort would be the organizational housing we might well choose if we were to actively oppose the apartment house. We might well find that other neighborhood associations would ally with us as well.

There are few systematic comparative studies of neighborhood organizations, so we can only speculate as to what accounts for their ad hoc growth, their persistence, and their decline.[30] Nor do we know much that is firm about what kinds of cities are the most fertile ground for neighborhood organization growth. It is reasonable to hypothesize that the older cities with more established neighborhoods would have more associations. San Francisco, it has been reported, has over 200 such groups ranging from a number of gay neighborhood associations to a Coalition of Arab Grocers.[31] The corollary is that the newer Sunbelt cities, with a less well-developed social infrastructure, would have fewer neighborhood associations. It also appears that middle-class neighborhoods would contain more such organizations than would either upper- or lower-class neighborhoods, as upper-class people tend to exercise the exit option rather quickly and lower-class residents are not so easily organized.

Good Government Groups

Here we have an example of a kind of interest group that develops as a response to the local political process itself. "Goo-Goo" groups, as some of their critics derisively call them, often aim to have local government adopt one or all of the elements of what we will describe in Chapter 6 as the reform package—for example, council-manager government, home rule, nonpartisan elections, and civil service reforms. Increasingly, good government groups have found themselves in the same coalition with environmentalists and neighborhood associations.

Good government groups provide a basis for political coalition apart from political parties or other established interests. They are notable for their image of civic virtue, conveyed by neutral sounding names like The Citizen's League of Pawtucket, The Richmond Civic Association, The Municipal League of Spokane, Citizens Union of New York City, and the New Boston Committee.

The League of Women Voters and the Parent-Teachers Association (PTA) are special cases of good government groups. The League of Women Voters has

---

[30]Harry Boyte, *The Backyard Revolution* (Philadelphia: Temple University Press, 1980).
[31]Fredrick Wirt, *Power in the City* (Berkeley: University of California Press, 1974).

considerable political presence in most cities, although it commonly restricts its activity to stimulating informed voting participation. One of the League's common programs is preparation and distribution of local candidates' responses to questions on the issues. Occasionally, after studying an issue, the League will move to advocacy. The PTA, of course, specializes in the area of education, but it also becomes involved in both city council elections and local referenda elections that affect education.

Quite similar in superficial appearance to the good government groups are the taxpayers' associations. As the name makes clear, they specialize in matters of local finance. Their general orientation is to keep pressure on local governments to spend less and more efficiently. But, unlike the other good government groups, the taxpayers' associations are usually front organizations for large business interests: the taxpayers with heavy investments in industrial and commercial property in the city.

Ad Hoc Groups

The wise local political map maker leaves a place for groups to be called together by particular issues. When Hutchinson, Kansas, fought over urban renewal, "Stand up for Hutch," a pro-renewal organization first appeared. When the issue had been won, the organization disappeared. Best understood as a political strategy than a stable political actor, the ad hoc group has many advantages for political action. It can, for example, provide the grounds for unaccustomed political bedfellows to get together. No embarrassing public explanations need be made if both labor and business groups support the Citizens Committee for Fiscal Conservatism, which supports the building of a downtown convention center. An ad hoc group can also assume a cloak of "objectivity," which permits it to court public support more effectively than can an established group with known biases.

Howard Jarvis and Paul Gann created an ad hoc group to pursue the California tax limitation amendment, Proposition 13, if you require evidence of the utility of this strategy.

Ethnic and Minority Groups

"You can always tell who has no power," I was once told by a successful politician. "They yell a lot." Ethnics and blacks have been highly visible participants in urban politics, but that does not mean they are powerful. The exercise of voice has occasionally been extended to the exercise of angry voice and, thence, to angry action. Still the results have been mixed. If we had only Hirschman's typology to guide us, we would expect such groups to at least exercise exit. But exit depends on economic ability. Asking why the poor do not move if they are not happy in the ghetto is a bit like Marie Antoinette's famous response to the question about the availability of bread. Nor is it particularly accurate to interpret their failure to exit as meaning that they are demonstrating loyalty. Such are the limits of the Hirschman typology.

The ethnic minorities still exist and, particularly in the older cities of the Northeast, exert their influence in local politics. Many others have over the generations become assimilated, while still others resist, retaining as much of their original identities as possible. America is rightly described as a nation of nations. New York City, for example, contains more Italians than Naples, more Greeks than Sparta, and more Puerto Ricans than San Juan. Most have been assimilated, if by that we mean brought within the basic habits, attitudes, and mode of life of the national culture. Although most American cities still have their "Little Italies" or "Germantowns," most of their number are thoroughly integrated into middle-class American culture. "Their political attitudes and behavior are scarcely distinguishable from those of the direct descendants of the arrivals on the Mayflower."[32]

Election studies do reveal some need to qualify the assumption of complete assimilation, however. Ethnicity has been observed to become a factor in non-partisan elections, wherein voters lack party labels to guide them. Some then resort to ethnic identification.[33]

The black experience in America has been substantially different from most other groups. Thomas Sowell, a prominent neoconservative critic of what he calls black "special pleading," has made an elaborate statistical comparison of economic and social progress of 12 ethnic groups in America from 1619 to the 1970s.[34] The conclusion of this effort is that the economic achievement pattern has been different but parallel for every ethnic group but one. This group, the descendants of African slaves forcibly brought here, is the only one that was not drawn here by a vision of a better life. Instead, they were brought here against their will and were substantially repressed for extended periods of time. "Its history, and not its color," Sowell thinks, "is the key to [slave descendants'] failure to advance."[35]

Sowell's is a different explanation from that preferred in the emergent field

[32]Robert Lineberry and Ira Sharkansky, *Urban Politics and Public Policy* (New York: Harper & Row, 1971), p. 69.

[33]See Willis Hawley, *Nonpartisan Elections and the Case for Party Politics* (New York: John Wiley & Sons, 1973), and Chester Rogers and Harold Armen, "Nonpartisanship and Election to City Office," *Social Science Quarterly,* Vol. 61 (March 1971), pp. 941–945.

[34]Thomas Sowell, *Essays and Data on American Ethnic Groups* (Washington, D.C.: The Urban Institute, 1978).

[35]Sowell distinguishes three categories of blacks: slaves, free blacks, and West Indians. Each had widely varying patterns of socioeconomic attainment. West Indian blacks show higher attainment levels than do whites, for example. Sowell interprets this to be substantial refutation of explanations that rely on biological inferiority of the black.

of sociobiology. According to Arthur Jensen, "success" is legitimately a function of a particular kind of intelligence—"conceptual intelligence" or "cognitive ability"—the kind of intellectual skill required to make complicated technical decisions or to do scientific work.[36] That kind of intelligence is inheritable, Jensen argues. Different genetic endowments are the explanation for lower levels of black achievement. Needless to say, that argument for "natural inequality" is controversial. But it is particularly attractive to certain neoconservatives. Philip Green, writing from the radical perspective has provided an elaborate critique of the methods, logic, and conclusions of the sociobiologists and Jensen, in particular. Green makes a convincing case that Jensen's are not scientific findings at all, but simple racial prejudice cloaked in the trappings of science.[37] By far the greatest weight of evidence acceptable to social scientists suggests that Jensen and the sociobiologists are incorrect.

It remains clear to most social scientists that blacks have found themselves victims of racial and economic practices that have long kept them in an inferior status. That there should be a group of unequals in a country that proclaims equality for all one of its central principles constitutes what Gunnar Myrdal many years ago called the "American Dilemma." Since the abolition of slavery, it has become the urban American dilemma: In 1910, 90 percent of the blacks lived in the poor rural South; today closer to 70 percent live in cities.

Black political participation is also somewhat different from other minority groups'. The general pattern for political participation is that those of lower socioeconomic status are less engaged in politics. Blacks and whites are almost identical in membership in local political organizations, and blacks participate in politics at slightly higher levels than do whites.[38] More important, perhaps, blacks evidence strong solidarity in their voting participation. A number of studies find black voters vote as a bloc in urban elections.[39] Their voting turnout increases further when there is a black candidate on the ballot, although this tendency is diminished somewhat when the elections are on a nonpartisan basis.[40]

Voting is but one form of political participation. The increasingly militant black leadership that emerged in the 1960s was inclined to argue that the vote was

---

[36]Arthur Jensen, "How Much Can We Boost IQ and Scholastic Achievement?"*Harvard Educational Review*, Vol. 39 (Winter 1969), pp. 1–23.

[37]Philip Green, *Pursuit of Inequality* (New York: Pantheon Books, 1981), esp. Appendix A, "Arthur Jensen's Methodology."

[38]Sidney Verba and Norman Nie, *Participation in America* (New York: Harper & Row, 1972), Table 2.1. For more current discussion of the explanations of black political participation, see Richard Shingles, "Black Consciousness and Political Participation: The Missing Link,"*American Political Science Review*, Vol. 75 (March 1981), pp. 76–91.

[39]Walton Hanes, Jr., *Black Politics: A Theoretical and Structural Analysis* (Philadelphia: Lippincott, 1972).

[40]Findings are based on a study of 1973 Atlanta electons; see William P. Collins, "Race as a Salient Factor in Nonpartisan Elections," *Western Political Quarterly*, Vol. 33 (September 1980), pp. 330–335.

an imperfect instrument for breaking down injustice. There is much in the literature of political science that supports this assessment. William Keech, for example, carefully analyzed voting as a political resource in Durham, North Carolina.[41]
He concluded that "the vote is a far more important instrument for achieving legal
justice than is social justice."[42] In other words, Keech found that the vote helped
blacks to gain equal treatment by the government, a substantial gain. But for
achieving equality of more fundamental kinds—including such things as comparable incomes on comparable jobs, opportunity for economic advancement, and
courteous and equal treatment by fellow citizens—the vote proved ineffective.
"The really striking gains of Durham's Negro minority have come through
resources other than votes."[43]

The recent history of black politics in America has been one of cultivation of
other resources in the exercise of the voice option. In the 1950s and early 1960s,
the essential stance was that of nonviolent pursuit of integration. Martin Luther
King quoted and imitated the protest strategies of Gandhi, both capturing white
support and mobilizing intense hostility. By the mid-1960s, both passive resistance as a strategy and integration as a goal were challenged by a new type of black
leader. Malcolm X, Stokely Carmichael, H. Rap Brown, and Eldridge argued that integration was less important than was black solidarity, and, as Brown
put it, "violence is as American as apple pie." The Student Nonviolent Coordinat-
ing Committee (SNCC) dropped the "Non." The militant and confrontive
strategies of the Black Panthers came to be identified with "black power." For
many of these black leaders, the ultimate goal was black separatism. In 1968, 30
percent of black college graduates believed in substantial black control of black
neighborhoods.[44]

Did rising black power sentiment cause the violence in the urban ghettos in
the summer of 1967? Was the violence to be understood as an extreme, though
intelligible, form of political voice? Neoconservatives like Edward Banfield
thought not. As he saw it in his *Unheavenly City*, there were various explanations
that he summed up in a chapter titled "Rioting Mainly for Fun and Profit," but
none was legitimate political protest. Other popular commentators explained the
riots in terms of "riffraff theory," in which it was suggested that (1) the "typical"
rioter was a tiny minority (1 and 2 percent) of ghetto residents; (2) most were
"riffraff," that is, unattached youths, people with criminal records, disoriented
migrants from the rural South, a few self-conscious radicals; and (3) the majority
of blacks deplored the rioting. However comforting this explanation was to

[41]William Keech, *The Impact of Negro Voting* (Skokie, Ill.: Rand McNally, 1968).

[42]Ibid., p. 105.

[43]Ibid.

[44]Angus Campbell and Howard Schuman, "Racial Attitudes in Fifteen Cities," in National
Adivsory Commission on Civil Disorders, *Supplementary Studies* (Washington, D.C.: U.S.
Government Printing Office, 1968), pp. 19, 26, 57.

middle-class whites, the more careful analyses did not confirm it. The best evidence suggests that between one-third and one-fifth of the ghetto neighborhood participated in the rioting. The "typical" rioter, by contrast to the stereotype, was slightly better educated, was more likely to have been born in the neighborhood, was employed and earning an income about equal to that of other ghetto residents, and was no more likely to have a criminal record.[45]

A large number of rioters, many of whom were not consciously black power advocates or responding to direct commands of militant leaders, nonetheless apparently shared that broad political perspective. Particularly, they shared a sense of grievance and persecution and a belief that drastic measures were necessary. This is not to say that rioting was chosen as a rational strategy. It would appear that the riots were more adequately characterized as only vaguely political statements, as "outbursts of righteous indignation."[46]

If rioting had been a rationally chosen strategy, it would have been on the implicit assumption that protest and even violence can secure attitude and policy change. Connecting protest action with political outcomes is a tricky exercise. Some public figures were anxious to show compliance, others were willing to comply but wanted to keep the face of firm stability. Eisenger's study of protest incidents in 43 cities led to the conclusion that in a slight majority of cases (54 percent), no concessions were made.[47] More directly in point, Susan Welch examined expenditure levels in cities that had major racial riots during the 1960s. She compared those expenditure levels with those of cities that had no riots. What she found more confirms backlash than gain. Riot cities significantly increased police expenditures, but not others.[48]

Black power gave way in the first half of the 1970s to a more fragmented approach. The assassinations of Malcolm X and Martin Luther King, the withdrawal of a number of militant leaders and the conversion of others—like Eldridge Cleaver, now a featured advocate of evangelical religion and retailer of his own line of men's jeans that emphasize male sexuality—as well as changing economic conditions have produced malaise. The disillusionment of some black groups with the perceived failure of the Carter presidency to be more supportive of black causes led to an active and somewhat successful effort by the Reagan Republicans to entice blacks into the party. The emphasis on individual, rather than group, effort, which was so prominent a component of the ethos of the early 1980s, found its voice in black leaders like Clarence Pendleton of the Urban League, President

[45]Robert Fogelson and Robert Hill, "Who Riots?" in National Advisory Commission, *Supplementary Studies.*

[46]Peter Lupsha, "Explanation of Political Violence: Some Psychological Theories versus Indignation," *Politics and Society,* Vol. 2 (Fall 1971), pp. 89–104.

[47]Peter Eisinger, "The Conditions of Protest Behavior in American Cities," *American Political Science Review,* Vol. 67 (March 1973), pp. 11–28.

[48]Susan Welsh, "The Impact of Urban Riots on Urban Expenditures," *American Journal of Political Science,* Vol. 19 November 1975), pp. 741–760.

Reagan's appointee to the Civil Rights Commission, who believes fervently that capitalism will solve what remains of a racial problem in America. The surest way to get out of the ghetto is to get rich, he contends. With increasing frequency, then, civil rights liberals of the 1960s have found a parting of the ways with their former black allies. It is perhaps not so surprising in retrospect. Black militance seldom went to a critique of capitalism; "we want our share of the pie" is considerably different from wanting cake. Still it would be an oversimplification to say that blacks are destined to become neoconservatives. Buoyed by the victories of black candidates for mayor in such cities as Chicago, Philadelphia, and Detroit, some black leaders have foreseen the opportunity to consolidate political power on a local base. Because such a large number of blacks have been among those who did not benefit from the economic "recovery" of the early Reagan years, black leaders have continued to speak as critics of neoconservative policies. The Rev. Jesse Jackson relied on just such an appeal as he gathered considerable black support for his bid for the Democratic Party's presidential nomination in 1984.

The New Arrivals

But the route to upward socioeconomic mobility in the early 1980s offers some new complexities. During the decade of the 1970s, new immigrants with different cultural origins arrived in the cities in numbers not seen since the turn of the current century (see Table 4.1). Asian, Latin American, and Caribbean refugees account for a large portion of the 14 million (6.2 percent) who are foreign born. More than half of those have settled in cities. And this figure is seriously understated because many Latin Americans are here illegally. Once again the city will provide the setting for the struggle to meet immigrant needs for scarce resources. The social and economic conflicts produced by these new waves of immigration will give our cities both a strong dose of revitalizing cultural richness and diversity, and some new social, economic, and political conflict. As Robert Nathan put it, "It's a vicious cycle. . . . Cities become blacker and more ethnic, jobs keep disappearing, crime increases. As this happens chances for rescue shrink."[49]

A number of incidents have resulted from this new migration. Blacks and newly arrived Cubans have raised tensions in Miami. Rioting occurred there in 1983. And the local Klan members took it upon themselves to drive a band of industrious Vietnamese shrimp fishers out of the coastal waters near Houston. But the basic political issues that are being raised relate to schooling, housing, and health care and whether these new arrivals will or should be assimilated in the manner of earlier arrivals.

[49]Robert Nathan, quoted in *U.S. News & World Report*, March 21, 1983, p. 49. Copyright, 1983, U.S. News & World Report, Inc.

TABLE 4.1 Racial and Ethnic Composition, Selected Cities, 1970 versus 1980

1. New York

	1970	1980
White	77.2%	60.7%
Black	21.1	25.2
Hispanic	15.2	19.9
Asian		3.3

2. Chicago

	1970	1980
White	66.6%	49.6%
Black	32.7	39.8
Hispanic	7.4	14.0
Asian		2.3

3. Los Angeles

	1970	1980
White	77.5%	61.2%
Black	17.9	17.0
Hispanic	15.0	27.5
Asian		6.6

4. Philadelphia

	1970	1980
White	65.8%	58.2%
Black	33.5	37.8
Hispanic	2.3	3.8
Asian		1.1

5. Houston

	1970	1980
White	73.6%	61.3%
Black	25.3	27.6
Hispanic	10.6	17.6
Asian		2.1

6. Detroit

	1970	1980
White	55.6%	34.4%
Black	43.6	63.1
Hispanic	2.0	2.4
Asian		0.6

7. Dallas

	1970	1980
White	74.3%	61.4%
Black	24.9	29.4
Hispanic	7.6	12.3
Asian		0.8

8. San Diego

	1970	1980
White	88.9%	76.2%
Black	7.6	8.9
Hispanic	9.0	14.9
Asian		6.5

9. Phoenix

	1970	1980
White	93.3%	84.3%
Black	4.8	4.8
Hispanic	10.9	14.8
Asian		0.9

10. Baltimore

	1970	1980
White	53.0%	43.9%
Black	46.4	54.8
Hispanic	1.0	1.0
Asian		0.6

11. San Antonio

	1970	1980
White	91.7%	78.6%
Black	7.1	7.3
Hispanic	44.9	53.7
Asian		0.6

12. Indianapolis

	1970	1980
White	81.6%	77.1%
Black	16.9	21.8
Hispanic	0.8	0.9
Asian		0.5

13. San Francisco

	1970	1980
White	71.7%	58.2%
Black	13.4	12.7
Hispanic	9.7	12.3
Asian		21.7

14. Memphis

	1970	1980
White	60.9%	51.6%
Black	36.9	47.6
Hispanic	0.4	0.8
Asian		0.4

15. Washington

	1970	1980
White	27.9%	26.9%
Black	71.1	70.3
Hispanic	2.0	2.8
Asian		1.0

16. San Jose

	1970	1980
White	94.0%	73.6%
Black	2.4	4.6
Hispanic	14.7	22.3
Asian		8.2

17. Milwaukee

	1970	1980
White	84.5%	73.3%
Black	14.6	23.1
Hispanic	3.9	4.1
Asian		0.6

18. Cleveland

	1970	1980
White	61.1%	53.5%
Black	38.3	43.8
Hispanic	2.1	3.1
Asian		0.6

19. Columbus, Ohio

	1970	1980
White	81.0%	76.2%
Black	18.4	22.1
Hispanic	0.6	0.8
Asian		0.8

20. Boston

	1970	1980
White	82.0%	70.0%
Black	16.3	22.4
Hispanic	2.6	6.4
Asian		2.7

21. New Orleans

	1970	1980
White	54.6%	42.5%
Black	45.0	55.3
Hispanic	3.8	3.4
Asian		1.3

22. Jacksonville

	1970	1980
White	77.0%	73.0%
Black	22.3	25.4
Hispanic	1.7	1.8
Asian		1.0

23. Seattle

	1970	1980
White	87.4%	79.5%
Black	7.1	9.5
Hispanic	1.6	2.6
Asian		7.4

24. Denver

	1970	1980
White	89.3%	74.8%
Black	9.1	12.0
Hispanic	13.4	18.8
Asian		1.4

25. Nashville

	1970	1980
White	80.1%	75.7%
Black	19.6	23.3
Hispanic	0.6	0.8
Asian		0.5

26. St. Louis

	1970	1980
White	58.8%	53.5%
Black	40.9	45.6
Hispanic	1.0	1.2
Asian		0.4

27. Kansas City, Mo.

	1970	1980
White	77.5%	69.8%
Black	22.1	27.4
Hispanic	2.7	3.3
Asian		0.8

28. El Paso

	1970	1980
White	96.9%	58.6%
Black	2.3	3.2
Hispanic	58.1	62.5
Asian		0.8

TABLE 4.1 (cont.)

29. Atlanta

	1970	1980
White	48.6%	32.4%
Black	51.5	66.6
Hispanic	1.0	1.4
Asian		0.5

30. Pittsburgh

	1970	1980
White	79.3%	74.7%
Black	20.2	24.0
Hispanic	0.8	0.8
Asian		0.6

31. Oklahoma City

	1970	1980
White	84.0%	80.0%
Black	13.6	14.6
Hispanic	2.0	2.8
Asian		1.0

U.S. Average

	1970	1980
White	87.5%	83.2%
Black	11.1	11.7
Hispanic	4.5	6.4
Asian		1.5

Note: Some of the decline in white share is because some Hispanics counted as white in 1970 are in other groups in 1980. Hispanics may be of any race. No figures on Asians available for 1970.

Source: "City Dwellers: Changes of a Decade," *U.S. News & World Report*, March 21, 1983, pp. 50–51. Copyright, 1983, U.S. News & World Report, Inc.

Preliminary evidence suggests that the new arrivals will be different from the earlier ethnics in important ways. Many of the refugees from Vietnam, Laos, and Cambodia, for example, may not be as interested in assimilation as were earlier immigrants. They are, after all, persons driven from their home countries by real or anticipated political repression.[50] More than that, they come from traditionally strong cultures that appear relatively operative despite the traumas of uprooting and immigration. Generalization on this point is difficult, however, because of wide differences among the groups themselves; many of the early-arriving Vietnamese, for example, were quite Westernized and urbanized even before they left their native country. By contrast, the Hmong were from isolated Laotian mountain villages. Assimilation of the Hmong does not appear imminent, as they are reportedly internally well structured and relatively isolated. Even their internal migrations within the country appear to be directed by traditional Hmong leaders. This closedness apparently affects their utilization of social services.[51] By contrast, the early arriving Vietnamese have made more consistent and effective contact, especially economically.[52]

The political strategies and resources employed by these groups are difficult to discern at this early stage. Teachers and social service professionals describe their leaders as generally skillful and effective. The Indochinese in particular are considered by many who work with them to be model immigrants—hard working, efficient, anxious to learn, and obedient. In the short run, they are the recipients of a variety of government programs designed to aid them. As might be imagined, that fact alone, in a time of shrinking budgets, fans some hostilities between the Indochinese and those others who are being pressured off governmental assistance.

Perhaps the more interesting aspect of the politics of the new immigrants is not so much what they are doing but how they are being used as part of the strategies of other groups. The Indochinese add to a labor pool. They provide a model of hard work to their American counterparts and are unaccustomed to the expectation that they should join a union. They are also likely to reinforce strong pro-American and anticommunist sentiments. For such reasons, they are welcomed by neoconservatives. Radicals would prefer the formulation that the new arrivals are exploited themselves and are being used to put pressure on the

[50]For an overview and further commentary on this point, see Ray Smith, "Indochinese Americans: A Case Study in Immigration History," paper presented to the Western Conference of the Association for Asian Studies, Berkeley, California, November 5–7, 1981.

[51]See Paul Strand and Woodrow Jones, "Health Service Utilization by Indochinese Refugees," unpublished manuscript, available through Social Science Research Laboratory, San Diego State University (1983).

[52]D. S. Massey, "Dimensions of the New Immigration to the U.S. and Prospects for Assimilation," *Annual Review of Sociology,* Vol. 7 (1981), pp. 57–85. For a recommendation that assimilationist assumptions be amended to include discussions of colonialist and class analysis in the study of recent arrivals, see Wen H. Kuo, "On the Study of Asian Americans: Its Current State and Agenda," *Sociological Quarterly,* Vol. 20 (Spring 1979), pp. 279–290.

American worker to serve more cheaply and quietly the interests of the ruling class.

So much for the essential features of the local political power map. Obviously, we must know much more about the unique features of any city before we can be certain of our map, but this is a beginning. Reviewing the catalog of basic actors in city politics in this way also suggests strongly how political resources are distributed in a strong skew toward those at the top. Our tracing of our likely success in opposing the apartment house being built in our neighborhood illustrates the point. The leading business and labor organizations would not likely take up our cause and might actively oppose it; our most powerful ally might well be within the urban bureaucracy; environmental and "good government" groups would be sympathetic but would probably not commit many of their scarce resources to us; black and ethnic groups could be courted, but they tend to be relatively resource poor. In short, the best guess is that if we fought this political battle we would lose. That is not saying the matter is unwinable, but only that extraordinary effort would be required. Realism dictates that we recognize a bias in the structure of the group process.

ELECTIONS: INSTITUTIONALIZED VOICE

Mention "political participation" to most Americans and they will immediately think of voting and elections. Our primary criterion for whether a political system is "democratic" is whether there are regular elections. Such associations are entirely proper. The history of Western civilization reveals a long struggle to overcome arbitrary, self-interested, authoritarian rule. The electoral process is a lasting monument to the enlightenment and political skill of our forbearers. Speaking in terms of their linkage functions, elections are institutionalized voice—an assurance that citizens will regularly be asked to pass judgment on the viability of their leadership.

But such affirmations cannot end the discussion of elections in America. A number of political scientists incline to the view that elections are not a particularly effective means of expressing oneself to government. Critics from conservative to radical find the electoral process less directive of government than the optimists suggest. Murray Edelman has summed up voting participation as functioning mainly to provide us with "symbolic reassurance," that is, a relatively contentless action by which we reaffirm our faith in the political order.[53] Certainly, those who would be effective, as the preceding review of group activity was designed to emphasize, must organize and mobilize themselves quite apart from the electoral

[53]Murray Edelman, *The Symbolic Uses of Politics* (Urbana: University of Illinois Press, 1964).

process. Voting is but one political resource; it is seldom adequate when used alone.

Voting Participation

It is difficult to collect systematic data on local elections as there is no national repository that collects them. Nonetheless there has been sufficient analysis over time to allow some firm generalizations. Perhaps the most striking observation is that only about one-third of the adult population actually votes in local elections. That is half the roughly 60 percent who customarily turn out for presidential elections.[54] Low local voting turnout is not offset by other forms of political activity either. Verba and Nie examined other modes of participation and found that 21 percent voted as their sole political act; another 20 percent participated in groups that had some political goals; 15 percent engaged in political campaigning. Only 11 percent were classified as complete political activists.[55]

Variation in local settings accounts for some city-to-city differences in participation. In general, social factors that affect attachment to the locality and some of the characteristics of the electoral and governmental structure appear to account for much of the variation in local political participation.

Social Factors That Affect Attachment to the City

Compiling the findings of a number of studies, one could construct a profile of a highly participative city. It would be relatively stable, with low mobility rates and higher social class composition, but also with a high level of ethnic consciousness, so that citizens would see clearly their personal and ideological stakes in government action, and conflict would be more intense than in most cities.[56]

This profile will come as a surprise to those who would expect higher rates of participation to occur where there is great homogeneity in the population and low levels of political conflict. That is precisely the image that many who have fled the city for quieter suburban havens seem to carry with them. Quite the contrary, the same factors that define the city accelerate the forces of political participation.

---

[54]Verba and Nie, *Participation in America*, Table 2.1.

[55]Ibid., Chap. 4.

[56]This profile is constructed from the findings of the following major studies: Robert Alford and Harry Scoble, "Sources of Local Political Involvement," *American Political Science Review*, Vol. 62 (December 1968), pp. 1192–1206.; Alvin Boskoff and Harmon Ziegler, *Voting Patterns in a Local Election* (Philadelphia: Lippincott, 1964); Howard Hamilton, "The Municipal Voter: Voting and Nonvoting in City Elections," *American Political Science Review*, Vol. 65 (December 1971), pp. 1135–1140; Robert Lane, *Political Life* (New York: The Free Press, 1959).

The Effects of Electoral
and Governmental Structure

The competitiveness of the political parties, the structure of the electoral process, and the form of government exercise an independent effect on voting participation in cities. Interestingly, that effect is clearly associated with the package of reforms that good government groups have championed since the founding of the American Civic League and the crusading of Richard Childs at the turn of the current century. That movement was designed to bring down "boss rule" based on "machine politics." We will discuss the reform movement more fully in Chapter 6. But for present purposes, let us just say that reform, when successful, led to lower levels of political participation.

The profile of a low-participation city is one with a council-manager form of government, a nonpartisan ballot, and a mayor and a council elected on an at-large basis and in which the political parties are weak and/or noncompetitive.[57] The aim of the reformers was to undercut the machine. It accomplished this, but at the cost of lower levels of participation. Of course, not all American cities have adopted the reform package. Eighty-five percent of the cities that have adopted the council-manager form also have nonpartisan elections. Of all major U.S. cities, 64 percent elect candidates without party identification. This result is exactly what the reformers intended—to weaken party organization at the local level. But without the mobilizing and identifying effect of party activity, the voters do not turn out in as great numbers. Nor, it should be noted, is the failure to turn out randomly distributed. The lower socioeconomic status residents stay out of politics in larger numbers.

The at-large election system, wherein council members are elected citywide instead of as representatives of a geographically specific area called a ward or district, also contributes to lower levels of political participation. Particularly, it discourages minorities of all kinds—racial, ethnic, or ideological. The at-large system has this effect because it requires that any candidate, say, a Socialist, win a majority citywide. Even if the city were 40 percent Socialist, there would be no representative of that view on the council, whereas in a ward system, they would win the council seats from the districts in which they had a majority.

Karnig investigated this effect as it relates to black representation.[58] He

---

[57]This profile is constructed from materials in the following sources: Hawley, *Nonpartisan Elections;* Gerald Pomper, "Ethnic and Group Voting and Nonpartisan Elections," *Public Opinion Quarterly,* Vol. 30 (Spring 1966), pp. 79–99; Raymond Wolfinger and John Field, "Political Ethos and the Structure of City Government,"*American Political Science Review,* Vol. 60 (June 1966), pp. 306–326; Robert Salisbury and Gordon Black, "Class and the Party in Nonpartisan Elections: The Case of Des Moines,"*American Political Science Review,* Vol. 54 (November 1963), pp. 584–592; Albert Karnig, "Black Representation on City Councils: The Impact of Reform and Socio-Economic Factors," *Urban Affairs Quarterly,* Vol. 12 (December 1976), pp. 223–242.

[58]Karnig, "Black Representation on City Councils."

examined the ratio between the black proportion of the population and their "share" of council seats in 139 cities. His finding was that by this abstract standard, blacks had only about half the council seats their numbers warranted. More than a third of the cities had no black council members at all. Both the at-large system of election and the location of the city in the South provided the major explanations for the cities with low ratios. In northern cities, the ratio is almost commensurate with blacks in the population (0.983). But in southern cities, that ratio drops to only about a third.

This discriminatory effect is an illustration of "institutionalized bias," that is, a systematic skewing of the political process that favors some interests and disadvantages others. It is not direct discrimination, but discrimination nonetheless. This pattern has not gone unnoticed by black and civil rights groups. The U.S. Supreme Court was asked in *Chavez* v. *Witcomb* (1975) to find at-large electoral systems unconstitutional.[59] It refused.

Is it necessary that all interests be represented in proportion to their existence in the population? Just putting the question this way suggests that no representative system is capable of that. Think of all the interests we have that are not even discussed as unrepresented. Who represents the vegetarian? Neoconservatives are particularly unimpressed by the idea that any minority needs to be represented in the governmental process in proportion to their existence in the population; this implies a quota system. Even if we could construct governing bodies that reflected the proper proportions of blacks to whites, it has been argued, we might thereby unbalance other interests. Finally, this viewpoint runs, we must acknowledge that one does not have to be a black, for example, to make rules that are fair to blacks and to others as well. The questions as finally raised are: How important is political participation? and How crucial is the linkage function in assuring democracy?

Liberals and radicals are inclined to think that participation is quite important, particularly as democracy presumes that the lower-status citizen should have equal voice. Political participation is important to assure a relatively close connection between what people want from their political system and what it does. It may be true that white representatives can protect black interests. But the real test of that is what Susan Hansen has dubbed "concurrence," that is, the degree of agreement on more substantive public issues between the general population and the decision makers.[60] Her study of sixty-four randomly selected American cities compared the responses of an "elite" with a "mass" sample when asked what were the principal problems facing the community. The broad requirement of democracy would be a high level of concurrence. That was found in a number of cities. In many cities the views of leaders and citizens differed sharply. Hansen's analysis of what factors are associated with higher levels of concurrence turned up the following: (1)

[59]415 U.S. 972.
[60]Susan B. Hansen, "Participation, Political Structure and Concurrence," *American Political Science Review*, Vol. 69 (September 1975).

Concurrence was higher in communities with partisan rather than nonpartisan elections. (2) Concurrence was higher in communities where there was more intense electoral conflict. (3) Concurrence was higher in communities where participation rates were higher. Participation appears very important in assuring representative governmental response.

Finally, it may be noted that economic conditions may independently affect belief in democracy and contribute to defining the impulses to participate. Ostheimer and Ritt, for example, say "our data provide support for the proposition that self-perceived financial decline is related to the weakening of attitudes most supportive of democracy."[61]

SUMMARY

When a city offers citizens problems, they may exit. Otherwise, they may express their discontent through the institutionalized means of elections or through their participation in other forms of political activity, or they may join groups that express voice for them, or, in most dire circumstances, they may engage in protest actions—all illustrations of Hirschman's "voice" option. If government still fails to meet the demand, they may finally choose to exit or to remain out of loyalty. Such is the general perspective of neoconservatism.

The connection of Hirschman's formulation with neoconservatism is better understood if we associate it with the work of John Tiebout. In his classic "pure theory of local expenditures," he suggested that we view the metropolis as a marketplace of local governments in which citizens "vote with their feet."[62] As both liberal and radical critics would point out, that formulation makes the central act of political participation one dimensional—the decision to move or not. Even so, many recent formulations by urban scholars have adopted that basic stance. Peterson, for example, while rejecting the most extreme formulation of the "pure theory," adopts the basic notion that migration based on tax and service is the central participatory decision: "individuals consider the relative costs and benefits of government services in choosing places of residence." He says, "If migrants calculate the costs and benefits of public services, local governments, to insure local prosperity, must anticipate the preferences of potential migrants."[63] This is the central reason for his conclusion that, "It is only a modest oversimplification to equate the interests of cities with the interests of their export industries."[64]

[61]John Ostheimer and Leonard Ritt, "Abundance and American Democracy: A Test of Dire Predictions," *Journal of Politics*, Vol. 44 (May 1982), pp. 365–387, 87.

[62]John Tiebout, "A Pure Theory of Local Expenditures," *Journal of Political Economy*, Vol. 64 (1956), pp. 416–424.

[63]Peterson, *City Limits*, p. 32.

[64]Ibid., p. 23.

Subsequent empirical work appears to support Peterson's position, at least, as regards the responsiveness of elected officials to the demands of advantaged groups. Entirely in keeping with the observations of this chapter, a study of the responsiveness of elected officials in fifty-one cities found that "wealthy cities with little party competition, a weak Democratic party, a centralized power structure, and few blacks represented in group activity are more likely to bias their policy responses in favor of advantaged groups."[65]

Liberals, particularly those associated with pluralism, contradict the idea that business interests must, or even do, occupy such a central place in the political life of a city. What Peterson points to as the dominating city interest is simply one of a number of competing groups. Group theory presumes that every significant interest in the city is represented by some voluntary or economic association. The power of these groups depends not on some reified notion of a "city interest" but is the result of its skill in cultivating and mobilizing its political resources. In this way, the content of policy reflects the relative power of the groups. The role of the political decision maker is to search for a compromise that all (or many) of the contending groups can accept. This means that political participation is important and multidimensional and must be kept free from single interest domination. That set of conditions is the minimal requirement of a "democratic" order; what the neoconservatives describe is not a democracy.

Radicals agree with the neoconservative description of the city as dominated by its upper-income residents and its basic industries. Radicals take as evidence of the class basis of the electoral system the institutionalized biases of the electoral system that favor the middle-class and stunt the participation of the lower socio-economic groups. But what to neoconservatives is a description of a system that optimizes individual freedom is to radicals a description of a system that subordinates, deceives, and exploits those who cannot afford to exercise the exit option. Exit can be exercised only by those who can financially afford it. The poor and increasing numbers of middle-class residents are cynically misinterpreted as exercising loyalty when, in reality, many have no choice but to stay and endure further exploitation.

---

[65]Paul Schneider and Russell Getter, "Structural Sources of Unequal Responsiveness to Group Demands in American Cities," *The Western Political Quarterly*, Vol. 36 (March 1983), pp. 7–29.

CHAPTER 5

Changing Patterns
of Conflict
and Coalition

Urban conflict is structured. Cities are diverse, their strategies varied and their resources unevenly distributed. But that is not to say that there are no stable coalitions in American cities. Contrary to the imagery of pluralism that coalitions come and go from issue to issue, contemporary urban scholars find relatively stable coalitions conflicting with other coalitions over extended periods of time. While stable, they are not static. There are long-term forces of change as well.

As we have been documenting throughout this book, it is the economic forces that are the most basic sources of transformation of American cities. It will be no surprise to find that when economic shifts occur, political coalitions will adapt, break down, or realign. Unfortunately, just a handful of studies exist to help us understand these processes, but they do suggest some broad outlines.

COALITIONS IN PUBLIC CHOICE THEORY

The basic logic of coalitional behavior has been well developed by public choice theorists, particularly those using "game" assumptions. Their aim is to set forth the minimal conditions for coalition formation in legislative bodies. If we may assume that the basic logic of coalitions is the same for less formal decision makers, then the logic is equally applicable to coalitional behavior among participants in urban politics.

Coalition building becomes a possible strategy in the format called n-person, zero-sum games, that is, conflict situations in which there are many players (n-persons) and a finite amount to gain (zero sum) for all players. In such conditions, we can define the minimum requirements for a player to choose to join with others. They are (1) individual rationality, by which is simply meant that an individual will join a coalition when he or she gets as much or more from doing so than not; (2) collective rationality, that is, the payoffs to the players will be more if they enter a coalition than if they do not; and (3) the sum of the payoffs to all the players being equal to the value of the "grand coalition," that is, the total payoff even if there were no coalitional formation.[1]

The main question the n-person game analogy seeks to answer is which coalitions will form? Which payoff configurations (i.e., how much for which coalitions) will rational, utility-maximizing players agree to? The answer that the theory suggests is simply that payoff that will bring the greatest return to all members of the coalition. However, as Abrams points out, stable coalitions (i.e., coalitions that no member has an incentive to leave and that cannot benefit from the inclusion of other members) are rare in this game format.[2] The most important implication of this is that these apparently simple, reasonable conditions set too stringent criteria for rational choice making. But the game situations that do allow application of these criteria are considerably more complex. For example, they are developed in what are called n-person nonconstant-sum games, such as the well-known "prisoner's dilemma."[3]

William Riker pioneered the effort both to achieve a closer proximation to political reality and to apply the theory of games to political situations. In his *The Theory of Political Coalitions*, he suggests the central construct of the logic of coalitional behavior is the "minimum winning coalition" (MWC).[4] The minimum winning coalition is defined as that coalition that would not be winning if any one of its members defected. Riker concludes that "in n-person, zero-sum games, where side payments are permitted, where players are rational, and where they have perfect information, only minimum winning coalitions occur."[5] By "side

---

[1]For a discussion of the origins, implications, and modes of symbolic expression of each of these conditions, see Robert Abrams, *Foundations of Political Analysis: An Introduction to the Theory of Collective Choice* (New York: Columbia University Press, 1980), pp. 215–234.

[2]Ibid., p. 232. The payoff configurations and coalitions that satisfy these three criteria are called the "core of the game." There are no stable coalitions possible because "all essential constant-sum, n-person games have empty cores," which is to say that there are no coalitions and payoff configurations that satisfy all three conditions.

[3]Ibid., pp. 191–193.

[4]William Riker, *Theory of Political Coalitions* (New Haven, Conn.: Yale University Press, 1962).

[5]Ibid., p. 32.

payments,'' game theorists mean something like a bribe, but without the element of moral judgment. It involves one player giving another an additional portion of the payoff to get the player to join or leave a particular coalition.

While the rule for a winning coalition takes a step toward realism, as Abrams says, ''it still does not aid very much in empirical prediction, since it allows for the possibility of a great many winners, without telling us which winning coalition will form.''[6] Moreover, the logic of Riker's concept MWC has subsequently been called into question by those who argue that MWCs may occur, but not necessarily.[7]

GROUNDS FOR COALITIONS IN CITY POLITICS

There remains a great gap between the rationalist model of coalition building and the realities of urban politics. Approaching the effort to describe coalitional behavior from a different perspective altogether, a number of urban scholars have sought to describe what they see in particular cities. They then use those generalizations as the basis for comparison over time and in other settings. These studies have begun with the effort to identify the common ground upon which a coalition of groups may form.

Locals versus Cosmopolitans

An early attempt by the sociologist Robert K. Merton characterized two competing coalitions he found in a study of a New Jersey city that he called Rovere.[8] The ''locals'' are those influentials who are raised mostly in the area, are economically and sentimentally rooted in the city, derive their political influence from an elaborate network of friends and associates built up over the years, and organize that influence through a variety of localistic organizations such as the Elks, the Rotary, or the Masons. Locals are loyal, given to voice rather than to exit. ''Cosmopolitans'' by contrast, are in, but not of, the particular city. They are cosmopolitan in the sense that they are oriented to the larger world outside. A local manager of a national chain store is a good example of a cosmopolitan. He derives his influence not from friendships but from the status commonly ascribed to one in his position. Cosmopolitans have a need for local influence to promote their

[6] Abrams, *Foundations of Political Analysis*, p. 236.

[7] See Robert Butterworth, ''A Research Note on the Size of Winning Coalitions,'' *American Political Science Review*, Vol. 65 (November 1971), pp. 741–748.

[8] Robert K. Merton, ''Patterns of Influence: Locals and Cosmopolitans,'' in his *Social Theory and Social Structure*, rev. ed. (Glencoe, Ill.: The Free Press 1957).

business interests, but they know that they are likely to be short-term residents. Merton describes the cosmopolitan as being less interested in boosting the locality and more involved with policies that ratify the integration of the city into the broader socioeconomic processes.

Thomas Dye used the local-cosmopolitan distinction to study sixteen suburban Philadelphia cities. He found that the locals were the dominant coalition in cities of relatively lower social and economic composition and that locals had distinct advantages in achieving influence and office. Interestingly, both locals and cosmopolitans were found to support a kind of social segregation. Both coalitions could agree that they "favor using zoning law to keep out of [the] community the type of people who usually build cheaper houses on smaller lots."[9]

Images of City Government

Oliver Williams and Charles Adrian have suggested another and more elaborate basis for coalition among urban political actors. Derived from their study of four cities, they supply a typology based on differing "images" of the proper role of government.[10] Table 5.1 contains a summary of the typology, the common membership of each coalition, and their usual policy preferences.

The four images are as follows:

1. Some people see the city government as an "instrument of community growth." This coalition is brought together by its central concern to promote the expansion of the economy and the population of the city. The most powerful interests in the city are likely to be growth advocates: bankers, newspapers and electronic media, utilities, city bureaucrats, and large property owners, for example. Typically, this coalition wants re-zoning of land for commercial use and for development and the extension of sewer and water lines to those building sites. Growth advocates may also favor policies to attract new businesses; they like advertising the city as an advantageous location and offering low taxes and other advantages for new businesses to relocate there.

2. The city government should "provide life's amenities." For these political actors, the primary function of local government is to keep the city a good living environment; their emphasis is on "the home environment rather than on the working environment—the citizen as consumer rather than pro-

---

[9]Thomas Dye, "The Local-Cosmopolitan Dimension and the Study of Urban Politics," *Social Forces,* Vol. 41 (March 1963), p. 244.

[10]Oliver Williams and Charles Adrian, *Four Cities* (Philadelphia: University of Pennsylvania Press, 1963), pp. 23–32, and Oliver Williams, "A Typology for Comparative Local Government," *Midwest Journal of Political Science,* Vol. 5 (May 1961), pp. 150–164.

TABLE 5.1   The Williams-Adrian Typology of Images of City Government

IMAGE	GENERAL EXPLANATION	COMMON ADHERENTS	TYPICAL PREFERRED PUBLIC POLICIES
1. Instrument of city growth	1. Central priority is that city's population and economy should grow	1. Bankers, local businessowners, newspapers, utilities, city bureaucracy.	1. Re-zoning land for industrial use; extension of sewer and water lines to potential factory sites; low taxes on land zoned industrial and on new plants.
2. Provider of life's amenities	2. Central priority is that city should be a desirable residence	2. Homeowner's associations, residential real estate brokers.	2. Exclusionary zoning; land-use control; industrial parks with light industry; heavy investment in parks, recreation and educational facilities.
3. Caretaker	3. Central priority services. Low tax advocate.	3. Philosophical, homeowners.	3. Opposition to most
4. Arbiter of conflicting interests.	4. No substantive control priority. Governments exist to settle disputes in accordance with principles of equity and justice.	4. Minority groups, others that have reinquished desire to govern in terms of their preferred images.	4. Open housing, equal job opportunity.

Source: Prepared from Oliver P. Williams and Charles R. Adrian, *Four Cities* (Philadelphia: University of Pennsylvania Press, 1963), especially pp. 23–26.

ducer.''[11] When public monies become scarce, the amenities seekers prefer expenditures on streets, parks, and recreation areas and improvement of educational facilities. Exclusionary zoning to keep out ''undesirables'' is commonly embraced as well. Amenities seekers do not necessarily oppose economic development; rather, they prefer particular kinds of development—light industry that produces no smog or a large labor pool of low-income workers is preferable. The ideal strategy of economic develop-

[11]Williams and Adrian, *Four Cities*, p. 25.

ment for the amenities advocate appears to be the industrial park composed, for example, of research centers of large corporations and high-technology firms. Amenities seekers were earlier associated with middle-income suburbs; more recently they have a strong voice in a number of Sunbelt cities.

3. Most cities have another coalition, composed of those who see city government more as a "caretaker." Those embracing the caretaker image take seriously the credo, "That government is best which governs least." Along with minimal government, they demand low taxes. They acknowledge that it is permissible for the city to patrol the streets, fight fires, and purify the water supply, but activities beyond those absolute essentials are unwarrantable. Two types of people make up this coalition; philosophical conservatives and the economically marginal. Conservatives may be in this position out of commitment, but the economic marginals are there out of personal necessity. The homeowner who may lose the house if his taxes increase, the elderly, and others on fixed incomes are good examples of caretakers-by-necessity.

4. Finally, Williams and Adrian identify a loose coalition of those holding an "arbiter" image of city government. To them the city should not embody one single, dominating interest but should function as an umpire among conflicting interests. City government exists to manage conflicts among competing interests, they believe, and it should do that in accordance with rules of fairness and equity. Often this image is held by those who have no hope of controlling city politics but simply want fair treatment and additional access to collective goods. The self-conscious ethnic and minority groups commonly coalesce in this form. It appears that larger cities come to be dominated by the arbiter image when it becomes clear that no one of the other coalitions can maintain control in its own terms. New York and Chicago, for example, appear to operate loosely within the terms of an arbiter image.

These images are not mutually exclusive or collectively exhaustive. Williams and Adrian acknowledge that they are "empirically, not logically, derived."[12] Nor are there any clear criteria for classification or synoptic measures contained in the original formulation. As is often the case with empirical political science, we have traded rigor for realism. Despite some of the limitations, the Williams-Adrian typology appears more comprehensive and refinable than do some others.[13]

---

[12]Ibid., p. 35.

[13]See, for example, the long discussion and apparent abandonment of the attempt to describe urban coalitional behavior in terms of "ethos" in Edward Banfield and James Q. Wilson, "Public-Regardingness as a Value Premise in Voting Behavior," *American Political Science Review*, Vol. 58 (December 1964) pp. 876–877; Raymond Wolfinger and John O. Field, "Political Ethos and the Structure of City Government," *American Political Science Review*, Vol. 60 (June 1966); pp. 306–326; and James Q. Wilson and Edward Banfield, "Political Ethos Revisited," *American Political Science Review*, Vol. 65 (December 1971), pp. 1048–1062.

A bit later in this chapter I will suggest a way in which this typology might be integrated with another to provide some of the historical perspective that typologies lack.

Salamon's Typology: The Private City, the Bureaucratic City, and the Policy-Planning City

Lester Salamon seeks to provide a new conceptual framework for urban political analysis that "acknowledge[s] the possible existence of different types of policy arenas within a single city" and that also makes the "substance of policy, the role of government, and not just the structure of institutions or the structure of power, the major focus."[14] These criteria are also met by the Williams-Adrian typology, but there are some important differences in Salamon's categories.

THE PRIVATE CITY

The dominant coalition of interests in this type of city "confines the government to a largely passive role as facilitator of private economic activity."[15] The private city is not inert. The process of economic growth necessitates governmental action to facilitate it—streets, water, services. What distinguishes the private city is the great extent to which governmental power is put in service of the private economy and the resulting ad hoc character of the accommodating governmental actions. Historican Sam Bass Warner describes Philadelphia in just these terms, and with increasingly unhappy outcomes: "Privatism suffered and abetted a system of politics which was so weak it could not deal effectively with the economic, physical and social events that determined the quality of life in the city."[16]

The private city vision is strongly present in most American cities. "Indeed . . . the 'private city' is easily the dominant form of city politics."[17] The image is particularly ascendant when the city is at the stage of historical development in which its economy is growing. It is present, but perhaps not dominant, at other times, although its focus may be on specialized policy arenas within city politics—those policy arenas that most directly affect the economic climate.

[14]Lester Salamon, "Urban Politics, Urban Policy, Case Studies and Political Theory," *Public Administration Review*, Vol. 37, no. 4 (July–August 1977), pp. 418–434, 18. Reprinted with permission from *Public Administration Review*, © 1977 by The American Society for Public Administration, 1120 G Street, N.W., Washington, D.C. All rights reserved.

[15]Ibid., p. 422.

[16]Sam Bass Warner, Jr., *The Private City: Philadelphia in Three Periods of Its Growth* (Philadelphia: University of Pennsylvania Press, 1968), p. 202.

[17]Salamon, "Urban Politics, Urban Policy," p. 424.

THE BUREAUCRATIC CITY

While the private city may be the most common form, it is not universal. The growing power of the urban bureaucracy has been noted in a number of cities. It is so powerful in some cities that it may be characterized as the dominating coalition. The bureaucratic city, then, is "a city whose policy is shaped in significant areas more by the internal operating procedure, professional norms, and organizational ethos of the bureaucracy, than by the conscious choices of the . . . elected officials, or even economic elites."[18] Oakland fits this type. A study of Oakland in the mid-1970s found that the key determinant of the amount of money spent on streets, libraries, and schools was more the result of internal bureaucratic rules than of conscious political choice.[19] The central rule of the bureaucratic model, according to the Oakland study, was the "Adam Smith rule"; that is, "When a customer makes a 'request,' take care of him in a professional manner; otherwise leave him alone."[20]

Bureaucratic dominance is not equally likely in all policy arenas. It is most likely in those policy areas that involve substantial service delivery functions, relatively weak and disorganized client groups, extensive professionalization, and that are well integrated with other levels of government. "Education, welfare, and law enforcement are prime candidates for this kind of pattern."[21]

The emergence of the bureaucratic city would appear to confirm the expectations of the public choice theorists. Yet the explanation provided by Salamon is considerably more complicated. He traces the origins of the bureaucratic city to five conditions:

1. Modern urban government has become increasingly more complex. As technical and administrative detail multiplies, elected officials and economic elites alike lack the detailed knowledge that is necessary to informed decision.

2. Bureaucrats, because they are inside, know best how to accomplish goals within the process.

3. Professionalization and unionization help to insulate bureaucrats from control by elected officials and others.

4. The enlargement of state and federal programs has given local administrators influential allies among their counterparts in the higher levels of government.

---

[18]Ibid.

[19]Frank Levy, Arnold Meltsner, and Aaron Wildavsky, *Urban Outcomes* (Berkeley: University of California Press, 1974).

[20]Ibid., p. 229.

[21]Salamon, "Urban Politics, Urban Policy," p. 425.

5. Agencies with strong client groups can benefit from the political power of those groups. Such external political support has been made particularly necessary and effective by the reform movement.

THE DEMOCRATIC (POLICY-PLANNING) CITY

The third image upon which a dominant urban coalition may form is what Salamon calls the democratic or policy-planning city. From his description, however, there appears little that is clearly democratic about this model. As he defines it, the image is of an effective policy-planning process; that is, the city "performs a more conscious steering role, taking the initiative to alter or anticipate existing trends in pursuit of some broader vision of the public good." An extension of the early impulses of the city planning movement, the modern vision has been "amply nourished in more recent years by the development of new decision-making techniques like systems analysis that permit better analysis of complex social realities and thus afford decision-makers better comprehension of the trade-offs involved in the decisions they make." Such modes of analysis, it is presumed, would be more knowledge based and analytical than group-oriented pluralism would be.

Salamon offers no illustrations of contemporary cities that are substantially policy-planning cities, but he finds in two works—one on New Haven and another on San Francisco—considerable insight into the problems of moving from the "private city" to the "policy-planning" model.[22] There are a number of conditions that must appear before the transition to the policy-planning type can occur: a divided business sector, an activated citizenry, and a strong political leader "with the will and capacity to mobilize a pro-redistributive electoral coalition sufficient to neutralize the bureaucracy and promote activist policies."[23]

Salamon acknowledges that it is possible that the policy-planning city may not emerge at all but rather constitute merely a "warmed over" version of the private city. Which occurs depends on who controls the new planning tools. For the policy-planning ideal to be realized as a completely distinct type, there must be a strong, independent planning agency with an ethic of equitable resource distribution. Finally, he admits that this expectation is contrary to much of the recent history of city planning: "Despite the avowed expectations of early reformers, planners have typically been forced to choose between impotence and cooptation,

---

[22]Raymond Wolfinger, *The Politics of Progress* (Englewood Cliffs, N.J.: Prentice-Hall, 1974); Fredrick Wirt, *Decision-Making in San Francisco* (Berkeley: University of California Press, 1974).

[23]Ibid., p. 426.

between splendid isolation and service to the goals of the city's economic powers-that-be."[24]

The (Single) Urban Interest

One final formulation of the structure of the urban political economy is to be found in the work of the orthodox economist Charles Tiebout. Understanding the city by analogy to "the firm," he posits the existence of a singular city interest—the attainment of "optimum size."[25] While firms seek to maximize profits, cities seek to attain the optimum size for the delivery of the bundle of services that the local government produces. Optimum does not mean just bigger and bigger. "Cities below optimum size seek to attract new residents to lower average costs. Those above optimum size do just the opposite. Those at optimum size try to keep their populations constant."[26] Unlike the other typologies discussed in this section, Tiebout simply ignores the diversity of goals of urban actors and the fact of conflict—thereby ignoring politics—to assume that at the core that there is one city interest and that one interest is different from the sum of its group and coalitional parts.

Political scientist Paul Peterson has used Tiebout's basic formulation in his *City Limits*.[27] But Peterson broadens the concept beyond the singular concern for the economic character of the city. Yet he does not move back to the conception of city politics as the result of the clash of local interests. "The interests of cities are neither the summation of individual interests nor the pursuit of optimum size." Instead, according to Peterson, "policies and programs can be said to be in the interest of cities whenever the policies maintain or enhance the economic position, social prestige or political power of the city taken as a whole."[28]

URBAN DEVELOPMENT AND CHANGING COALITIONS

Among the many criticisms that are possible of each of the formulations just discussed, one is most persistent and probably most profound. All are ahistorical and static, even though all acknowledge the importance of explanations that takes

---

[24]Ibid. For some additional discussion and the addition of three types of cities—progressive conservative, community conservative, and liberal pragmatist—see Dale Rogers Marshall, ed., *Uban Policy-Making* (Beverly Hills, Calif.: Sage Publications, 1979), pp. 20–23.

[25]"A Pure Theory of Local Expenditures," *Journal of Political Economy*, Vol. 64 (1956), pp. 416–424.

[26]Ibid., p. 419.

[27]Paul Peterson, *City Limits* (Chicago: University of Chicago Press, 1981). See particularly Chap. 2.

[28]Ibid., p. 20.

forces and directions of change into account. Intuitively, we all expect that the private city of today may be overtaken by amenities seekers tomorrow, or some such pattern. But there is no developmental theory that has wide currency among urban political economists. Once again, however, we can make suggestions. A synthesis of the major features of each of the typologies would lead to the following pattern:

Stage 1.   Caretaker. Small American towns with relatively stable populations, little prospects for growth, and severely limited revenues are likely to be dominated by the caretaker image.[29] Their leadership is likely to be local rather than cosmopolitan. Whether located in rural America or in an earlier historical period, these towns keep government to a minimum. Eagle, Nebraska, for example, in the early 1960s debated the legitimacy of paving the main street.

Stage 2.   Economic Growth. In reaction to the sense of stagnation (some of the residents prefer to call it "stability"), there may emerge a group of economic boosters who organize the community growth coalition. "Young people leave Eagle [Nebraska]," it was argued, "because the town is dead. The only jobs are in Lincoln or Omaha. And there's no excitement here except the beer joint." The growth coalition that forms in this early stage is an activist version of the private city image. The boosters must be active to attract an economic base. As they succeed, they may become more passive, seeking to protect some notion of optimum city size.

Stage 3.   The Challenge of the Poor and the Amenities Seekers. Economic growth is a mixed blessing. It brings into the city both more poor, working class, and racial and ethnic minorities and also more white-collar, professional, and managerial amenities seekers. Either or both may challenge the private city image. A new housing project in Eagle brought an influx of young newcomers. The main street got paved, and a park and a swimming pool were built as the caretaker image broke down. But this pattern is not restricted to small towns. San Diego, the consummate Sunbelt city, was dominated by a growth coalition with a private city vision during the postwar period during which it developed rapidly. But the diversification of its economic base to provide a more stable economy led the town to expand its universities and seek headquarters operations and research and development arms of major corporations and electronic industries. Such diversity brought with it amenities-seeking professionals, a self-selected number who came

---

[29]For a careful study of such a small town in upstate New York, see Arthur Vidich and Joseph Bensman, *Small Town in Mass Society* (Garden City, N.Y.: Doubleday, 1958).

to San Diego partly because of its favorable climate and low densities. The amenities seekers rose to prominence during the 1960s around environmentalist concerns and were a large part of the dominating coalition in San Diego politics. Mayor Pete Wilson, young, articulate Ivy League law school professional, was the amenities seekers' self-image.

The challenge of the blue-collar and racial and ethnic groups was slight in San Diego. Strong antiunion sentiments and practices stayed in place in this recent history. But not so in most of the older, larger cities that emerged in the age we have called industrial capitalism. Ethnics dominated city politics in the era of the "boss" and his "machine." The successes of the reform movement returned many such cities to the pattern of the private city image once more. But, more usually, the conflict among the growth oriented, the amenities seekers, and the poor led to the next stage.

Stage 4.   The Arbiter Image. As the city becomes so large and diverse as to defy control by any single coalition, the city may come to act in the terms of Williams and Adrian's "arbiter of conflicting interests" image. Each of the previously strong coalitions gives up its efforts to dominate the politics of the city and rests content with the hope that it will get equity and fairness. It is in this stage that the bureaucratic city pattern may flourish. The very multiplication of rules and procedures designed to assure fairness makes the city administrator the center of the local political process.

But the arbiter stage is highly unstable. It is easily perceived as, or may indeed be, deadlocked or dominated by intense single interest groups and constituencies or, still differently, as subverted by bureaucratic self-interest. To some, it may be the essence of pluralistic democracy; to most others it is discomforting malaise. Pressures to change produce an uncertain future, but the path apparently diverges in one of two directions.

Stage 5.   Either the Policy-Planning City or the Private City Revisited. The need for more centralized power to make relatively comprehensive decisions to allow the city to adapt to forces not under its control produces pressures in one of two directions. The first is a refinement of the bureaucratic city. The policy-planning city has yet to take firm hold, although tendencies appear. But as Salamon himself recognizes, there are a great many barriers to its realization. Given the historical tendency of cities to revert periodically to the control of the growth oriented, it would appear that the safe money would be on a recurrence of the private city model in those cities well situated to integrate themselves into the economic order of the multinational era of capitalist development. The choice is centrally between whether city planning will be done in the public sector (the policy-planning city) or the private sector. It is worth hypothesizing that the older,

Northeastern cities will be more attracted to the policy-planning image, whereas the newer Sunbelt cities will tend to revive the private city. In the transition period characterized by fiscal stress, it appears that the policy-planning and private city types overlap.

STAGES OR THE DIALECTIC?

However illuminating this historical developmental pattern of urban conflict, it glosses over the much more detailed processes of change. It also leaves us with the implication that history marches in a progressive straight line. As might be expected, Marxist analysis would suggest that if we were to look more carefully, we would find the dialectical process. That does seem fairly implied. If we take the private city image as essentially the capitalist "thesis," what we see in these developmental stages is the differentiation of opposing blocs. These blocs—caretakers, amenities seekers, and racial and ethnic minorities—do not quite appear as full "antitheses" based on oppositional class consciousness, but slightly more narrow clusters of class-related interests. Nonetheless, they achieve some measure of power and effect a synthesis of the private city image with their own. The contemporary coalitional confrontation between the policy-planning city and the private city may be seen as the current form of that classlike struggle.

More specifically, radical analysis of the structure of urban conflict in the contemporary period relies on the assumptions of "uneven peripheral development" discussed in Chapter 3. Norman and Susan Fainstein, for example, describe the structure of political conflict in "declining cities" and in "converting cities."[30] The "declining cities" are those experiencing a racially based legitimation crisis. Recall that by "legitimation crisis" we mean the withdrawal of voluntary public compliance with the dominant norms. Historically specific, this crisis emerged in the period 1965 to 1974. Conflict occurred at that time in the form of sit-ins, takeovers of government offices, and struggles over occupancy of land and buildings. Government attempted to meet the situation with additional jobs and services and with redevelopment efforts. The politics of disinvestment determined who would control the shrinking resources.

The "converting city" results from fiscal crisis, which the Fainsteins date 1975–? In the converting city, the aims of government shift to improving fiscal management, dismissing redundant employees, and improving the city as a place for private investment (i.e., improvement of the conditions for accumulation). The structure of conflict that results in each of the types is schematized in Figures 5.1 and 5.2.

[30]Norman Fainstein and Susan Fainstein, "Restructuring the American City: A Comparative Perspective," in Norman Fainstein and Susan Fainstein, eds., *Urban Policy Under Capitalism* (Beverly Hills, Calif.: Sage Publications, 1982), pp. 161–189.

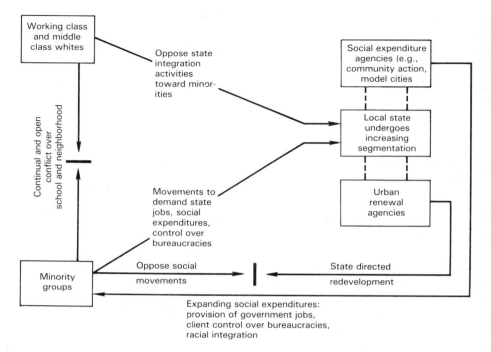

Political situation: legitimation crisis (racial definition); government efforts to integrate minority groups and simultaneously to displace them from core areas
Mode: direct confrontation, politicization of socioeconomic conflicts
Outcomes: increased social expenditures, integration of minority groups into local state, urban renewal of CBD and environs

FIGURE 5.1 Dominant form of political conflict, declining cities, 1965-1974. (*Source:* Norman I. Fainstein and Susan S. Fainstein, *Urban Policy Under Capitalism* (Beverly Hills, Calif.: Sage Publications, 1982), pp. 182–183. Copyright © 1982 by Sage Publications. Reprinted by permission of Sage Publications, Inc.)

The mode of conflict clearly differs between the two types: In the declining city, it is direct confrontation, whereas in the converting city, private allocation of resources displaces political allocation.

In the declining city the issues are primarily concerned with the distribution of government-controlled resources. The outcome in these cities may include gains for the low-income residents, but "within the local political economy, opponents of governmental expansion may diagnose the outcome as a "cave-in" to pressure, resulting in a 'negative business climate.' "[31] In the converting city, the issues focus on the concern for using the power of local government to facilitate the growth process. Racial issues are downplayed. More specifically, controversies shift to such concerns as rent control, coop and condominium conversion, and

[31]Ibid., p. 182. Also see Manuel Castells, *City, Class and Power* (London: Macmillan, 1978).

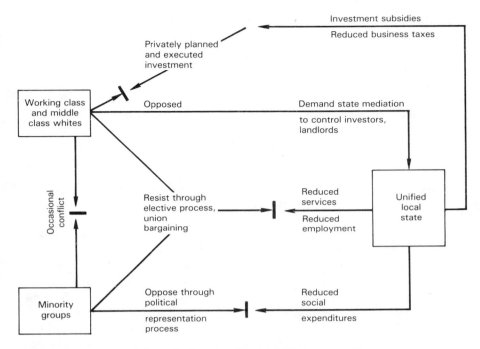

Political situation: accumulation/realization crises (fiscal definition), government efforts to improve fiscal management, encourage private investment
Mode: privatization, shrinkage of political sphere; state mediates between capital and community; institutionalization of conflict in an (expanded) interest-group politics
Outcomes: cutbacks in public employment, services, social expenditures; disciplining of municipal workers; displacement of working and middle classes through private means

FIGURE 5.2 Dominant form of political conflict, converting cities, 1975–. *(Source:* **Norman I. Fainstein and Susan S. Fainstein,** *Urban Policy Under Capitalism* **(Beverly Hills, Calif.: Sage Publications, 1982), pp. 182–183. Copyright © 1982 by Sage Publications. Reprinted by permission of Sage Publications, Inc.)**

historic site preservation and whether the emphasis of governmental redevelopment activities should be aimed at downtown expansion or neighborhood stabilization. The almost inevitable outcome in the converting city is that the poor and even the middle class lose control of the inner city.

The Fainsteins emphasize that the converting city comes to look more like European cities, particularly because the lower-income population is forced to the periphery. This tendency is evident in New York's outer boroughs and in areas adjacent to strip highways in Denver, Daly City, and Oakland.

In sum, in this formulation the focus is less on discrete clusters of interests than it is on the traditional concern of Marxism—class conflict. The fundamental struggle in the contemporary period is one in which the dominant class is seeking to re-establish its position and continue its pursuit of accumulation.

SUMMARY

Neoconservative contributions to our understanding of urban coalition building are minimal at this point. The logic of coalitional behavior in legislative bodies, however, may be adaptable to coalitional decision making in urban politics.

Among the several typologies developed by urban scholars to describe recurrent coalitional patterns, the most commonly used have been (1) the distinction between locals, who ground their political power in their intimate connections with the city, and cosmopolitans, who are powerful because of the status ascribed to them; (2) the Williams and Adrian formulation of conflict among those desiring "growth," those seeking "amenities," those preferring government to minimize its action to "caretaker," and those expecting government to be an "arbiter" of city conflicts; and, finally (3) Salamon's formulation of three types of cities, depending on the image of city government that prevails among those who hold substantial power in the particular city: the "private city," the "bureaucratic city," and the "policy-planning city."

When we seek to understand the broad historical patterns that describe the rise and break-up of particular coalitions, a five-stage developmental process appears: From the small-town (1) "caretaker" image there emerges a challenging (2) "growth"-oriented coalition, who prefers a "private city" mode of government. (3) The poor and the amenities seekers challenge the dominance of the pro-growth forces producing a compromise (4) arbiter image of government that incubates the "bureaucratic city." But the instability of this stage gives way to condition (5), which will either be a return to the growth-oriented "private city" or the "policy-planning" type.

Finally, the pattern of historical development of American cities, and particularly the kind of conflicts emerging in the 1980s, suggests the Marxist formulation that "class"-based conflict is the central force causing historical development to take a dialectical pattern.

CHAPTER 6

*Urban
Institutions
and
Leadership*

These people are all talking about the same things:

"All life is a game of power," Michael Korda.

"I am not a crook," Richard Nixon.

"I seen my opportunities and I took 'em," George Washington Plunkett of Tammany Hall.

"Win . . . through intimidation," Robert Ringer.

"Power tends to corrupt. Absolute power corrupts absolutely," Lord Acton.

"We derive our ultimate authority from the people. And we carry an obligation to make sure that in carrying out our responsibilities, we do so at a price they can afford," Ronald Reagan.

"L'état c'est moi," Louis XIV.

"There go my people. I must catch up with them for I am their leader," Gandhi.

All these people are talking about political power. Their differences suggest some of the reasons why the entire history of Western civilization, not just the modern history of the American city, is full of tension about the proper scope, basis, and organization of governmental authority. When power is institutionalized, we call it authority. It has been institutionalized to prevent the abuses of a Louis XIV. For a variety of reasons, in the contemporary era, governmental authority is strongly criticized by neoconservatives, liberals, and radicals alike. When we see a lapel button that says "Question Authority," it may be worn by a radical angry at the arbitrary exercise of power by educational authorities or by a conservative member of the Libertarian Party.

In practically all human associations, a relatively few leaders operate the system in the name of all the members. They alone have the detailed knowledge of the organization; the great majority know little or nothing about it. In modern democracies, we place our reliance on a "legal-rational" basis of authority as a means of assuring that personal ambition will not overwhelm public good. But the struggle is perennial. In other words, authority is like a lemon. It is a perfectly good fruit that has gotten a bad name because of unscrupulous advertisers.

Let us begin this section with the clear recognition that political institutions are not neutral. Neither are they automatically corrupt because they are not neutral. Historically, we have sought to create institutions that are biased against the arbitrary and selfish behavior of incumbents, that assure a measure of freedom and equality for the largest number of members of the society. Our institutions are a visible index of our success and of our failure to achieve such high purposes. In this chapter, we will describe the basic governmental institutions and the political conflicts about them within American cities. At a minimum, what we will observe is the role of government as a manager of conflict. Recall that, by definition, government exists to regulate conflict. In addition, though, we will see how some interests and coalitions effectively control government for periods of time, how some consistently place their own in the principal offices, and how some build their own biases into the very structure of the conflict resolving process.

Local political institutions and leadership will be developed first historically. The history of "bossism" and "reformism" is too instructive to be ignored. Second, the basic institutions of local politics will be described. Third, the effect of current problems—notably fiscal stress—on city governmental institutions will be assessed. Fourth, the modern version of the reform movement will be identified. And, finally, we will examine the literature that seeks to discover a "power structure," that is, leaders outside the public sector who overpower the authority structure and undermine the democratic process.

BOSSISM AND THE REFORM TRADITION

A great many Americans reserve a special lofty scorn for city politics. The "shame of the cities" to them is still that the cities fell prey to "bossism," that is, control by a "machine" dominated by "grafters and crooks" who lined their pockets with tax monies and ignored the public good. Although no major city now appears to be dominated by such a ''boss''—the death and dissolution of the Daley machine in Chicago apparently ending an era—good cathartic fits of virtuous civic indignation can still be aroused by invoking the shadowy hand of bossism. When the modern Sunbelt city of San Diego voted on a 1981 proposal to change the election system from an at-large basis to district representation, the local newspaper warned that such a change ''might revive machine politics.''

The most careful analysis makes it clear that bossism was the result of particular historical conditions that have passed. James Scott, comparing the emergence of political machines in various countries, concludes that the city boss and his machine was a ''conservative response to rapid social change.''[1] Scott does not necessarily mean ''conservative'' in its ideological sense; rather, he intends to imply that machines minimized what might have been extraordinary turmoil had such moderating social structures been lacking.

The boss and machine era arose in response to the rapid urbanization created by the conditions of the era of industrial capitalism (Civil War to New Deal, as discussed in Chapter 3). The primary fact is that between 1860 and 1920, the urban population rose from 6.2 million to 54.2 million. The largest portion of that new population was poor, drawn from rural America and Europe to the prospects of employment in burgeoning industries. They placed unprecedented demands on city governments that were relatively underdeveloped.[2]

City governments at the time were disorganized. It was common to have a very large number of elected offices, large and unwieldy councils, a number of independent boards, and a weak executive. Another precondition for the emergence of machine politcs was the fact that an increasing number of business operators needed the cooperation of city government and in many cases were willing to pay directly for it. Some of these business people wanted simply to be left alone by government, but others saw in the expanding city an opportunity to make fortunes building the streets, sewers, bridges, buildings, and other urban facilities. Further, the new city dwellers were predominantly poor people with great dependency needs. They were the pool of cheap labor of their time. But there was no public welfare system. Even short-term unemployment or sickness might be a personal disaster. Finally, the new arrivals had but one assured political resource: the vote. Their use of that resource was simple and direct: The ward captain, local member of the political machine, provided for their needs—jobs, short-term loans, personal favors; in exchange, the poor gave the boss their vote.

---

[1] James Scott, ''Corruption, Machine Politics, and Political Change,'' *American Political Science Review*, Vol. 63 (December 1969), pp. 1154–1156.

[2] This discussion draws heavily on Fred Greenstein, ''The Changing Patterns of Urban Party Politics,'' *The Annals of the American Academy of Political and Social Science*, Vol. 353 (May 1964), pp. 2–13. Copyright © 1964 The American Academy of Political and Social Science and reproduced by permission.

The political organization that emerged to facilitate this "equilibrium of incentives" had some consistent characteristics from city to city, including

1. A disciplined party hierarchy directed from the top.
2. The party controlled the nomination process.
3. The party leadership often did not hold office itself.
4. Party leaders were usually of lower social class origins.
5. Party loyalty was maintained with a mixture of material rewards and non-ideological psychic rewards such as ethnic recognition and friendship.[3]

Machine politics was a conservative response to rapid urban growth because it opened alternatives to either ideological political organization or violence. It accomplished this by increasing the legitimacy of the city government to its poor residents by providing them with a route to survival, integration, and even upward social mobility. Because the votes of all—regardless of ethnicity or color—were equally valuable to the machine, it minimized class conflict.[4] Although it is clear that the machine rested on the political support of the poor, it is not clear that the poor were consistently the recipients of favorable social policies. Raymond Wolfinger, speaking specifically of New Haven, observed that an individual's support of the machine may be rewarded with individual favors but seldom with the kinds of changes that aid the poor as a group.[5] That is because machine politicians usually formed close alliances with those local interests who wanted, for example, weak enforcement of housing codes and were mostly uninterested in the quality of public services. Wolfinger argues that the poor gain little from such alliances: "where money talks, the poor are silent," even when the politicians come from among them.[6]

THE REFORM MOVEMENT

Early resistance to the machine was ineffective. In the 1870s, the Reverend Charles Parkhurst put on sporty black and white checkered trousers and took the crusade of his City Vigilance League into New York's bars and brothels. He was

---

[3]This is a bloodless description of a colorful phenomenon. There is a rich historical literature that provides needed flavor and an important sense of local variation. See Milton Rakove, *Don't Make No Waves, Don't Back No Losers* (Bloomington: Indiana University Press, 1976).

[4]For discussion of some of the additional, latent functions of the urban machine, see Robert Merton, "The Latent Function of the Machine," in Robert Merton, ed., *Social Theory and Social Structure* (New York: The Free Press, 1957), pp. 71–81.

[5]Raymond Wolfinger, *The Politics of Progress* (Englewood Cliffs, N.J.: Prentice-Hall, 1974), p. 120.

[6]Ibid.

colorful. But it was the spirit of pragmatic reform of the progressive era that eventually produced the conditions in which a serious reform movement could emerge. The so-called "muckraking journalists," particularly Lincoln Steffans, exposed "urban corruption." A collection of his articles, *The Shame of the Cities,* is a classic of muckraking journalism and one of the first studies of urban power structure. There Steffans shaped Americans' perceptions that it was "moral weakness" of both citizens and politicians that had corrupted our cities. He proceeded city by city: "St. Louis exemplified boodle; Minneapolis, police graft; Pittsburgh, a political and industrial machine; and Philadelphia a general civic corruption. . . ."[7] Beginning in 1869, *The New York Times* began to editorialize against its local machine, Tammany Hall. The *Times* editorial cartoonist Thomas Nast began to build a national reputation for his drawings decrying Boss William Tweed and his organization.

As is often the case, the early stages of reform rely on radical leadership. Upton Sinclair, for example, was a socialist. His book, *The Jungle,* exposed the extraordinarly unsanitary practices of the meat-packing industry. And although the book gave impetus to the movement to regulate the industry, he was unhappy about its overall impact. Sinclair, by his own testimony, had intended "to frighten the country by a picture of what its industrial masters were doing to their victims." He had aimed at the public's head and heart, but he lamented that "by accident I hit it in the stomach."[8] A number of progressive scholars shared Sinclair's distrust of capitalism—Charles Beard and Thorstein Veblen, for example. And, in fact, socialism had a greater impact on cities than is commonly assumed. In 1911 some seventy-four cities and towns had elected socialist mayors or other municipal offices. While most of these were small Midwestern cities, they included Berkeley and Watts in California; Schnectady, New York; and Milwaukee, Wisconsin.[9] By 1920 only two cities—Davenport, Iowa, and Milwaukee, Wisconsin—retained their socialists. The radical influence had been broken.

As is also often the case, radicals lost their centrality to the reform movement at the point at which ideals had to be translated into concrete proposals for change. The organizing, packaging, and selling of a "reform package" was the accomplishment of the National Municipal League. Founded in 1894, it was anxious to end the boss era, but it was hardly radical. Some sense of why that is so can be gleaned from a brief sketch of NML's founder, Richard S. Childs.

Childs was the son of a successful New York City businessman. Graduating from Yale in 1904, he began a long business career of his own. He started as an advertising executive in Bon Ami Company (founded by his father) and at different

[7]Lincoln Steffans, *Shame of the Cities* (New York: Hill and Wang, 1957), pp. 10–11.

[8]Upton Sinclair, "What Life Means to Me," *Cosmopolitan,* Vol. 61 (October 1906), pp. 591–601.

[9]James Weinstein, *The Decline in Socialism in America: 1912–1925* (New York: Random House, 1967), pp. 116–118.

times was executive vice president of Lederle Laboratories and a director of American Cyanamid Corporation.

As his background suggests, Childs was importantly different from the more visible figures of urban reform. He disagreed often with Lincoln Steffans even though attracted to the latter's moral ardor: "There was another prophet of doom, Lincoln Steffans! As a reporter of municipal corruption, superb; as a diagnostician, all wet! For he sneeringly belittled our Model City Charter and our efforts to simplify the complex and preposterous mechanism of the democratic process."[10] Childs found the progressive attack on big business particularly abhorrent. When asked if he supported Sinclair's and Steffans' proposals for public ownership of municipal utilities, he replied "No. After all, I was the son of a capitalist."[11]

Childs recognized the advantages of presenting reform not as an ideology, or abstract discussion of principles, but as a concrete set of proposals for institutional change. The National Municipal League has been the central vehicle for creating and selling the "reform package." The League made the reform movement national in scope. It has accomplished this by acting as a research center, consultant, and conference organizer for municipal officials. It still disseminates its viewpoint widely through its publication of the *National Civic Review* (formerly the *National Municipal Review*). Most central to our immediate concerns, the League keeps up to date a "Model City Charter," recommending an "ideal" form for local institutions. Even when a city does not adopt the specific provisions of the charter, one can be sure that its principles have been a focal point of discussion. And that impact persists. When the Charter Convention convened in San Diego to discuss possible amendments to the city charter in 1971, on the desk of each delegate lay a Model City Charter.

Once the rhetoric is cut away, the central goal of the reform movement was to accomplish a massive power shift. The reformers wanted to remove the reins of government from representatives of the urban poor and place them in the hands of a rising middle class. While in many instances the middle class was composed of the second and third generations of formerly poor immigrants, their world view was considerably different.[12] Far from acknowledging that it was power the reformers sought, they couched their appeals in calls for "higher-quality officials," "professionalism," and an election system that found "the one best candidate." A second goal of the reform movement was to undercut the effectiveness of the party organization on which the boss relied. They pursued a two-pronged attack: one on "politics" and the other on the "bureaucracy." The attack on politics was based

[10]Richard S. Childs, "Civic Victories in the United States," *National Municipal Review,* Vol. 44 (September 1955), p. 398.

[11]Richard S. Childs, quoted in John East, *Council-Manager Government: The Political Thought of Its Founder* (Chapel Hill: University of North Carolina Press, 1965), p. 27.

[12]Richard Hofstadter characterizes the differences as between "old world political style" and indigenous "Yankee Protestant political style" in *The Age of Reform* (New York: Alfred A. Knopf, 1955), p. 9.

on the argument that politics, and particularly party politics, had no real place in local government: ''There is no Republican way to pave a street, no Democratic way to lay a sewer line.'' The attack on the bureaucracy was not at all like the more contemporary one. As the reformers saw it, the scope of administration should be expanded. Matters that were formerly decided politically must be decided by ''neutral,'' ''competent,'' ''professionalized'' bureaucracies. The Civil Service system was to improve city administration by preventing the boss from appointing his political ''cronies.'' In this way, government could become more ''efficient and economic.'' As reform developed, it also came to favor the grouping together of units of government in metropolitan consolidation or regional government efforts. By contrast to the success of the internal reform recommendations, the proposals to consolidate local governments attracted little support and resulted in only a few institutional changes—Dade County–Miami, for example.

LOCAL POLITICAL INSTITUTIONS

The three crucial features of the reform package have come to be (1) the council-manager form of government and (2) nonpartisan elections, which are (3) at-large, that is, elected from the city as a whole rather than from districts. Let us first compare the barest structural features of the council-manager form with the other two predominant types of city government organization—the commission form and mayor-council form.

Council-Manager Form

There are certain features of the council-manager plan that occur consistently, distinguishing it from other forms of city government (see Figure 6.1).[13]

1. A popularly elected city council with legislative powers is created. There are some variations among council-manager cities as to the size and method of selection of the council, but in general, the number of council members is small, usually nine or fewer. The council is characteristically elected at-large and on nonpartisan ballots.
2. A chief administrative officer or city manager is chosen by the council. As a general rule, managers are chosen because they have specialized, professional training or experience in urban administration. They serve as long as the majority of the council is satisfied with their work.

[13]The following description relies heavily on the summary of Carl A. McCandless, *Urban Government and Politics* (New York: McGraw-Hill, 1970), pp. 173–175.

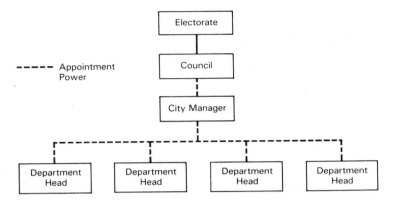

FIGURE 6.1   **The council-manager form of government**

3. The other major administrative officers, department heads, and the like are appointed by the manager and serve at the manager's pleasure.
4. There is often a presiding officer for the city council who is given the title of mayor. He or she is a regular voting member of the council but usually possesses no more administrative authority than any other council member; the mayor simply presides at meetings. The only other functions of the mayor are ceremonial.

In terms of our previous discussion of reform, we would find that the council-manager form approximates the organizational ideal of the modern corporation. By separating politics from administration, its proponents believe that it promotes greater efficiency and economy than do the alternative modes of urban governmental organization.

Mayor-Council Form

Slightly more than 50 percent of our cities are governed by the form of organization known as mayor-council (see Figure 6.2). The usual characteristics of this plan are

1. A mayor who is the chief executive of the city and who is popularly elected.
2. A city legislative body called either a council or a board of aldermen who are popularly elected. Most often the city council members are elected from districts or wards. This, however, need not be the case.
3. Additional administrative officers may either be popularly elected or appointed by the mayor. Where appointed by the mayor, these officials usually

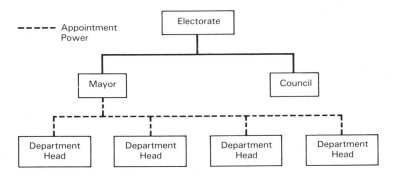

FIGURE 6.2   The mayor-council form of government

    must be approved by the council. These administrative officers are responsible for the day-to-day operation of the city government.

4. In very small cities, there may be one or more municipal courts with the mayor acting as judge; but in the larger cities, judges are either popularly elected or are appointed by the mayor with council approval. As the oldest form of local government, the mayor-council form resembles the national government. The fact that the structures are more separated than they are in the council-manager form suggests a kind of "separation of powers" in it. Here, as elsewhere, the idea of "separation of powers" is more accurately thought of as sharing of powers. The mayor has the veto power and the power to address the council, is often able to exercise a strong position of political leadership, and is generally charged with the supervision of administration. On the other hand, the council controls the purse strings and ratifies appointments by the mayor. Many charters provide that the mayor can be removed by the council before the regular term expires. The federal government analogy does not apply to council sessions, however, for these are administered by the mayor.

    As mayor-council government has evolved over a long period of time, it has adapted to the particular environment of the city in which it is set and has been transformed by specific issues and controversies within that city. As a result, there are important variations in the form from city to city. Two variations are most common: the weak mayor form and the strong mayor form. In essence, the weak mayor is one who has very little control over the several elements of the local administration. There may be a large number of elected administrators and many boards and commissions that are only tentatively responsible to the mayor, in this situation, there is little possibility that the mayor can achieve administrative coherence and secure control. Because the mayor can neither appoint nor remove key administrative officers, he or she is unable to direct any of them to fit their statements and policies into a single pattern of broad policies of his or her design.

In the strong mayor version, there is considerably more administrative integration. The mayor is able to exercise control over other administrative departments and officers because they are appointed by the mayor rather than elected. If they defy the mayor's will, they can be removed from office. However, the mayor appoints with the approval of the council and is also limited by the fact that not all municipal officers, even in the strongest mayor systems, are appointed. City treasurers, prosecuting officers, and comptrollers often are elected, even within a strong mayor system. In those cities in which the strong mayor has responsibility for preparation of the budget and also has a full-time professional administrative officer to assist in this job, the strong mayor system comes to look very much like the reform ideal. The mayor resembles an elected manager.

We should not form the impression, however, that the leadership capacity of the mayor's office is determined by the structure of government. Strong personalities can make a strong mayor. Highly developed party organization can make a strong mayor. The city of Chicago would have to be classified organizationally as a weak mayor system. But the political organization and personality of Mayor Richard Daley produced a mayor's office with considerable power.

Commission Form

In the wake of a tidal wave that severely damaged the city in 1900, Galveston, Texas, adopted a charter that calls for a government form significantly different from the other two. The commission form became the darling of the early reform movement; by 1917, 500 cities had adopted it. But since the 1920s, when the council-manager form began to fire the ardor of the reformers, the number of cities with governing commissions has steadily declined.

The most obvious difference in the commission form from the other two is that it does not embody a concept of separation of powers and does not provide for a chief executive officer (see Figure 6.3). It usually takes the following form:

1. A group of elected commissioners—usually from three to seven—exercise both legislative and administrative authority. Collectively, the commissioners act as a policymaking body, much as a city council does.

2. Often the commissioners appoint one of their number to act as mayor. This person is regarded simply as the first among equals and seldom has any additional powers. He or she presides at commission meetings and performs ceremonial functions in the name of the city.

3. Each individual commissioner is elected to serve as head of one specific

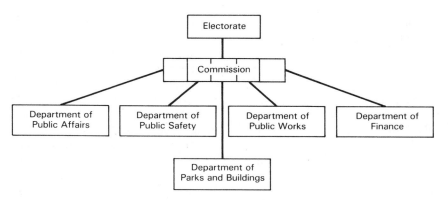

FIGURE 6.3   The commission form of government

administrative department of the city, presumably because each is best qualified to administer that department. Acting in this capacity, each commissioner hires employees in his or her department, prepares estimates of budgetary needs, decides matters of administrative policy, and, in general, functions as a department head just as he or she would in any other form of government.

THE POLITICAL EFFECTS OF REFORMED GOVERNMENT

Reformed government is dramatically different from bossism. Put most simply, reformed government is an institutional expression of neoconservatism. Most commentators on the reform movement would agree with Scott Greer's assessment that "the ideology of the reform movement rested upon assumptions congenial to the business interests who were a main resource of reform campaigns."[14] That essentially meant that reform willingly traded off a concern for democratic ideals of equality and participation for efficient and economical administration. Good government, it was assumed, was organized like a good business. When the council-manager plan was under consideration in Dallas in 1930, a newspaper asked, "Why not run Dallas itself on a business schedule by business methods under businessmen. . . . Dallas is the corporation. It is as simple as that.'"[15] Put

[14]Scott Greer, "Dilemmas of Action Research on the 'Metropolitan Problem,' " in Morris Janowitz, ed., *Community Political Systems* (Glencoe, Ill.: The Free Press, 1961), p. 187.

[15]Cited in Harold Stone, Don Price, and Kathryn Stone, *City Manager Government in the United States* (Chicago: Public Administration Service, 1940), p. 27. Original source is given only as the *Dallas News*.

another way, reformed government was seen by its adherents as the best institutional housing for the "private city" coalition. As time passed, it became apparent that unanticipated by the reformers it was an equally ideal setting for incubating the "bureaucratic city."

For a time it appeared as though the reformers had substantially triumphed. By 1941, there were 315 cities (15.5 percent of all cities over 5,000 population) that had adopted the council-manager plan. That number was 1,245, or 43 percent, by 1966. But the pattern of adoptions makes clear that there was continuing resistance to reform of this kind. For example, the largest cities remained unreformed—about three quarters of the cities with populations of 500,000 or more stayed with the mayor-council form.[16]

Richard Childs was convinced that reform had succeeded. "Testimony covering over 500 elections," he said, "demonstrates that politics without politicians is actually with us."[17] Actually, the reform program shifted the focal activities from the electoral and legislative (city council) arenas to the administrative (city manager). Reformers sought to separate policymaking from administration; the effect of their efforts was to make the manager the chief politician—a "politican for hire" as Norton Long called them.[18] There are various reasons for this power shift. One is that the full-time, professionally educated manager develops expertise beyond that of the (likely) amateur, part-time council members. City managers are enabled to be more expert partly because they have a virtual monopoly on information developed within the bureaucracy and a staff to help interpret and digest it all. All lines of communication converge in the manager. The council must depend on the manager for information. The long-term effect is easily that the manager controls the flow of information and the agenda and subordinates the council. But there are more reasons for manager centrality than this. Council members can use the manager to avoid taking clear positions on controversial issues. If the council can maneuver the manager into being out front on an issue that divides the constituency, then the council avoids the heat; its members can take credit later if the manager handles the situation well. If the manager fails, they can even make political capital by firing the manager. This is undoubtedly why large cities have not been attracted to the council-manager form. A large, diverse city will experience a great many intense political conflicts. Managers are fired often under those circumstances.

The political effects of the at-large and nonpartisan election features of the reform package were also designed to undermine the machine and maximize the power of an emerging middle class.

[16]International City Managers Association, *Municipal Yearbook, 1967* (Chicago: The Association, 1967), p. 103.

[17]Richard S. Childs, "Civic Victories in the United States," p. 303.

[18]Norton Long, "Politicans for Hire," *Public Administration Review*, Vol. 25 (1965), p. 19. Also, see R. J. Stillman, "The City Manager: Political Helping Hand or Political Hired Hand," *Public Administration Review*, Vol. 37 (1977), pp. 659–670.

Nonpartisanship.   Electing officials on a ballot that does not indicate the party affiliation of the candidate made it difficult for the machine to get its members to vote the straight party ticket. In the heyday of the machine, even the illiterate voter had no problem. If he could identify a picture of an elephant or a donkey and mark an "x" beside it, he was voting for all the candidates of the party. The nonpartisan ballot was the reform antidote.

The result of nonpartisan elections is that voters who have the time, interest, and resources to develop their own information about candidates stay involved. Those not so motivated, disproportionately the poor and less educated, become confused and disengaged from participation. Many reformers would argue that there is a certain appropriateness to those who know less not participating in the political process. Reformers proposed to improve the quality of local government and to raise its standards to better conform to middle-class ideals, but careful studies suggest that nonpartisanship undermined its own stated ideals. By weakening political parties at the local level, it left few clear sources of partisan information and campaign competition diminished, contributing to the lack of clarity of modern campaigns. The result, unanticipated by reformers, is that the more knowledgeable voters are to be found in partisan electoral systems: "Partisanship seems to be the concomitant of aware, issue-oriented voting rather than its antithesis."[19]

At-Large Elections.   At-large elections are those in which all candidates run citywide. No one represents a particular district or area of the city. Reformers argued that this would minimize concern for narrow interests and would produce more statesmanlike concern for the general public interest. They, of course, also aimed to cut the machine leadership off from its ability to deliver what particular groups wanted. And they expected to get a larger number of middle-class office holders—"best men" as Childs was fond of saying.

At-large elections result in majority sweeps of office. Minority groups—that is, black, Italian, hillbilly, Vietnamese, Hmong, with a solid but small percentage of population—may have difficulty placing a representative on the city council. In San Diego, for example, blacks make up about 9 percent of the population and are located primarily in the southeastern part of the city. The city election system is a hybrid, calling for nomination from districts but a runoff at-large. The experience of San Diego was that black candidates winning the southeast district election would lose citywide. Not until a strong Republican organization chose to appoint nonwhite members (often conservative) did the all-white council disappear. And San Diego is not atypical. In Boston, the old "ward" system gave minority interests better representation than did the at-large system. Among the 110 council

[19]Heywood Saunders, "Cities, Politics and Elections: Partisan and Nonpartisan Elections," *Municipal Yearbook: 1971* (Washington, D.C.: International City Managers Association, 1971), p. 19.

members elected in 25 years under the ward system, there were 12 Jews, 9 "Yankees," 4 Italians, and 1 black. After enacting an at-large system, the numerical majority Irish and Italians made a clean sweep. The first 45 council members elected after that were Irish or Italian.

But does the at-large system produce these results in all cases or only in particular cities? Susan MacManus has done aggregate data analysis of 243 central cities.[20] When she imposed statistical controls for a variety of socioeconomic characteristics of cities, she found that the connection between electoral format and black representation "virtually disappears."[21] But Richard Engstrom and Michael McDonald reanalyzed that data using some differing methodological assumptions and reaffirmed the traditional view "that at-large elections, at least in comparison with district-based electoral systems, tend to 'underrepresent' black people."[22] For the moment, the long-standing view of the effect of electoral arrangements on minority representation appears to hold.

In general, then, the reformers delivered much of what they promised. That gets even clearer when we examine the policy differences between reformed and unreformed cities. The analysis of Robert Lineberry and Edmund Fowler makes a strong case that reform institutions minimize governmental responsiveness to groups and interests in the population.[23] But the trade-off for less responsiveness is "efficiency and economy." They also found that reformed cities spent comparatively less, and especially spent less on the kinds of social policies desired by the poorer segments of the population. Another study adds that civil rights groups got more of the policy responses they desired from unreformed cities.[24]

Reform clearly had its impact, though, like all such efforts, it produced a number of unanticipated consequences. Both those effects and growing restiveness for greater equality produced strong counterreform tendencies during the 1960s and 1970s. Adoptions of the council-manager form practically stopped, and some strong efforts developed to repeal at-large electoral processes. And, as will become clear in the next section, while more blacks and women found their way into office, there was very little impact on urban institutions made by the counterreformers.

[20]Susan MacManus, "City Council Election Procedures and Minority Representation: Are They Related?" *Social Science Quarterly*, Vol. 59, (1978), p. 159.

[21]See also Leonard A. Cole, "Electing Blacks to Municipal Office: Structural and Social Determinants," *Urban Affairs Quarterly*, Vol. 10 (1974), pp. 17–39, and Albert Karnig, "Black Representation on City Councils: The Impact of District Elections and Socioeconomic Factors," *Urban Affairs Quarterly*, Vol. 12 (1976), pp. 223–256.

[22]Richard Engstrom and Michael McDonald, "The Election of Blacks to City Councils: Clarifying the Impact of Electoral Arrangements on the Seats/Population Ratio," *American Political Science Review*, Vol. 75 (June 1981), p. 352.

[23]Robert Lineberry and Edmund Fowler, "Reformism and Public Policies in American Cities," *American Political Science Review*, Vol. 61 (September 1967); pp. 201–216.

[24]Albert Karnig, "Private Regarding Policy, Civil Rights Groups, and the Mediating Impact of Municipal Reforms," *American Journal of Political Science*, Vol. 19 (February 1975), pp. 91–106.

THE OFFICIAL DECISION MAKERS

The struggle to reform the cities was also an effort to put better people in office. What is better to one may be worse to another, however. So we can put aside reformist views for the moment and simply describe what studies of urban politics have found to describe accurately the personnel of city politics. Particularly, we will focus on two concerns: What are the social and economic backgrounds of those who find their way into local public office? and What are their decisional characteristics?

Two ongoing theoretical questions become more clear as we proceed. First, we again confront concerns about the representational role of decision makers in a democratic society. Almost every scholar of representation agrees with James Mill that it is the "grand discovery of modern times." But even the most systematic thinkers on the subject acknowledge that the meaning and practical requirements of "political representation" are illusive.[25] The leading contemporary concern in city politics appears to surround the tension between the need for democratic representativeness and the need for expertise.

In addition, our concern for political economy will lead us to scrutinize the relations between business leadership and public decision making.

Councils

Reformers would be relatively pleased with the composition of city councils. Council members in the 1950–1960 period closely approximated their meaning of "best man." Studies of council behavior sketched the broad profile of a "typical" council member in that peiod. He was a white, middle-aged male, with a business or professional occupational background; he was relatively well educated and was most likely to have an upper-middle income; he had been active in civic associations and was most likely a Republican.[26] Deviations from the typical were associated with differences in the social rank and class composition of the particular city. The most comprehensive examination of city councils, the San Francisco Bay Area study, found that in cities with large working-class populations, the lower limit of the social stratum from which political leaders were recruited extended downward at bit farther—including occasional union officials, public

[25]See Hanna Pitkin, *The Concept of Representation* (Berkeley: University of California Press, 1967), p. 3. Also, see Heinz Eulau and Kenneth Prewitt, *Labyrinths of Democracy* (Indianapolis: Bobbs-Merrill, 1973), Part 5.

[26]Brian Downes, "Municipal Social Rank and the Characteristics of Local Political Leaders," *Midwest Journal of Political Science,* Vol. 12 (November 1968), pp. 514–537, and Oliver Williams et al., *Suburban Differences and Metropolitan Politics* (Philadelphia: University of Pennsylvania Press, 1965).

school teachers, craftsmen, and skilled laborers.[27] As Prewitt sums the matter up, "Some social strata, those located toward the upper end of the stratification system, contribute more than their share. . . . Other strata, those in the lower echelons, are substantially underrepresented." Prewitt also notes that it is not just the lower-status groups that are not represented but also the very wealthy. The politically active instead "reflect the religious, ethnic, occupational, and to a lesser degree educational diversity of a metropolitan middle-class."[28]

Much popular discussion suggests that the egalitarian spirit of the 1960s changed all this—that government, especially local government, came under the control of the black and ethnic minorities and women. Although some change occurred, it was far less than dramatic. A 1978 study of all 243 central cities of the SMSAs found 166 blacks and 60 Hispanics in city office.[29] Computing an "equity score" by subtracting the percentage of the city's minority population from the percentage of council seats held by minorities, it was found that blacks remained substantially underrepresented (−9.358). Hispanics had fared only slightly better (−8.847).[30] Variations within this pattern are also instructive. Underrepresentation of minorities is greatest in reformed cities and cities of the South. In fact, underrepresentation follows the Sunbelt pattern rather than being restricted to the Old South. "Although racial prejudice may be less of a cultural characteristic of western cities, cities in that region, more than in any other, almost uniformly have adopted the reform features of city government, and that region ranks second in the inequity of representation."[31]

A more recent and detailed examination of Sunbelt city representation patterns also assessed progress in the representation of women on city councils. Data gathered in cities of 25,000 or more in Arizona, California, Colorado, New Mexico, and Texas add that women of both majority and minority groups are less equitably represented than the least represented males.[32] "Clearly," the study concludes, "local politics is an Anglo and a male game." The figures on which that conclusion is based are congruent with the earlier study. Of the total membership of city councils in the Southwest, over 82 percent are held by Anglos and 87 percent by males. Among women, Anglo women win about one-third of the number of seats that their number in the population would justify. Black women

---

[27]Kenneth Prewitt, *The Recruitment of Political Leaders: A Study of Citizen-Politicians* (Indianapolis: Bobbs-Merrill, 1970), p. 47.

[28]Ibid.

[29]Delbert Taebel, "Minority Representation on City Councils: The Impact of Structure on Blacks and Hispanics," *Social Science Quarterly,* Vol. 59 (June 1978), pp. 142–152.

[30]Ibid. Table 1, p. 145.

[31]Ibid., p. 146.

[32]Albert Karnig and Susan Welch, "Sex and Ethnic Differences in Municipal Representation," *Social Science Quarterly,* Vol. 60 (December 1976), p. 467.

gain about 16 percent and Mexican-American women about 11 percent of their proportional rate.[33]

COUNCIL ROLES

As with any office, there are a variety of ways in which an individual incumbent can translate the duties. A role is simply a mental construct of what are the expected and customary attitudes and activities of the role player. To use the terminology of most studies of the role behavior of city councilpersons, most perform their representational roles more as "trustees" than as "delegates." A "delegate" feels bound to vote the interests of the immediate constituency, even if they conflict with his or her own views. A "trustee," by contrast, casts his or her role as voting his or her own conscience and best judgment, even if it means offending the constituency. The San Francisco Bay Area study is fairly representative in its finding that fully 60 percent of those councilpersons interviewed described themselves in terms of the trustee role, 18 percent saw themselves as delegates, and 22 percent presented a mixed case.[34]

COUNCIL DYNAMICS

Decision-making processes are much more complex than is suggested by the notion of role. Councilpersons, like their counterparts in any organizational setting, do not simply enact roles, they become involved in a process of negotiation and renegotiation of themselves and their obligations. They do this in a setting that produces powerful forces for change—a small group. Unfortunately, this aspect of council behavior has been neglected. The most provocative studies to date were also a part of the San Francisco Bay Area project. Heinz Eulau and Peter Lupsha, using sociometric analysis, discovered three types of council structure: unipolar, bipolar, and nonpolar.[35] A unipolar council is one in which all members tend to vote together; there are strong pressures to maintain a consensus. Bipolar councils exhibit a relatively permanent division between two factions, although such structures usually have "swingers" who shift back and forth. A nonpolar council has no such recurrent patterns—it may be multipolar or too amorphous to characterize.

The most interesting findings regarding the internal dynamic of city councils are

[33]Ibid., p. 468.
[34]Eulau and Prewitt, *Labyrinths of Democracy*, p. 407.
[35]Ibid., Chap. 9.

1. Councils usually have "opinion leaders" who function both as "catalyst of the mass mood and as transmitter of elite messages," thereby taking leadership in structuring and integrating the council.[36]
2. Contrary to some expectations, swing voters are not at all respected by fellow council members. They are likely to be thought of as "wishy-washy" or undependable, not as independent.
3. The most conflicted city councils evidence the most declarations of friendship: "The antagonistic atmosphere of the group as a whole seems to call out strong friendship(s) . . . in the council's subgroups, but not across subgroup lines."
4. There is no apparent relationship between expertise and decision-making structure. Subject matter experts may be found in all three types of decisional structure.

So much more must be known before we can make additional use of this construct. What environmental conditions predispose toward particular decisional structures? What is the approximation of council member behavior to public choice theory assumptions? How much impact does role definition play as compared with situational factors? When we can answer some of these questions, we may begin to understand how councils might adapt to, say, fiscal stress or expanding revenues or how they might react to criticism from the press or proposed new guidelines from federal agencies. Perhaps, even more ambitious, we might someday know what the effects of coalitional change are on the city council decision-making structure. For example, is a strong private city coalition likely to produce a unipolar council? When amenities seekers are in large enough proportion to the population, does the council become bipolar?

Mayors

Mayors are in a tough spot. We Americans have a vision of chief executives as people of vision and action as well as considerable administrative skill. Particularly in those moments in our history in which there is need for decisive action to meet changing conditions, we tend to look to individual leadership skills to save the day. Business leaders are nearly always projected as prototypes in such periods. Lee Iacocca comes to set the standard of executive leadership. But, for a number of reasons, American mayors cannot respond as business leaders or even,

[36]Heinz Eulau, "The Informal Organization of Decisional Structures in Small Legislative Bodies," *Midwest Journal of Political Science*, Vol. 13 (August 1969), pp. 341–366. Published by The Unversity of Texas Press. Copyright © 1969 The University of Texas Press and reproduced by permission.

indeed, is it likely that they can act as would a governor or president. In fact, both the formal powers of office and the political clout of the mayor varies markedly. Most commentators find that mayors seldom match our high expectations for leadership. One commentator thinks that is more the result of the legal setting than of individual failings: The root of the problem "lies in the considerable fragmentation of authority and dispersal of power characteristic of the formal governmental structure of American urban areas."[37]

The fragmentation of formal authority of the mayor's office creates great variety from city to city. In general, the range is from a strong to a weak formal power position. Mayors move toward the strong side of this continuum as they are allowed more of the following advantages: (1) election as mayor rather than election as a councilperson and then election as mayor by the council, (2) veto power over council decisions, (3) control over the council agenda and organizational structure; (4) some role in the budgetary process, (5) appointment of key department heads and other officials, and (6) a longer term of office than other councilpersons.

Beyond the formal authority of the office, mayors show widely differing levels of skill as political entrepreneurs. The ability to develop and use the political resources available to them enables some to make the most of a weak mayorship or squander possibilities in a position of strong formal authority. Mayor Yorty of Los Angeles, for example, was widely regarded as a weak mayor in a weak mayoral system. His successor, Tom Bradley, is credited with considerably more achievement. Mayor Richard Daley of Chicago was set in a weak mayor structure of authority, but few doubted the availability of his political resources or his skill in using them.

MAYORAL ROLES

There have been a number of formulations of the role definition and performance of American mayors, but perhaps the most comprehensive is that of John Kotter and Paul Lawrence.[38] All big-city mayors are expected to perform certain functions: to keep order, to focus public opinion on city needs, to umpire important disputes, for example. But how the mayor performs these and other functions will be importantly shaped by the context of the particular city. Kotter and Lawrence emphasize the following: (1) the city itself, that is, what we have called urban

[37]Alexander George, "Political Leadership and Social Change in American Cities," *Daedalus*, Vol. 97 (Fall 1968), p. 1196.

[38]John Kotter and Paul Lawrence, *Mayors in Action* (New York: John Wiley & Sons, 1974. Copyright © 1974 John Wiley & Sons. Reprinted by permission of John Wiley & Sons. Other interesting formulations are Jeffrey Pressman, "Preconditions of Mayoral Leadership," *American Political Science Review*, Vol. 66 (June 1972), pp. 520–528, and Roger Starr, "The Mayor's Dilemmas: Power and Powerlessness in a Regional City," *Public Interest*, Vol. 16 (Summer 1969), pp. 10–23.

environment, the mix of economic, social, and political characteristics that provide both opportunities and constraints on mayoral action; (2) the formal structure of city government; (3) the distribution of power in the community. The configuration of interest group politics and what we discussed as their coalitional behavior in Chapter 5 will also set some broad terms within which a mayor defines a role; and (4) the mayor's personal characteristics.

Observing a variety of mayors in the conduct of their daily affairs, Kotter and Lawrence characterize their actions generally as deciding what to do (agenda setting), getting and managing resources (network building and maintenance), and doing it (accomplishing tasks).

Agenda Setting   We have already discussed the political importance of agenda setting. Who sets the agenda calls the tune. Kotter and Lawrence found that the agenda-setting behaviors of the twenty mayors they studied could be described along a one-dimensional continuum: At one end of this continuum, the agenda-setting process is "reactive," that is, "short-run oriented, individual or part oriented, continuous and sometimes 'irrationally' unconnected." This end of the range is what Charles Lindblom has called "muddling through." At the other extreme, the process is "proactive, middle- to long-range oriented, citywide or holistic oriented, periodic, and logically interconnected."[39] This end of the continuum is what Lindblom calls the "rational-deductive" planning model. It is said to be "used by leaders in the military and large corporations."

Mayors were found to cluster into four agenda-setting types along this continuum. The first agenda-setting type was exemplified by major Victor Schiro of New Orleans. His ideas about what needed doing were mostly the result of people coming to him with problems. His daily schedule consisted mostly of ceremonial functions: "Occasionally there were openings of new businesses," Schiro said, "and they invited the mayor to cut the ribbon." Such mayors concentrate on short-run concerns like the cleanliness of the streets. The second agenda-setting type focuses less on daily concerns and more on monthly or yearly projects. The mayors of the third type went even farther in their futuristic concerns, creating 5-, 10-, and 15-year agendas as well as midrange ones. Milwaukee Mayor Henry Maier illustrates this type. Observing Maier's typical day, the researchers found his time was divided almost equally between proactive concerns such as meeting with economic planners and cultivating support for such activities among the council members and the same kind of reactive, discreet, short-run problems that so occupied Mayor Schiro. No mayors fit the fourth type, although former Mayor Eric Jonsson of Dallas is put forth as an illustration of what the model might look like. Jonsson began a process in 1965 to consult citizens and leaders to set community goals. Based on that input, he created some 100 goals of various

[39]Ibid., pp. 49–50.

durations, broken down into functional areas and containing some detail as to costs, timing, and needed action to achieve each goal.

Network Building and Maintenance   Mayors are more or less self-conscious and vigorous in maintaining contact with groups, individuals, and coalitions. Power bases must be cultivated among the local constituents and within the state and federal bureaucracies for maximal mayoral effectiveness. A schematized illustration of such a network is contained in Figure 6.4. It shows the network maintained by Mayor H. Roe Bartel of Kansas City around 1957.

We may easily connect such patterned bases of power with our previous

FIGURE 6.4   Bartle's network in 1957. (*Source:* **John Kotter and Paul Lawrence,** *Mayors in Action* **(New York: John Wiley & Sons, 1974), p. 66. Copyright© 1974 John Wiley & Sons. Reprinted by permission of John Wiley & Sons.)**

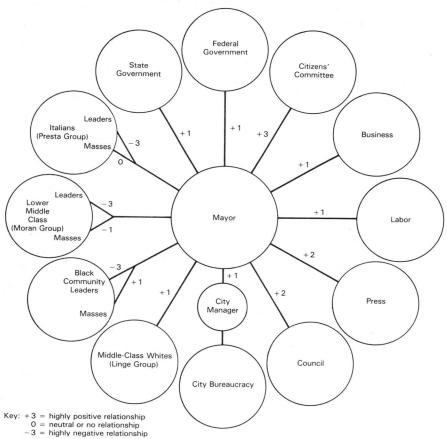

Key: + 3 = highly positive relationship
    0 = neutral or no relationship
  − 3 = highly negative relationship

discussion of local coalitions. The Bartel network, for example, would suggest that Bartel was the mayor of a "private city" coalition.

Accomplishing Tasks   To get policies implemented, mayors must have the cooperation of the bureaucracy. Individual mayors also may vary in their effectiveness in moving administrators toward their policy objectives. Having sufficient staff assistance and powers of appointment and removal over key members of the bureaucracy are the central formal powers that secure mayoral control. But it is likely to be more informal entrepreneurial skills in cultivating and mobilizing resources to assure responsiveness that will tell. Mayor Richard Lee's use of jobs, contracts, and patronage as resources to achieve urban renewal in New Haven makes a good illustration of the assertive mayor. Maintaining such a strong role becomes increasingly difficult for a mayor as the "bureaucratic city" coalition gains power.

Combining all these elements of mayoral role definition, Kotter and Lawrence identify five different types of mayors:

1. *Ceremonial.* These mayors use the type 1 agenda-setting process, use personal appeal in approaching network cultivation, and have little staff to aid in task accomplishment; therefore, they also rely on an individualistic approach to task accomplishment.

2. *Caretaker.* These mayors also use a type 1 agenda-setting process, but they are more active with network building and rely somewhat on both bureaucratic process and individual effort to get things done.

3. *Personality/Individualist.* Using a type 2 agenda-setting process, these mayors use personal appeals to the public at large rather than carefully cultivating a network.

4. *Executive.* These project-oriented mayors use a type 2 agenda-setting process, vigorously cultivating networks and using the bureaucratic process heavily.

5. *Program Entrepreneur.* Using type 3 agenda setting, this type of mayor is also active both in network building and task accomplishment.

All such typologies reflect the value commitments of their academic creators. This one is no exception. One has the clear impression that the mayors get "better" as the number gets higher. The image of the better mayors is equally clearly analogous to the image of a good business executive. That is not surprising as Kotter and Lawrence write from the perspective of their academic positions at the Harvard Business School. So the implicit recommendations of this study are much like the ideology of reform. They dispose toward institutionalizing neo-conservative biases.

MAYORAL RECRUITMENT

Mayors come from much the same social and economic backgrounds as do councilpersons. Karnig and Welch found that 88 percent of the Sunbelt mayors were Anglos and that 94 percent were male.[40] But there have been some dramatic breaks with the traditional patterns of recruitment in particular cities. Harold Washington was elected the first black mayor of Chicago in 1983. Chicago had been the last major city maintaining the vestiges of an old-style machine. But with the death of Richard Daley, the machine began to decline, and the city's first woman mayor, Jane Byrne, failed to keep it intact. So in a campaign that emphasized race as an issue and that threatened to divide the national Democratic party leadership along racial lines, Washington was the victor. It is essentially the growth of the black population in particular cities that has accounted for more blacks in the mayor's office. Carl Stokes of Cleveland, Kenneth Gibson of Newark, and Richard Hatcher of Gary were among the first black mayors. But a large black population is not the sole explanation. Black mayors have been elected in cities with overwhelmingly white poplations—Berkeley, California; Boulder, Colorado; College Park, Maryland; Grand Rapids, Michigan; and Chapel Hill, North Carolina, for example. That list fairly shouts its explanation, however, as all are university towns.[41]

Women have also made some gains in achieving mayoral office, although there is a substantial literature that suggests that public attitudes regarding the "proper role of women" has not altered enough to remove entirely the cultural barrier to electoral success.[42] But there is some evidence that sexual stereotyping will break down with the experience of female competence in public office. Kathy Whitmier was elected first woman mayor of Houston in 1977, and as a result of her performance in office, there have been discernible positive shifts in citizen attitudes toward having women in office.[43]

City Managers

The formal responsibilities of the manager usually include (1) seeing to it that the policies set by the council are implemented; (2) preparing and submitting a

[40]Karnig and Welch, "Sex and Ethnic Differences," 467–468.

[41]For a discussion of the problems facing black mayors, see Michael Preston, "Limitations of Black Urban Power: The Case of Black Mayors," in Louis Masotti and Robert Lineberry, eds., *The New Urban Politics* (Cambridge, Mass.: Ballinger, 1976), and Charles Levine, *Racial Conflict and the American Mayor* (Lexington, Mass.: D. C. Heath, 1974).

[42]See Sharyne Merritt, "Winners and Losers: Sex Differences in Municipal Elections," *American Journal of Political Science,* Vol. 21 (November 1977), pp. 731–744; Ronald Nedlund, Patricia Freeman, Keither Hamm, and Robert Stein, "The Electability of Women Candidates: The Effects of Sex-Role Stereotypes," *Journal of Politics,* Vol. 41 (May 1979), pp. 513–524.

[43]Susan MacManus, "A City's First Female Officeholder: 'Coattails' for Future Female Officeseekers?" *Western Political Quarterly,* Vol. 34 (March 1981), pp. 88–99.

budget to the council; (3) appointing, supervising, and removing the major department heads; and (4) making recommendations on policy to the council. Depending on how the manager determines his or her role, this matter of making policy recommendations sets the stage for the manager to become a political leader.

MANAGERS' ROLES

Managers play three roles: managerial, policy, and political.[44] The managerial role, of course, is involved with the relationship of the manager to the city bureaucracy, including supervision and control of personnel and policy administration. By policy role, we mean the manager's relationships with the city council, particularly as he or she is the source of policy recommendations. The political role includes efforts as a community leader and as representative of general community interests before the council, the city at large, and other governmental units. Different managers emphasize one or another of these roles, depending on a variety of factors, from their own personality characteristics, the professional training they received, and their adaptation to the particular urban setting. But let us not forget that the manager's office was the result of the reform movement that emphasized the need to separate politics from administration. The bias of the office is against overt politicking.

Traditionally, managers have been most at home in their administrative role.[45] This attitude reflects basic professional training that is likely to have emphasized efficient management, delivery of public services, personnel administration, and detailed financial accounting. On the other hand, Ronald Loveridge's study of managers in the San Francisco Bay Area found that those managers who were likely to take a stronger political role were those who majored in the social sciences in college and who pursued graduate training in public administration.[46]

POLITICAL ECONOMY
AND INSTITUTIONAL BIAS

The long developing interpretation in this chapter has been that reform government institutionalized the biases of neoconservatives, especially those that view gov-

---

[44]Diel Wright, "The Manager as a Development Administrator," in Robert Daland, ed., *Comparative Urban Research* (Beverly Hills, Calif.: Sage Publications, 1969), p. 218. Also see Ronald Loveridge, *City Managers in Legislative Politics* (Indianapolis: Bobbs-Merrill, 1971).

[45]Wright, "The Manager as a Development Administrator," p. 236.

[46]For an assessment of the manager role, see R. J. Stillman, "The City Manager: Professional Helping Hand or Political Hired Hand?" *Public Administration Review*, Vol. 37 (1977), pp. 659–670.

ernment as best when it most closely approximates the personnel, organization, and standards of decision making of the large-scale business organization. As we have examined the council-manager form and the personnel of contemporary city governments, we have found that reform has in some measure succeeded, but not without some variation and with a number of unanticipated consequences—most important, laying the groundwork for the rising power of the bureaucracy.

The 1960s produced a great deal of rhetoric for fundamental change, but little of the action went to the reform of urban institutions. Some campaign contribution laws and efforts to control lobbying appear to be the major exceptions. Nonetheless, the most power-poor minorities have found their way into office in slightly larger numbers—particularly black men and Anglo women. Radicals would argue that such failures to confront the institutional biases of city government is a characteristic failure of liberals. But there is little evidence that the rising radical consciousness of the period made careful analysis of alternative modes of political organization.

But in the late 1970s and early 1980s, there emerged a renewed effort to understand the ideological character of urban institutions and decision makers. As the normative theories in the fields of city management and urban planning became more sophisticated, scholars began to look past the administrative claim of "neutral competence" to ask what values and ideological stances planners and managers actually held and what broad political function they served.[47] A neo-Marxist analysis written by two British scholars, Joe Cullen and Paul Knox, argues that urban planners and managers have become the "social gatekeepers" of an essentially capitalist society. The gatekeeper function is to suppress political opposition and to pursue program development that creates new opportunities for private interests.[48] As they put it, "By acting as social gatekeepers, planners are performing a function as part of the 'internal survival mechanisms' of a capitalist system of production and organization, so that the decisions they make (and the ideology which underlies these decisions) are aimed at furthering the continuing dominance of the status quo."[49]

But surely such a singular view of the relationship of capitalism to the values and actions of urban decision makers is overstated. Cullen and Knox do recognize more subtle dynamics. But another empirical investigtion of the values and ideological commitments of planners and managers provides a strong sense of that diversity. Terry Edwards and Thomas Galloway developed a "two-value model of political ideology" and sampled the city managers and city planning directors of 309 U.S. cities with populations of 40,000 or more.[50] The two-value model was

---

[47]Planners and managers are often discussed together in this literature, which is appropriate because both positions were the creation of the reform movement.

[48] " 'The Triumph of the Eunuch': Planners, Urban Managers and the Suppression of Political Opposition," *Urban Affairs Quarterly,* Vol. 17 (December 1981), pp. 149–172.

[49]Ibid., p. 154.

[50]"Freedom and Equality: Dimensions of Political Ideology Among City Planners and Managers," *Urban Affairs Quarterly,* Vol. 17 (December 1981), pp. 173–193.

derived from the widely accepted formulation that "all major varieties of political orientation will have to take a . . . position with regard to two values . . . freedom and equality."[51]

Dichotomizing each of those variables—freedom and equality—they created a fourfold classification scheme: socialism (high freedom and high equality), capitalism (high freedom and low equality), communism (low freedom and high equality), and fascism (low freedom and low equality). Their raw findings are reproduced in Figure 6.5.

Managers and planners were, of course, the twin offspring of the reform movement, but the stereotypical characterization of them is that managers are capitalistic and planners socialistic. Reality, as always, is more complex. Edwards and Galloway found such a view only weakly supported. What is most striking is the degree of diversity of ideological commitment. As they note, their findings suggest a healthy degree of value pluralism in these fields. However, the radical interpretation is given some degree of support by these findings because "neither set of practitioner groups can be viewed generally as active or leading protagonist for the value of equality in local governance." In fact, they suggest the low value accorded equality is "disturbing given the centrality of these values in democratic theory."[52]

There are apparently some notable differences between those who could be classified as ideological in their orientation and those who are nonideological. Again, contrary to some popular stereotyping, it is not the nonideological who exhibit superior comprehension of and devotion to "professional" values; this study finds only one important difference between the ideological and nonideological—the ideological regard the value of equity more highly. Also "the ideologues tended to be more 'rational' on 3 of the 19 (test) items." And, finally, among the managers only, the ideological ones were more "self-regarding" and younger than their nonideological counterparts.

THE NEW REFORM: INSTITUTIONAL CHANGE AS A RESPONSE TO CONTEMPORARY PROBLEMS

Although there is no modern counterpart to the reform movement, a series of problems have created pressures on local governmental institutions that dispose them to move farther toward the ideals of the earlier reform movement. The most important set of forces we have already discussed in Chapter 2, namely, the

[51]Milton Rokeach, *The Nature of Human Values* (New York: The Free Press, 1973), p. 169.
[52]Ibid., p. 188.

Cross Tabulation of Equality and Freedom (percentages)

A. Managers

Freedom

Equality		High	Neutral	Low		
		High	**Neutral**	**Low**		
	High	(Socialist) 17.0	5.2	(Communist) 0.7	23.0	(31)
	Neutral	(Nonideological) 17.0	17.0	3.7	37.8	(51)
	Low	17.8 (Capitalist)	20.0	1.5 (Fascist)	39.3	(53)
		51.9 (70)	42.2 (57)	5.9 (8)	100.0	(135)

B. Planners

Freedom

Equality		High	Neutral	Low		
		High	**Neutral**	**Low**		
	High	(Socialist) 20.6	4.4	(Communist) 1.1	26.1	(47)
	Neutral	(Nonideological) 21.7	8.9	2.8	33.3	(60)
	Low	16.7 (Capitalist)	16.1	7.8 (Fascist)	40.6	(73)
		58.9 (106)	29.4 (53)	11.7 (21)	100.0	(180)

Note: The value rankings were cross tabulated as follows: high (1-6), neutral (7-12), and low (13-18). A respondent was deemed ideological only if both values were either high or low.

FIGURE 6.5 Ideologies of planners and managers: Cross-tabulation of equality and freedom. (*Source:* **Terry Edwards and Thomas Galloway, "Freedom and Equality: Dimensions of Political Ideology Among City Planners and Managers,"** *Urban Affairs Quarterly,* **Vol. 17 (December 1981); p. 179. Copyright © 1981 by Sage Publications. Reprinted by permission of Sage Publications, Inc.)**

transformation of the national and international economy, leading to the spatial redistribution of productive and employment activity from the industrial Northeast to the Sunbelt. The most visible effect of these broad changes is fiscal stress.

Fiscal Stress and Retrenchment

Whether a city has an expanding or a contracting economic base, it is likely to experience governmental fiscal stress. Declining cities will experience erosion of tax bases along with an increase in dependent populations as unemployment increases. Growing cities will experience a sudden need for new capital expenditures and increasing costs of maintenance and replacement, along with pressures on the standard services, and often without new revenues.

The two events that have most focused public attention on the financial problems of cities was the New York City fiscal crisis and the passage in California of Proposition 13, which limited property tax. The New York City situation provides the model for understanding political and economic adaptation to changes in fiscal status. The experience with Proposition 13, and its ''sons'' in other states, provides some understanding of how the public mood provides constraints on public decision makers as they seek to meet public financial needs. That effect is discussed below in connection with the institutional consequences of taxing and spending limits. In broad outline, these developments parallel the earlier reform movement goals—they are the New Reform.

New York City: A Model Fiscal Crisis

Despite the celebrated uniqueness of New York, we can sort out the key elements in its fiscal crisis to use as a model, a standard against which to compare other cities.[53]

Dramatically Fluctuating Resource Levels. Available revenues had increased steadily by increments averaging 7.9 percent a year from 1961 to 1965 in New York. Then began a period of ''windfall increases'' from 1966 to 1970, during which time inflation and increases in local, state, and federal aid led to an annual increase of about 14 percent each year. Windfall growth ended as intergovernmental growth slowed and the local tax base eroded. From 1971 to 1975, operating revenue growth averaged 12.8 percent, down though not dramatically

[53]Much of the formulation of this section derives from Charles Levine, Irene Rubin, and George Wolohojian, *The Politics of Retrenchment: How Local Governments Manage Fiscal Stress* (Beverly Hills, Calif.: Sage Publications, 1981).

from the previous years. The overall revenue growth picture worsened during the post–1975 "crisis" period.

The major feature of this fluctuation, the rapid growth of revenues available to cities, is clearly not unique to New York, as Table 6.1 shows.[54]

TABLE 6.1   Local Revenue Sources: Inside SMSAs, 1976–1977
(in millions)

SOURCES	AMOUNT	AVERAGE ANNUAL CHANGE, 1976–1977
A. General revenue	$140,926.6	12.7%
1. Intergovernmental	58,937.1	15.7
a. From state	45,286.1	13.9
b. From federal	13,651.0	25.6
c. From revenue sharing	3,213.5	NA
B. Own source	81,898.5	11.1
1. Taxes	61,361.1	10.6
a. Property	48,462.7	9.9
b. General sales	4,688.7	15.8
c. Selective sales	2,550.4	14.3
d. Income	3,542.2	14.9
2. Charges and miscellaneous	20,628.4	12.4

Source: U.S. Bureau of the Census, *Census of Governments,* Vol. 5, *Local Government in Metropolitan Areas* (Washington D.C.: Government Printing Office, 1980), Table 9.
NA — Not available.

Shifting Dominant Coalitions.   During the period of stable incremental growth (1961 to 1965), the comptroller had been the center of a pattern of fairly strict fiscal conservatism, applied with the full approval of the largest economic interests. With increased social unrest came additional federal aid, much of which required matching funds from local revenues. A large portion of this money was controlled by the mayor. John Lindsay in particular was able to use that windfall money to bypass the more conservative political interests and to shape the expenditure of the monies to attract the political support of the active minorities—especially blacks and Hispanics.[55]

As the rate of increasing revenues slowed and the crisis emerged (1975), the governmental response was to selectively cut a few programs and also to increase

[54]Also see John Bowman, "Urban Revenue Structures: An Overview of Patterns, Trends and Issues," *Public Administration Review*, Vol. 41 (January 1981, speical issue), pp. 131–149.

[55]S. David and P. Kantor, "Political Theory and Transformations in Urban Budgetary Arenas: The Case of New York City," in Dale Rogers Marshall, ed., *Urban Policy-Making* (Beverly Hills, Calif.: Sage Publications, 1979).

taxes, many of which were on business, and, further, to step up borrowing. As the fiscal crisis deepened, the city was pressed to respond to its business interests once again. The creation of the Emergency Financial Control Board (EFCB) and the Municipal Assistance Corporation (MAC) in effect stepped outside the traditional governing institutions. The authority exercised by those entities was partially at the expense of the mayor. The most prominent member of those bodies was Felix Rohatyn, an investment banker who spoke as a "superchief executive" of the city, calling for a massive governmental effort to rebuild our threatened cities. In Mayor Beame's place, "bankers, real estate interests, and other businessmen became more prominent in the new leadership structure."[56] This new dominant coalition insisted on curtailment of union power and cut back on the "open admissions" policy of the City University of New York.

Put into the terms of our typology of urban coalitions, the New York City situation opens with the fiscal mechanisms of the city under the control of a private city coalition. The 1960s saw a challenge to that coalition's power, through a strong mayor, by an "amenities-seeking" coalition of the minorities and poor. The superior resources of the private city coalition enabled it to repel that bid and restore its power.

It is this formulation that has led John Kenneth Galbraith and a number of others to characterize the "crisis" as "the revolt of the rich against the poor." That, of course, is the liberal interpretation. Marxists would simply prefer to style what we see as class conflict, whereas neoconservatives tend to the view that business people stepped in just in time to save the city from fiscal incompetents who were pursuing personal political gain mindless of the economic "bottom line."

Fragmentation of Formal Authority.　Already highly fragmented, New York City government became even more so during the 1960s.[57] Particularly a problem were the agencies that were funded by the city but did not report directly to the mayor, such as the transit system and the Health and Hospitals Corporation. The poverty program added importantly to the decentralization of power as well. And the collective bargaining structure reduced the possibilities of mayoral control even farther. As a result, when retrenchment became necessary, city government lacked the comprehensive control of its internal structures to carry it out.

Administrative Response.　More accustomed to incremental decision making with an assumption of moderate revenue growth, administrative responses

[56]Levine, *Politics of Retrenchment*, pp. 27–28.
[57]D. Haider, "Sayre and Kaufman Revisited: New York City Government Since 1965," *Urban Affairs Quarterly*, 15 (1979), pp. 123–145.

went through several stages of adjustment. Levine and his associates define the stages as follows:

1. Denial and delay (1970–1975). Hoping that the traditional revenue pattern would be restored, administrators cultivated skills of artful budgetary manipulation. Operating expenses were put in the capital budget and capital improvements and maintenance were delayed.
2. Stretching of resources and resistance of agencies and clients to cutbacks (1975–1978).
3. Deeper, more targeted cuts (1978–1980). Resource stretching had featured across-the-board cuts, spreading out the burdens.

Such strategies proved not to restore the faith of the financial community. Finally, when Mayor Koch announced a new round of cuts in 1980, it involved deep cuts in all agencies except for the police. These cuts involved layoffs as well as attrition; more than half came from the school system. Programs were to be combined, hospitals were shut down, schools were closed. The proposal represented a cutting strategy that was more targeted and selective.

Outcomes.   Many of the areas that had experienced rapid growth during the early 1970s were cut back, including higher education, the courts, health, and the Housing Authority subsidy. Some of the other activities that had also grown rapidly escaped, such as corrections, transportation, the Transit Authority subsidy, Health and Hospitals Corporation, and medical assistance payments.

The budgetary process shifted to reflect greater concern for short-run needs than for the long term. The effect has been a slow deterioration of the city's capital plant. The rate of breakage of water mains has increased, several major bridges are in poor condition, and the elevated West Side Highway collapsed.[58] A broken water main in August 1983 caused an electric outage in the garment district at the height of the district's fashion display and clothing purchase season.

The city budget also reflects shifting political power. There has been a turn away from emphasis on programs for the poor and more emphasis on programs that maintain a healthy business climate. Power has also shifted somewhat from the city's municipal unions to business groups, but as Levine points out, "These shifts have been gradual and do not represent a total reversal. . . . But the direction of change is clear, and the changes appear to be long run."[59]

[58]D. Grossman, *The Future of New York City's Capital Plant* (Washington D.C.: The Urban Institute, 1979).
[59]Levine, *Politics of Retrenchment*, p. 34.

   The patterns of New York City are remarkably generalizable. Levine, Rubine, and Wolohojian schematized these factors in Figure 6.6. They then examined fiscal retrenchment in Oakland, Cincinnati, Baltimore, and Prince George's County, Maryland. Of course, there were important variations between such diverse cities. Oakland, for example, an atypical Sunbelt city, exhibited some major differences: Like New York, their fiscal base erosion had been long term, they have a large minority population and high unemployment. But Oakland's adaptation to fiscal stress (accelerated by the passage of Proposition 13) included (1) no external borrowing, (2) no imposition of new taxes and a sensitivity to business opposition to certain taxes, (3) quick recognition of the problems, and (4) no denial stage, among others. Oakland's strong city manager form of government "helped to eliminate much of the period of delay and budget manipulation," but it did not alter the "duration and severity of fiscal stress . . . [or] the pattern of retrenchment responses."[60] The differences appear to be traceable largely to the interest group structure that resembled that of the private city throughout.
   In sum, the New Reform is created by cutting back revenues to local governments. Like the old reform movement, the major effect is to bring to political power those whose ideologies are more compatible with the business interests and to assure that the city adapts its policies to keep the business climate healthy. Like the old reform movement, New Reform seeks to adapt city institutions so as to assure a "bias" in behalf of business values. Let us trace some of the institutional transformations that are part of the New Reform.

FIGURE 6.6   Major variables and theoretical linkages. (*Source:* Charles Levine, Irene Rubin, and George Wolohojian, *The Politics of Retrenchment: How Local Governments Manage Fiscal Stress* (Beverly Hills, Calif.: Sage Publications, 1981), p. 35. Copyright © 1981 by Sage Publications. Reprinted by permission of Sage Publications, Inc.)

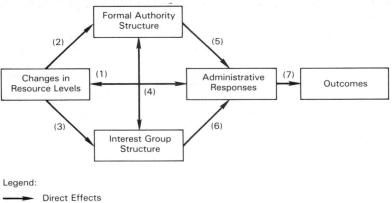

Legend:

———▶   Direct Effects

( )   Theoretical Linkages

   [60]Ibid., p. 82.

INSTITUTIONAL CONSEQUENCES
OF THE NEW REFORM

Institutional change in the multinational era (post–World War II) has generally been in the direction of reform assumptions. The New York City fiscal crisis and the passage of Proposition 13 in California represent acceleration of what had previously been a longer, less dramatic pattern of institutional reform. Some of the most important are taxing and spending limits, shifting powers in intergovernmental relations, and the building-in of business organization, practices, and personnel. All have the effect of more severely constraining local autonomy.

Taxing and Spending Limits

Perhaps the most obvious institutional change of the New Reform has been the legislation imposed by state initiative on the ability of its local governments to expand its revenues through tax increases. In 1978 there were forty-four tax and expenditure initiatives on the ballots of twenty-seven states.[61] As Table 6.2 shows, voters approved eight of thirteen tax limitation measures and four of seven expenditure limits.

While it was clearly the intention of the tax reformer to cut back the amount of money available to local authorities, there is some preliminary evidence, gathered in the immediate aftermath of their passage, that they may not be

TABLE 6.2   States Voting on Taxing and Spending Initiatives, 1978

TAX LIMITS		EXPENDITURE LIMITS	
Alabama	Passed	Arizona	Passed
Arkansas	Failed	Colorado	Failed
Florida	Failed	Hawaii	Passed
Idaho	Passed	Michigan	Passed
Illinois	Passed	Nebraska	Failed
Massachusetts	Passed	Oregon	Failed
Michigan	Failed	Texas	Passed
Missouri	Failed		
Nevada	Passed		
North Dakota	Passed		
Oregon	Failed		
South Dakota	Passed		
Texas	Passed		

succeeding. A study of Phoenix, Boise, and Portland noted that "all three experienced significant increase in general revenue since the tax revolt."[62] Much of the explanation of that increase was as a result of money transferred from the federal government in connection with housing and urban renewal expenditures.

Shifting Power in Intergovernmental Relations

The New Reform era has transformed American intergovernmental relations. Always a complex system, the contemporary period of federalism is more so. More than complex, the shifting and mingling of local, state, and national autonomy leaves us with little of the traditional theory of federalism intact. Traditionally, we had thought of federalism in terms of "dual sovereigns," that is, with neither the states nor the federal governmental having the right to interfere in matters left to the other. That era is sufficiently obsolete as to lead Paul Peterson to conclude, "We no longer have a theory of federalism."[63] But we certainly have a practice of federalism. And in the contemporary period, much of that practice has involved shifting responsibilities for service delivery and costs between levels of government. The reason for such shifts is often to improve efficiency, say, when taxes can be more equitably raised and disbursed at another level of government. But the shifts also occur as a matter of politics.

The reactions to fiscal stress in the late 1970s illustrate the local government responses and some of the consequences. Faced with budget cutting requirements, local governments chose to transfer certain services to other levels of government. Cincinnati, for example, divested itself of its courts, its university, and its city hospital.[64] Both Baltimore and Prince George's County, Maryland, shifted the costs of social services to the state of Maryland.

Shifting services is only half the picture; the other half is increasing local dependence on state and especially federal aid. Well into the period of multinational capitalism, the pattern of state and federal aid favored suburban development. As of 1965, per capita aid to cities and suburbs was nearly identical in dollar amount—$78 per person. But since those fateful mid-1960s, that aid shifted in the direction of cities of over 500,000 population. The period 1964 to 1973 saw per capita aid from the federal government increase 25 percent more and state aid increase 28 percent more in those larger cities than in suburbs and smaller cities.[65] Figure 6.7 shows how important intergovernmental revenue was as a source of support for cities.

---

[62]Ibid., p. 117.

[63]Paul Peterson, *City Limits* (Chicago: University of Chicago Press, 1981), p. 66.

[64]Levine, *Politics of Retrenchment*, p. 190.

[65]Advisory Commission on Intergovernmental Relations, *Fiscal Balance in the American Federal System* (Washington D.C.: Government Printing Office, 1967), p. 84.

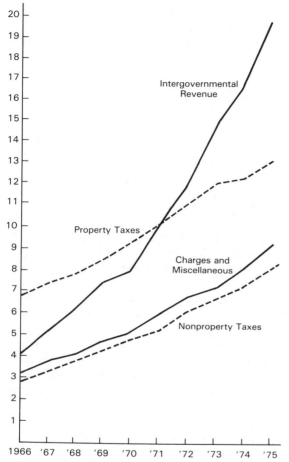

FIGURE 6.7 Trends in city general revenue from selected major sources, 1966–1975 (billions of dollars). (*Source:* U.S. Bureau of the Census, *City Government Finances in 1974–75* (Washington, D.C.: Government Printing Office, 1976), Figure 1, p. 2.)

The increased aid allowed the cities to continue to perform most of their normal functions and at normal levels despite fiscal stress. The most benign interpretation was that state and national authorities came to collect the revenues rather than the localities. But, in fact, the effect was to cut back the scope of power of the cities. As Levine observed "state and federal agencies added strings, mandates, and maintenance of effort requirements as conditions for receiving money," and the result was, "there can be little doubt that one effect of fiscal stress was to reduce local autonomy."[66] The limited city becomes even more limited with the New Reform.

[66]Levine, *Politics of Retrenchment*, p. 191.

Building-In Business Organization

The long-term effort of the reform movement has been to make the government organization more like that of private business. That effort has been increasingly successful in the multinational era. Increasingly, staff assistants to mayors and managers are expected to emulate corporate decision-making styles; budgeting followed the business modes of program planning budgeting system to zero-base budgeting; and "businessman" became the favorite occupational designation on the nonpartisan ballot. But perhaps one of the most central organizational contributions of the New Reform is the increasingly ubiquitous appearance of "public authorities" within local government organizations.

Introduced before in the discussion of business as an interest group (Chapter 4), the amount of money under the control of these semipublic agencies has tripled in the decade of the 1970s.[67] State and local authorities—authorized by state statute—spent more than $14 billion per year on operations, and they invested some $10 billion a year in new capital facilities in 1974. By way of comparision, in that same year the capital budget expenditures of New York and California state governments were $893 million and $1.8 billion, respectively. Another way to understand the magnitude of public authority fiscal importance is to recognize that public authorities constitute the largest category of borrowers in the tax exempt bond market. They raise more money for investment than do either all state or all local governments.[68] Clearly, this level of investment exerts a strong influence on the patterns of development of the economy and nation.

Evaluating the effects of public authorities, Annmarie Hauk Walsh raises the kind of questions of one who has grown skeptical of the superiority of business organization, business methods, and business executives to conduct local government. She contends, in fact makes it the central thesis of her analysis of public authorities, that even though they are "supposed to act in the general interest of the state, region or city, frequently [they] do not."[69] Walsh's reasons for such a conclusion can be taken as a criticism of the pattern we have called the New Reform. She essentially suggests that the reliance on public authorities is undemocratic. "In a democracy, public resources should be allocated among competing projects by open and farsighted political processes." Businesslike approaches that claim—and are generally perceived—to be free of the narrow and sometimes "nasty" aspects of American politics may also escape constructive pressures at work in the political arena. As for public authorities (and business executives), "because of their institution, they overemphasize financial returns. . . . They bias government in favor of physical infrastructures for short-term economic return." More theoretically, their "ideologies of laissez-faire, localism, au-

---

[67]Annmarie Hauck Walsh, *The Public's Business* (Cambridge, Mass.: The MIT Press, 1978), p. 6. Copyright © 1978 The MIT Press and reproduced by permission.
[68]Ibid.
[69]Ibid.

tonomy and limited politics converge to limit the forms and ambitions of public enterprise.'' And, politically, they ''preserve the power of groups with narrow and specialized aims, and . . . relieve the [authorities] themselves of obligations to respond to broader interests.''[70]

Need we once again remind ourselves that such views are from a critical liberal perspective? The neoconservative generally welcomes the New Reform pattern. To a great extent, the New Reform is the result of substantial neo-conservative effort. Radicals, finally, might also welcome these developments, if only because they clarify by laying bare the strong hold that capitalism has over Americans. Such a recognition is the necessary prelude to counteraction.

Before concluding this discussion of local institutions and leadership, there is one last concern that requires attention. It has been one of a few topics that has shaped our understanding of American city life. In many ways, the following discussion is an attempt to summarize in its broadest terms the state of urban political economy.

IS THERE A POWER STRUCTURE?

We were introduced to the community power structure debate in the discussion of "pluralism" in Chapter 2. Let us place that discussion in the context of our concern for political economy and urban political leadership. The central concern is simply, Is there an informal structure of power that rules in its own self-interest outside control by the general public?

Everyone will recognize that it is part of the "conventional wisdom" of most cities that such a small group of "big boys run this town." But like most inside dope, it requires verification before the prudent political participant acts on it. The effort to verify that elite hypothesis preoccupied urbanists for about fifteen years, from the early 1950s to the mid-1960s and then was practically abandoned for fifteen years after that. Reviewing the natural history of the debate over power structures, we find once again that much of the underlying basis of dispute is a result of unstated ideological commitments of the researchers and their interpreters. Specifically, it would appear that the assumptions of radical political economy were being vindicated by Floyd Hunter and the "Reputational" school. Pluralists, we have already pointed out, made the liberal response. Elaboration will make this point more clearly.

The Radical Thesis: An Elite Governs

Radical sociologist C. Wright Mills described a national power elite in the mid-1950s.[71] It was composed of the "military-industrial complex," and it cir-

[70]Ibid.

[71]C. Wright Mills, *The Power Elite*, (New York: Oxford Press, 1959).

cumvented and dominated the institutions of democratic government. Floyd Hunter, at about the same time, was also finding an elite in Atlanta. Hunter's *Community Power Structure* opened the modern debate, defined the "reputational" approach to the study, and spawned a number of subsequent studies.[72]

The reputational technique starts with the commonsense assumption that if you want to know who is in charge of a city, you ask people who ought to know. The muckracking journalist, Lincoln Steffans, had taken this direct approach.[73] Hunter formalized it for his own research. First, he obtained lists from civic organizations: a list of business and financial leaders from the Chamber of Commerce, a list of "local political leaders who had at least major governmental committee chairmanship status" from the League of Women Voters, and lists of the socially prominent from newspaper editors and other civic leaders. These lists gave Hunter a total of over 175 names. He then asked a panel of fourteen judges, chosen because of their long-standing acquaintance with activities in a variety of institutional sectors of the city, to say who were the top leaders on his lists. Hunter reports that the fourteen judges "revealed a high degree of correlation in their responses," giving him a roster of forty people who were most mentioned. The top twenty-seven were then interviewed and asked to pick the top ten city leaders from the list of forty. In this way Hunter narrowed his lists to the most influential.

Atlanta, as Hunter found it, was run by a small group of powerful men. As he describes them, they interacted socially, and they determined the outlines of policy for the city informally and behind the scenes. The Atlanta elite was not an equal opportunity organization: "The test for admission to this circle of decision-makers," Hunter contended, "is almost wholly a man's position in the business community."[74] The domination of business people has been the common finding of those other scholars who have used Hunter's methods in other cities.

The second important characteristic of Hunter's elite was that they were not publicly accountable. The more visible institutional leaders—mayors, council members, bureaucrats—implemented elite policy, took the heat for it, but were actually an "understructure" of power; "organizational leaders are prone to get the publicity; the upper-echelon economic leaders the power."[75]

Finally, Atlanta's power structure was not benevolent; rather, it ruled in its own self-interest. And since it had the upper hand, its major policy goal was simply to prevent drastic change. Again quoting Hunter, "When new policy is laid down it must be consistent with the general scheme of old policy and should not radically change basic alignments of settled policy . . . so that the basic equilibrium in the social systems of the community may undergo as little disruption as possible."[76]

[72]Floyd Hunter, *Community Power Structure* (Chapel Hill: University of North Carolina Press, 1953), pp. 79, 86–87, 209.

[73]See M. Kent Jennings, *Community Influentials* (New York: The Free Press, 1964).

[74]Hunter, *Community Power Structure*, p. 79.

[75]Ibid., pp. 86–87.

[76]Ibid., p. 209.

Hunter's methods and findings have been replicated in a number of cities throughout the country.[77]

The Liberal Antithesis: Pluralism

Although a number of political scientists were enthusiastic about Hunter's work, there soon developed a reaction. A research group headed by Robert Dahl of Yale began to crystalize systematic criticism of the reputationalists, and they created an alternative method for the examination of community power.

The pluralist's repudiation of Hunter's work was complete. Raymond Wolfinger called it a "dry hole" as "it requires a factual assumption that is obviously false; its findings are often invalidated and never confirmed; and its product conveys very little useful information about a local political system."[78] This harsh conclusion was based on three major criticisms of the reputational technique. First, the critics urged that reputation for power is not the same as real power. Since the exercise of power requires action, the critics argue that one should observe some power-directed action before proclaiming a power holder. If a person's work is banking, the researcher should assume that the banker will spend his or her time in the bank and not in manipulating the city's politics "until the banker's activities and participations . . . indicate otherwise."[79]

Second, the critics object that the reputational technique contains the embedded assumption that the structure of city decision makers is stable over time and from issue to issue. Cities are too large and complex for any single elite to be so omnipresent. In any case, the assumption takes as a given what is the subject to be studied. Nelson Polsby, one of Dahl's graduate students at the time, insisted on the alternative assumption that "power may be tied to issues, and issues can be fleeting or persistent, provoking coalitions among interested groups and citizens, ranging in their duration from momentary to semi-permanent."[80]

And, third, the critics attack the assumption that there is an ordered system of power that has simply to be discovered. By asking the question, "Who rules this city?" the reputationalist researcher puts the interviewee in the position of answering a "Have you stopped beating your wife yet?" kind of question. Virtually any response short of total unwillingness to answer supplies the researcher with a

---

[77]The community power literature is too large to sample adequately here. For a good critical review of the reputational studies with bibliography, see Nelson Polsby, *Community Power and Democratic Theory* (New Haven, Conn.: Yale University Press, 1963). For a more recent evaluation and bibliography, see Terry N. Clark, *Community Power and Policy Outputs: A Review of Urban Research* (Beverly Hills, Calif.: Sage Publications, 1973).

[78]Raymond Wolfinger, "A Plea for a Decent Burial," *American Sociological Review*, Vol. 27 (December 1962), p. 845.

[79]Nelson Polsby, "How to Study Community Power: The Pluralist Alternative," *Journal of Politics*, Vol. 22 (August 1960), p. 481.

[80]Ibid., p. 478.

power structure. Dahl and his associates insisted on a research design that enabled the finding of unstructured power. "If anything there seems to be an unspoken notion among pluralists that at bottom nobody domintes in a town, so that their first question is not likely to be 'Who runs this community'' but 'Does anyone at all run this community?' ''[81]

The pluralist alternative to the study of local decision making is "issue area analysis." They pioneered the approach in a study of New Haven. The major steps in their alternative research design were as follows:

1. *Select key issues.* The pluralist researcher's first task is to designate which issues have been most important in the city's recent past. This decision has almost always proved controversial because of the difficulty of determining criteria for choice. The New Haven study used "one or another, or a combination" of four criteria: (a) the number of people affected by the issue outcome, (b) how many different kinds of community resources were distributed by the outcome, (c) what amount of resources were distributed by the outcome, and (d) how drastically the outcome of the issue altered the distribution of community resources.[82]

2. *Designate the stages in the resolution of each issue.* Issue area analysts insist that the researcher specify each major arena of public decision making in which an issue is resolved. Dahl, for example, designated eight such stages of official decision making on the issue of redevelopment between 1950 and 1959. Included were the creating of the redevelopment agency, and the redeveloping of the Church Street area, for example.[83]

3. *Observe actual decisional behavior at each stage.* Pluralists actually observed the behavior of the participants at each stage. The New Haven study attempted quantitative expression of the influence of particular actors by observing "the number of successful initiations or vetoes by each participant" and the number of failures.[84]

In this way, a numerical score was compiled, changing from one decision-making stage to the next. According to Dahl, any particular participant could be considered influential if "the relative frequency of his successes out of all successes is higher, or the ratio of his successes to his total attempts is higher than other participants."[85] Dahl did not use this quantitative data without referring to

[81]Ibid.

[82]This problem is discussed at greater length in Fredrick Frey, "Comment: On Issues and Nonissues in the Study of Power," *American Political Science Review,* Vol. 65 (December 1971), pp. 1081–1088.

[83]Robert Dahl, *Who Governs?* (New Haven, Conn.: Yale University Press, 1961), pp. 333–334.

[84]Ibid.

[85]Ibid.

the settings in which the actors decided; in other words, Dahl used qualitative supplementary materials.

By proceeding in this way, the pluralists were seeking to determine whether power was in fact structured and dominated by an elite few, as Hunter and his followers had insisted. An important summary figure, then, is the number of participants who are effective in one issue area and "overlap" several issues.

Dahl's substantive findings were a complete contrast to Hunter's. Hunter did not calculate an overlap figure, but presumably it is near 100 percent. Dahl found only a 6 percent overlap. Dahl found no ruling elite, but shifting coalitions from issue to issue. Within this pattern "only the Mayor was a member of all the major coalitions, and in each of them he was one of the two or three men of highest influence."[86] Also in contrast to the Atlanta study, it was concluded that New Haven's economic and social leaders had relatively little direct influence on government decisions. As we have already noted, such findings could scarcely be more congenial to liberals. The radical analysis was on the defensive from this point on.

The Continuing Search for Synthesis

The differences between reputationalists and pluralists might be explained in other ways. They studied different cities at different points in time located in different regions of the country. As the research multiplied in other settings, however, there emerged a growing consensus among urban scholars that the anomolous findings were the result of divergent methodologies of the researchers. A number of others added that the methodologies differed in ways that suggested differing ideological commitments of the researchers.[87]

Critics of the pluralists appeared immediately. Those with radical political commitments saw a number of flaws in Dahl's methods and findings. The most influential of the writings that found fault with pluralist research and recommended new forms of synthesis came from Peter Bachrach and Morton Baratz. In several critical essays and an analysis of the poverty program in Baltimore, they offered an analysis that they believed avoided the deficiencies of the pluralists.[88]

According to Bachrach and Baratz, the major failing of the pluralist methodology was its failure to take account of the "other face of power" or what they called "non–decision making." Focusing on actual decision-making behavior, as the pluralists do, they say, "takes no account of the fact that power may be,

---

[86]Ibid., p. 200.

[87]David Ricci, *Community Power and Democratic Theory* (New York: Random House, 1971).

[88]Peter Bachrach and Morton Baratz, "Two Faces of Power," *American Political Science Review*, Vol. 61 (December 1962), pp. 948–949, and *Power and Poverty* (New York: Oxford Press, 1970).

and often is, exercised by confining the scope of decision making to relatively 'safe' issues.''[89] Non–decision making is a complex and abstract conception that is probably best understood in illustration. The central concern is to show that people who are outside the circle of active decision makers can operate in such a way as to convince them to limit themselves to consideration of alternatives that the ''non–decision makers'' find acceptable.

I got an illustration of the non–decision-making process on my first job as an assistant professor at a small, liberal arts university. Shortly after arriving on campus, I sat in on a discussion in the faculty club among members of the drama department. I was an interloper; they were selecting the plays to be produced in the upcoming year. As I listened, it occurred to me that they were choosing some very safe, unimaginative material. Tactfully, I thought, I raised that point. A senior member of the committee explained to me later that most of them (the active decision makers) would rather be working with more avant-garde plays but knew it was not a good idea to try that. Why? Because the year before I arrived, the president of the university (the non–decision maker) had canceled a controversial play two days before it was to open. The president's only explanation was that it would offend the university's constituency. The president was not physically present, nor did he actively communicate with any member of the committee, yet his past actions caused the active decision makers to anticipate his reactions. They limited themselves to the consideration of ''safe'' alternatives.

The strong implication here is that if there were an elite, this is how they would often have their effect—as non–decision makers. Bachrach and Baratz found evidence of non–decision making in Baltimore's community action program. More specifically, they said that blacks were deflected from translating their grievances into issues: ''In short, the prevailing mobilization of bias blocked black leader's attempts to arouse their would-be constituents to political action and thereby assured that blacks would remain 'locked out' of the political system.''[90]

While most would agree that the central insight—the existence of a non–decision-making process—may often be quite correct, there are few who believe that Bachrach and Baratz have successfully defended the finding of a willful power structure. Paul Peterson, for example, suggests that Bachrach and Baratz, in the Baltimore study, stretch the concept of non–decision making so far that it includes its opposite. For example, Peterson points out that the mayor's decision to establish a biracial task force is labeled ''an extremely effective nondecision'' in the Baltimore study, while it appears to be an important victory for black leaders. Along with a number of others, Peterson concludes that the elite findings are still not verified. Speaking particularly of the Baltimore situation, he concludes, ''Fundamentally, the ruling-elite hypothesis is unable to cope with the signal ac-

---

[89]Bachrach and Baratz, ''Two Faces of Power.''
[90]Bachrach and Baratz, *Power and Poverty*, p. 97.

complishment of antipoverty programs—the opening up of local political systems to previously excluded groups."[91]

Other researchers have tried to synthesize the pluralist-elitist dichotomy by proceeding with systematic comparative study based on more elaborate conceptualization. A promising illustration of this kind of research was undertaken by Agger, Goldrich, and Swanson.[92] They studied four cities, two in the West and two in the South. Their assumption was that the elite-pluralist dichotomy was oversimplified. They posited four types of power structures. They classify local political regimes in terms of these criteria: (1) whether there is a broad or narrow distribution of power among citizens and (2) whether the political leadership's ideologies are divergent or convergent. So, if there is a high level of agreement among a particular city's leaders on their ideology and very little power exercised by the citizens, they would call that structure a "consensual elite."

A third attempt at synthesis has been made by those who would go beyond the question of who governs to ask what difference it makes. The study of public policy more asks what are the consequences than it does who has power. But in the process of answering that question, they characteristically use previous studies or create other indicators to determine whether the decision-making structure of a particular city is centralized or decentralized. In other words, many of the policy studies have simply ignored the fact that the pluralist-elitist debate was left unresolved and have developed their own measures.[93]

Although each of these directions has some advantages, meeting particular objections raised in criticism of the community power studies, none has emerged as acceptable to a broad range of researchers. Perhaps the best single synthesizing formulation has been that of Clarence Stone.[94] He suggests that we turn our attention to the underlying system of social stratification to discover and adequately characterize the concern for non–decision making. The missing element in the community power puzzle, Stone argues, lies in discovering "Why, when all of their actions are taken into account, do officials over the long haul seem to favor upper-strata interests, disfavor lower-strata interests, and sometimes act in apparent disregard of contours of electoral power?"[95] His answer is what he calls

[91]Peterson, *City Limits,* pp. 87–88.

[92]Robert E. Agger, Daniel Goldrich, and Bert E. Swanson, *The Rulers and the Ruled,* rev. ed. (North Scituate, Mass.: Duxbury Press, 1972).

[93]Clark, *Community Power and Policy Outputs* and Terry N. Clark, "Centralization Encourages Public Goods, but Decentralization Encourages Private Goods," Research Paper 39 of the Comparative Study of Community Decision-Making, Department of Sociology, University of Chicago, 1972. For a different approach, see Michael Aiken and Paul Mott, eds., *The Structure of Community Power* (New York: Random House, 1970). And for a synthesis on these two approaches, see Larry Long and Charles Bonjean, "Community Power and Policy Output: The Routines of Local Politics," *Urban Affairs Quarterly,* Vol. 17 (September 1981), pp. 3–21.

[94]Clarence Stone, "Systemic Power in Community Decision–Making: A Restatement of Stratification Theory," *American Political Science Review,* Vol. 74 (1980), pp. 978–990.

[95]Ibid., p. 978.

"systemic power," that is "that dimension of power in which durable features of the socioeconomic system . . . confer advantages and disadvantages on groups . . . in ways predisposing public officials to favor some interests at the expense of others."[96]

Examining the role of business in cities, for example, Stone points out how his formulation is different from the ruling elite studies. The ruling elite studies are unable to explain why business is so effective in urban redevelopment issues, for instance, and so much less so in some other issues. He suggests that business interests prevail in some issues because "governments are drawn by the nature of underlying economic and revenue-producing conditions to serve those interests.[97] This appears to be a hopeful new beginning, but as yet there has been little research explicitly using the conception of "systemic power."[98]

Nonetheless, several works by radical researchers conceptualize and find evidence for systemic power. G. William Domhoff revisited New Haven in the mid-1970s to re-evaluate the pluralist assumptions. Domhoff turned up a number of documents that cast doubt on the claim that New Haven was as Dahl had claimed it to be. Domhoff found that the local leadership in New Haven was, at the time the pluralists worked, integrated into a national economic and political elite structure.[99] In fact, Domhoff argues that most cities are. "Chambers of Commerce, civic improvement associations, community foundations, research bureaus, United Funds, community service organizations, and newspapers" are the organizations that make up the "local policy-planning and opinion-molding network" that connects local leaders with "the national urban policy network."[100]

While Domhoff identifies the system, John Gaventa has conceptualized and studied the systemic, or "indirect," mechanisms by which the powerless come to support and even believe in the appropriateness of elite power.[101] Gaventa finds evidence among the poor of Appalachia, for example, that many "internaliz[e] . . . the values, beliefs, or rules of the game of the powerful" as a means of escaping the conscious recognition that they are powerless.[102] Their objective condition does not change, but they are better able to bear it by becoming fatalistic, self-depreciating, or apathetic about the situation.

[96]Ibid., p. 980.

[97]See, also, Charles Lindblom, *Politics and Markets* (New York: Basic Books, 1977).

[98]Another interesting new beginning, although in an entirely different direction is John Bolland, "Networks of Community Action: Toward a Reconceptualization of Community Leadership and Decision-Making," paper delivered at the annual meeting of the American Political Science Association, Denver, Colorado, September 1982.

[99]Clarence Stone, *Who Really Rules? New Haven and Community Power Reexamined* (New Brunswick, N.J.: Transaction Books, 1978).

[100]Ibid., p. 174.

[101]John Gaventa, *Power and Powerlessness: Quiescence and Rebellion in an Appalachian Valley* (Urbana: University of Illinois Press, 1980). Gaventa extends the formulation of Steven Lukes, *Power: A Radical View* (London: Macmillan, 1974).

[102]Gaventa, *Power and Powerlessness*, p. 17.

SUMMARY

This chapter has traced the systematic biases introduced into American city politics by a great variety of governmental institutions. Far from being neutral, institutions reward certain values and individuals while making it difficult for others. The broadest terms of bias in the modern era have been the association of reform, both old and new, with the values of capitalism. It is for that reason I have consistently associated reform with neoconservatism. It could be accurately pointed out that many self-styled liberals can be found among the reformers. That is as we might expect, for many liberals are capitalists as well. It is perhaps one of the failures (or strengths) of liberalism that its emphasis on procedure leaves it to others to define the tangible outcomes.

The New Reform, occasioned by the "fiscal crisis" of American cities, has had the effect of expanding the power of neoconservatives. It has brought to political power leaders who are sympathetic to pleas for governmental action to protect and promote the economic base of the city. This development is, of course, lamented by liberals and radicals alike.

It is, perhaps, the clarity of business power that has led to a resurgence of interest in studies of "community power structure," dormant for some fifteen years. Pluralist findings of the 1960s appear increasingly assailable in the 1980s. Neoconservatives and radicals tend to agree that there is a dominant set of interests in most cities, but they differ as to how that power is organized and whether it should exist at all. Academic study in this area still seeks an adequate synthesis.

CHAPTER 7

*Conflict
over
Urban Performance*

City governments, like all governments, exist to regulate conflicts by making policy. Whether they do it well or badly is the ultimate test of their performance. As cognoscenti in urban politics by now, you correctly anticipate that we will find systematic conflict over the adequacy of urban policies. But that may not be taken as prima facie evidence that local governmental institutions are failures. It may or may not be a governmental failure that no one wants to pay higher taxes but everyone wants better quality services. It may or may not be a governmental failure that wealthy neighborhoods have better maintained streets than do ghettos. To some extent, our governments are ourselves; they cannot relieve us of conflicts that we have not resolved internally—those conflicts they simply mirror. Understood in this way, conflict is the necessary, though painful, prelude to improvement.

Neoconservatives are just a bit restless with such liberal sounding formulations. With equal truth, they would remind us that a very large number of urban conflicts are precisely the result of governmental failure. When Johnny graduates from a public high school and a state university and is a cultural illiterate, this is at least partially a performance failure of government. When governmental budgets grow and the quality of services decline, we gain little in blaming ourselves. Neoconservatives have not been shy about bringing conflict, either.

This chapter provides a summary overview of the exploding literature on public policy as it relates to American cities. We will begin by setting some terms;

then we summarize the performance levels of American cities in world perspective. Finally, we review some of the central issues in conflict over whether and why these performance levels are adequate—that will, of course, once again reveal systematic ideological differences. The central reason for discussing performance here is to connect it with politics. Differing political patterns have been associated with different policies throughout the book, and this chapter will complete that picture. Comprehensive understanding of the public policy process, policy implementation, policy impact, and evaluation is beyond the scope of this work.

UNDERSTANDING LOCAL GOVERNMENTAL PERFORMANCE

Government seeks to resolve conflicts by making policy. Policy has five major components. First, there is a decision that relates to a particular object or set of objects; that is, policy sorts out some specific part of the environment to be affected. Second, there is a desired course of events that the object should follow. Third, there is a selected line of action that is chosen to bring about the desired course of events. Fourth, there is a declaration of intent, or some statement from those making the policy as to what they want done. And, finally, there is an implementation of intent.[1]

The leading effect of public policy is that it rewards some and punishes others. No serious student of politics believes the myth of government neutrality. And no one really thinks that governments ought to be neutral either. All organizations implement bias. American public policies reflect our biases against murder and for helping the blind and disabled. The politics of public policy results from the fact that many biases are not widely shared. That is, of course, why we have traced the systematic bases of conflict throughout this book.

If we recognize that individual policy preferences are often the result of one person getting something out of government that another person pays for, we have taken a step toward understanding why some policy biases are not widely shared. It is this recognition that policies have differing distributional effects that led Theodore Lowi to distinguish three basic types of policies: regulatory, distributive, and redistributive.

1. *Regulatory policies* grant and withhold options to particular groups and interests. When a public utilities commission raises rates, it is, among other things, exercising a regulatory function.
2. *Distributive polices* are those that allocate funds for a variety of accepted goals. When local government buys land and builds a park, it is creating a

[1]Austin Ranney, "The Study of Policy Content: A Framework for Choice," in Austin Ranney, ed., *Political Science and Public Policy*, (Chicago: Markham, 1968), p. 7.

public good from the public treasury as well as illustrating a distributive policy.

3. *Redistributive policies* are the most controversial. They are policies in which something is taken from someone and is given to someone else. Done by private parties, this is sometimes called stealing. But we all know enough about Robin Hood to realize that it is not always exactly that. Redistribution policies may reflect emerging consensus on the requirements of justice in a society, as when many agreed that blacks had been systematically discriminated against and deprived of both money and status unjustly. The only public policy remedies that one could create were redistributive. Needless to say, those from whom something is taken to give to someone else are likely to complain. It is in connection with this range of policies we would most expect to find conscious class differences (in the Marxist meaning) as the basis of conflict.

Governmental policymaking raises a number of questions: Why are particular policies chosen? What is the role of political considerations in policy choice? Who benefits and who pays? What is the actual effect (impact) of a policy? And how can public policies be evaluated? These have become the central concern of policy studies. Rather than trace answers to each of these questions, let us instead use a single, broad concern: urban performance.[2]

To focus on the performance of cities is to look primarily at outcomes. Throughout most of this book, our focus has been on the processes and conflicts that occur in the creation of policy. Now, we at last ask, How well do American cities meet citizen needs? As Fried and Rabinowitz sum it up, "The performance approach starts with the outcomes of urban processes—the differences among cities in the way people live and the quality of urban life—and attempts to identify the impact of these intercity variations of differences in politics."[3] Knowledge of policy outcome gives us the raw material with which to assess the products of urban political economy. This can best be done in the perspective of worldwide comparison and relative "development."

THE PERFORMANCE OF AMERICAN CITIES IN WORLD PERSPECTIVE

We must first recognize that the performance levels of cities throughout the world are affected by more factors than their political economies—historical traditions, social structures, race relations, regional migration trends, differing value pat-

---

[2]This formulation and much of the material contained in the following section is from Robert Fried and Francine Rabinowitz, *Comparative Urban Politics: A Performance Approach* (Englewood Cliffs, N.J.: Prentice-Hall, 1980).

[3]Ibid., p. 7.

terns, and the like all have a formative effect. But it is quite clear that economic development provides some of the broadest reasons for differential urban performance. In other words, poorer cities (measured in lower gross national product) perform less well than do wealthier ones. Stockholm, New York, Paris, Vienna, Athens, Belgrade, and Johannesburg all have relatively high per capita GNPs and high urban performance levels,[4] whereas Santiago (Chile), Bogota, Dakar, Peking, Calcutta, and Kabul have low per capita income and low urban service levels. But this is not to say that wealthy cities provide higher performance levels in general. There are striking differences between the performance of cities even within the group of capitalist democracies. In other words, "the correlation between modernization and the quality of urban life is only moderately high."[5]

A second, but important, point to bear in mind as we proceed to describe urban performance in aggregate terms is that local governments have only a small part of the responsibility for these policy outcomes. American cities are, as we have noted several times, authority and resource dependent. They have minimal control of the largest corporate resources within their boundaries, and city governments exercise highly fractionated powers. If the city of Youngstown performs poorly, it is more because of business decisions made by Youngstown Sheet and Tube managers than by city officials.

When aggregate performance measures are used, American cities show a mixed picture, yet one that is consistent in its tendencies. Table 7.1 summarizes the areas of high and low performance.

TABLE 7.1 The Performance Record of American Cities

Comparative High Performance	*Comparative Poor Performance*
High standard of living	Personal and property safety
Relative absence of status differences	Infant health care
Public works and facilities	Municipal corruption
Cost of living	Family breakdown, drug addiction
Regulation of traffic and pollution	Racial inequalities
Some forms of social disorganization	Conditions of the poor and minorities
(for example, suicide)	Unemployment
Modern taxation	
Services and amenities for middle-	
and upper-income groups	
Shopping facilities	
Citizen participation	
Due process and protection of	
individual rights	

Source: Robert Fried and Francine Rabinowitz, *Comparative Urban Performance* (Englewood Cliffs, N.J.: Prentice-Hall, 1980), p. 86.

[4]Ibid., Table 4.1.
[5]Ibid., p. 84. For a discussion of the conception of "modernization," see Chap. 3.

This set of results is based on aggregated results of compiling a large amount of data grouped into social indicators of each of the performance areas. From the outset, then, it is clear that American cities do relatively well, providing high levels of income, public works, regulation of traffic and pollution, and so on. But in other service areas, the record is much poorer and is comparatively weak when compared on a world scale. For example, conditions for the relatively poor are not what one would expect in a country with such a high GNP. That observation is not simply a matter of figures; it has been the common observation of travelers for years. Richard Lewellen-Davies, a prominent British planner, remarked, "For most Europeans it is hardly believable that a society as wealthy as America could tolerate the physical squalor of the inner-city slums, let alone accept the human degradation that they represent."[6]

But most Americans are apparently relatively content with overall city performance levels. An opinion survey by Gallup International found that Americans were more likely to express satisfaction with their urban surroundings than were the residents of any other country, except Canada.[7] This survey also found few significant differences among whites, blacks, and Latinos. Although the minorities tended to give their neighborhoods a relatively lower ranking than did whites, there were no strong differences given to their ratings of various public services. For example, in rating police protection, 85.9 percent of the total sample were satisfied, whereas 76.9 percent of the blacks and 81.8 percent of the Latinos were. Of course, these generalizations mask some important variations among cities from service to service.

Let us just sample some of the data on which the objective performance rankings rest. If we were to ask how good is the housing provided in American cities, we might specify a number of criteria for assessing that. One important measure is "crowding." Table 7.2 shows that in terms of crowding, the housing in American cities when viewed in the aggregate is not highly congested and is quite comparable with housing densities in Europe and Scandinavia. Most of the housing stock is privately provided. That becomes clear when we examine the comparative efforts of cities to provide public housing. Table 7.3 shows that American cities have done little to provide public housing, though some cities have done more than others.

A number of indicators could also be used to describe the relative safety of cities. If we use homicides per 100,000 people, American cities are disproportionately represented among the unsafe (see Table 7.4).

As Fried and Rabinowitz say after surveying a variety of statistical indicators of public safety, "we find that American cities are less safe in terms of violent

[6]Richard Lewellen-Davis, "The American City Through English Eyes," *Daedalus* (Fall 1972), pp. 185–186.

[7]George Gallup, "Human Needs and Satisfactions: A Global Survey," *Public Opinion Quarterly* (Winter 1976–1977), pp. 467.

TABLE 7.2 Comparative Urban Housing: Crowding (Persons per Room), Around 1970

High Comfort (.5–.6)	Moderate Comfort (.7–.9)	Moderate Overcrowding (1.0–1.9)	Extreme Overcrowding (2.0+)
Göteborg	Rome	Tokyo	Algiers
Stockholm	Venice	Osaka	Bombay
ATLANTA	Geneva	Cracow	
Hamburg	Bologna	Warsaw	
CHICAGO	Lausanne	Bari	
LOS ANGELES	Bern	Birmingham	
DETROIT	HONOLULU	England	
London	MIAMI	East Berlin	
Manchester	Zürich	São Paulo	
PHILADELPHIA	Cologne	Lisbon	
Montreal	NEWARK	Prague	
Toronto	WASHINGTON	Belgrade	
Brussels	NEW YORK	Vienna	
Copenhagen	Frankfurt	Moscow	
Oslo	Helsinki	Yokohama	
Bonn	Paris		
Bradford	Athens		
Edmonton			

Source: Robert Fried and Francine Rabinowitz, *Comparative Urban Performance* (Englewood Cliffs, N.J.: Prentice-Hall, 1980), p. 52.

Note: U.S. cities are capitalized for convenience.

crime than are any other cities in the advanced world and less safe than many cities in the Third World!''[8]

Concerning community health, one of the widely accepted indicators of relative health is the infant death rate. Here, once again, we find that the statistics show a huge gap between the richer and poorer countries and a moderately good performance in American cities (see Table 7.5).

Turning to indicators of comparative governmental performance, perhaps the most discussed single indicator is comparative taxation. By comparison to the other Western democracies, Americans pay less tax. The range is from high taxes in Scandinavia and the Netherlands to low tax burdens in such cities as Beirut, Hong Kong, and Madrid. Government takes about 41 percent of the gross incomes of mechanics in Amsterdam and 51 percent of the gross incomes of personnel managers in Stockholm, for example; this amounts to about double the taxes paid by comparable occupational categories in the United States.[9]

[8]Fried and Rabinowitz, *Comparative Urban Politics*, p. 33.
[9]Ibid., pp. 58–59.

TABLE 7.3   Comparative Public Housing Effort: Public Housing Units per 1000 Residents, Around 1970

Less than 5	5–14	15–24	25–34	35–44	55–64	75–84	85+
KANSAS CITY	HONOLULU	BOSTON	Geneva	Copenhagen	Naples	The Hague	Birmingham, England
HOUSTON	DENVER	BIRMINGHAM	NEWARK	Turin	Venice	Bologna	Sheffield
INDIANAPOLIS	DALLAS	Berne	Tokyo				Stockholm
LOS ANGELES	CINCINNATI	ATLANTA	Yokohama				Munich
MILWAUKEE	CHICAGO	Perth					Amsterdam
OKLAHOMA CITY	BUFFALO	Stockholm					London
OMAHA	Basel	Lausanne					Milan
PHOENIX	BALTIMORE	NEW ORLEANS					Rotterdam
SAN DIEGO	LOUISVILLE	PITTSBURGH					Vienna
Edmonton	MEMPHIS	Rome					Hong Kong
	MIAMI	Zurich					Bradford
	NEW YORK						
	PHILADELPHIA						
	PORTLAND						
	SAN FRANCISCO						
	SEATTLE						
	ST. LOUIS						
	WASHINGTON						
	Singapore						

Source: Robert Fried and Francine Rabinowitz, *Comparative Urban Performance* (Englewood Cliffs, N.J.: Prentice-Hall, 1980), p. 118.

Note: U.S. cities are capitalized for convenience.

TABLE 7.4 Comparative Personal Safety in Cities: Homicides per 100,000 People, 1970s

Relatively Safe Cities			*Relatively Unsafe Cities*
0–2.4	*2.5–4.9*	*5–9.9*	*More than 10*
Bern	Sydney	BOSTON	WASHINGTON
Toronto	Montreal	Rotterdam	BALTIMORE
Amsterdam	PITTSBURGH	MILWAUKEE	CLEVELAND
Madrid	Nagoya	PORTLAND	ST. LOUIS
London	PROVIDENCE	HONOLULU	Pretoria
West Berlin	MINNEAPOLIS	BUFFALO	ATLANTA
Oslo	Osaka	SAN DIEGO	NEWARK
Calcutta	Palermo	Amsterdam	SAN FRANCISCO
Bombay	SEATTLE	Copenhagen	PHILADELPHIA
Mexico City	Warsaw	Munich	ALBUQUERQUE
Antwerp	Bonn		CHICAGO
Rome	Vienna		CLEVELAND
Tokyo	Edmonton		BALTIMORE
Essen			DALLAS
Yokohama			MIAMI
Sheffield			HOUSTON
Hong Kong			Taipei
Bradford			NEW YORK
			MEMPHIS
			DETROIT
			NEW ORLEANS
			ATLANTA
			Rio de Janeiro
			Athens

Source: Robert Fried and Francine Rabinowitz, *Comparative Urban Performance* (Englewood Cliffs, N.J.: Prentice-Hall, 1980), p. 34.
Note: U.S. cities are capitalized for convenience.

The fiscal health of American cities is quite variable and, as Table 7.6 indicates, not easily distinguishable from the cities of the economically advanced nations, if we use per capita municipal debt as our indicator. It is worth noting that New York City is not alone in having a relatively large debt among the cities of the world.

Surveying a very large number of indicators, like the ones we have just sampled, Fried and Rabinowitz find a mixed performance in American cities. The mixture is relatively easily anticipated after a review of American city politics. The strong hold of the "private city" image, the continuing reform pattern that institutionalizes the preferences of the middle and upper classes, and the "systemic bias" of governmental decision makers in a similar direction all suggest that the content of policy would skew as shown in Table 7.1. The basic struggles in the industrially advanced countries appear to be "over priorities, over the relative

TABLE 7.5 Comparative Infant Death in Cities: Infant Death Rate per 100,000 Live Births, 1970s

9–9	10–19	20–29	30–39	40–49	50–59	60–69	70–79	80–89	90+
Taipei	Tokyo	ATLANTA	Panama	Buenos Aires	Havana	New Delhi	Accra	Quito	Freetown (127)
Bern	East Berlin	DENVER	Bangkok	Bucharest		Manila	Mexico City	Colombo	Tunis (99)
	Hamburg	DETROIT	Milan	Tashkent		Lisbon	Rio de Janeiro	Bombay	Cairo (141)
	Kiev	NEW ORLEANS	Turin	Athens			São Paulo	Madras	Alexandria (106)
	Kyoto	Baghdad	Sofia	Budapest			Ahmedabad	Naples	Belo Horizonte (105)
	Leningrad	Barcelona	Bologna				Bogotá		Istanbul (114)
	London	West Berlin	Palermo				Brasilia		RECIFE (229)
	LOS ANGELES	Birmingham, England	Belgrade						
	Madrid	CHICAGO							
	Osaka	Moscow							
	Paris	Munich							
	Yokohama	NEW YORK							
	Amsterdam	PHILADELPHIA							
	Copenhagen	Prague							
	Oslo	Rome							
	Göteborg	Saigon							
	Stockholm	Warsaw							
	Geneva	Vienna							
	Zürich	Brussels							
	Sydney	Leipzig							
	Melbourne	Dublin							
	Bonn	Manchester							
	Hong Kong	Glasgow							
	Singapore	Vienna							
	Bradford								
	Edmonton								

Source: Robert Fried and Francine Rabinowitz, *Comparative Urban Performance* (Englewood Cliffs, N.J.: Prentice-Hall, 1980), p. 40.

Note: U.S. cities are capitalized for convenience.

TABLE 7.6   Comparative Fiscal Health: Per Capita Municipal Debt, 1970s

$0–499	$500–999	$1,000–1,499	$1,500+
Lille	CLEVELAND	London	Rotterdam
Barcelona	Montreal	Frankfurt	Manchester
Lyon	Toronto	Palermo	Stockholm
Bordeaux	DETROIT	Birmingham	Rome
Portland	Oslo	Nottingham	Bern
Vienna	Munich	Zürich	NEW YORK
SAN DIEGO	Dortmund	Glasgow	Amsterdam
Nice	Genoa	Göteborg	
PITTSBURGH	Cologne	Sheffield	
MIAMI	DALLAS	Naples	
MINNEAPOLIS	Copenhagen	ATLANTA	
HONOLULU	BALTIMORE	Bristol	
Stuttgart	DENVER	Bradford, England	
Oska	SAN FRANCISCO	Edmonton	
Vancouver	PHILADELPHIA		
Kyoto	Milan		
CHICAGO	Bonn		
NEWARK	The Hague		
NEW ORLEANS	BOSTON		
HOUSTON	LOS ANGELES		
Tokyo	Frankfurt		
Turin	Yokohama		

Source: Robert Fried and Francine Rabinowitz, *Comparative Urban Performance* (Englewood Cliffs, N.J.: Prentice-Hall, 1980), p. 60.
Note: U.S. cities are capitalized for convenience.

scope of the public and private sector, and over the allocation of public sector funds.'' They sagely point out that there is no guarantee that ''wealthy countries will prefer schools over race tracks, hospitals over sailboats, or milk over alcohol.''[10]

CONFLICTS OVER PERFORMANCE

Policy is made to meet individual and collective needs and to solve conflicts. Conflict continues simply because we disagree as to what are our needs and what is the best means by which to obtain them. But conflict is inherently a discomforting phenomenon. Perhaps overgeneralizing, but nonetheless moving toward an important insight, Richard Sennett has argued that middle-class Americans are so-

[10]Ibid., p. 82.

cialized to avoid conflict and develop a "guilt-over-conflict" syndrome when it inevitably occurs.[11] As observers of the political process, we need not accept that cultural anticonflict bias. Conflict is in and of itself neither good nor bad. Its effects on individuals and cities may range from destructive to creative. Some conflicts certainly do leave cities torn apart, with all their leaders compromised, the integrity of social organizations in doubt, and the personal rapport between operating elements of the community destroyed. An atmosphere of mutual suspicion immobilizes the decision makers and the government drifts. This is the nightmare scenario, but equally often, it is not what happens, even when the conflict becomes rancorous. In other circumstances, conflict is cathartic; the participants need only to blow off steam by airing their grievances with one another and with particular policies. Once the tension has been released, there is a return to confidence in the established policies and leaders with no governmental structure or policy changes made. Finally, but most important, some conflicts are creative. They bring to the surface long-repressed grievances, stimulate the emergence of new leadership, and make innovation possible. In city politics, as with life in general, there is no creativity without conflict.

The intensities and strategies of the participants in conflict certainly play a large role in determining whether conflict will be destructive or creative. For present purposes, let us distinguish three types of conflict: latent, conventional, and rancorous.

Latent.   A conflict is latent when for a variety of reasons it is felt but not yet articulated politically. Frey has called these "suppressed" issues.[12]

Conventional.   A conflict is conventional when "established means of political expression are used to influence the outcome."[13] That is, the participants have genuine and strongly felt differences, but they put their faith in the established processes and leaders to find a resolution. There is a strong sense of the justice of the process and, as a result, a feeling of obligation to abide by decisions even though there are winners and losers. Conventional conflicts are settled by stable "routinized" processes.[14]

Rancorous.   A rancorous conflict is more intense and calls the fairness and justice of the process into doubt. When participants feel that the biases of

[11]Richard Semett, *The Uses of Disorder* (New York: Alfred A. Knopf, 1970).

[12]Frederick Frey, "Comment on Issues and Nonissues in the Study of Power," *American Political Science Review,* Vol. 65 (December 1971), p. 1088.

[13]William Gamson, "Rancorous Conflict in Community Politics," *American Sociological Review,* Vol. 31 (February 1966), p. 71.

[14]Ira Sharkansky, *The Routines of Politics* (New York: Van Nostrand Reinhold, 1970).

established institutions treat them unfairly, this is a perfectly understandable reaction. Most often, however, the passion of the moment causes the conflict to be framed less in terms of the fairness of institutions and more in generalities and personalities. Opponents in rancorous conflicts usually see one another as "playing dirty" and "vicious."

It is, of course, the rancorous conflict that has the greatest potential for rapid and profound change—either destructive or creative—though, on balance, it is clearly the case that most policy decisions are made in the less visible routines of conventional political conflict. And it is apparent that most of the "systemic bias" of the culture manifests its effects in conventional conflict. Whether conflict will be latent, conventional, or rancorous in any particular city is apparently a function of a number of factors in the environment of that city. Changes in the economic structure of the city, demographic shifts, altered patterns of political coalition, and cleavage all may produce the conditions for rancorous conflict. Because of its intensity and visibility, the rancorous conflict has received a good deal of study, and it has been found that, despite the obvious connection between unique characteristics of the environment and rancorous conflict, such conflicts follow a similar pattern regardless of the unique characteristics of the city or the particular policy.

The Dynamics of Rancorous Conflict

It is the peculiarity of social controversy that it sets in motion its own dynamics; these tend to carry it forward in a path which bears little relation to its beginnings,"[15] wrote James Coleman in an early, but still quite relevant, piece of research on community conflict. In a rancorous conflict, it is emotional reaction rather than rational, gamelike calculation that governs the moves and counter-moves, but they are nonetheless structured. In the broadest terms, a rancorous conflict shows three developmental tendencies. First, the issue moves from specific charges to more general ones. Second, in that process, new and different issues are added to the original ones. And, third, the controversy moves from disagreement to antagonism.

Those developments occur in the seven-stage process abstracted in Figure 7.1. The full development of the controversy depends on the existence of a reservoir of grievances, that is, a number of suppressed issues that have been put aside, but that nonetheless accumulate. Rancorous conflicts are analogous to the familiar personal quarrels in which we have all participated, so let us illustrate the process in those terms. We have all fought with friends and relatives, so we know that no matter how much we have in common, no matter how much we love each other, no matter how "irrational" we think it is to fight, we cannot stop ourselves.

[15]James Coleman, *Community Conflict* (Glencoe, Ill.: The Free Press, 1957), p. 2.

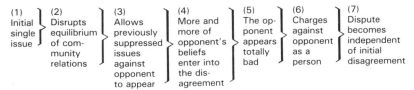

FIGURE 7.1 Coleman's seven stages of rancorous conflict development. (*Source:* James Coleman, *Community Conflict* (Glencoe, Ill.: The Free Press, 1957), p. 11. Reprinted with permission of the Free Press, a Division of Macmillan, Inc. Copyright© 1957 by The Free Press.)

The reservoir of grievances is the largest reason for this dynamic. There are always irritations: He dresses sloppily; she crowds me in bed; he uses my comb; she drives too fast; he is too friendly with other women; she doesn't appreciate my sense of humor; he undervalues my intellect. Most such problems seem either petty at the time or not something that can be easily faced, so we pride ourselves on our magnanimity as we graciously overlook them; but we do not forget. And their weight grows over time; the reservoir of grievances presses against the dam of rationality. Then, one day—usually it has not been a particularly good day—you find your comb is full of someone else's hair (stage 1) and you explode.

The explosion is all out of proportion to the precipitating event, or "triggering mechanism," as the event was called in describing the ghetto riots in the "long, hot summer" of 1967. But the triggering mechanism is simply the chink in the dam that allows the contents of the reservoir to gush out (stages 2 and 3).

As you attack the comb abuser, you are shocked to discover that he shows no signs of repentance. Oh no. Instead, he begins to recite from his reservoir of grievances against you. The only thing to do is let this ingrate know how long suffering you have been, so you begin to recite your other complaints (stage 4). He counters by doing the same, and soon you begin to realize what a totally rotten person you have been dealing with (stage 5), so you tell him so (stage 6).

If, after one of you stalks out in anger, the disruption does not heal in a short time, the effects are long term and structural. That is, the participants to the fight come to formulate their responses to issues in terms of their dislike for one another. "He's a supporter of Harold Washington? That settles it for me; I'm voting for the next person who runs against Washington, no matter who it is" (stage 7). The dispute has become independent of the initial disagreement, and it generates responses on subsequent issues.

We should not take any analogy too seriously. There are a number of differences between private disputes and public ones, but the essential dynamic is quite similar and the consequences important. Especially important is the implication that rancorous conflicts may mark the changing of coalition dominance within a city. The transition from a dominant private city coalition to an amenities-seeking coalition and back again is likely to be marked by rancorous conflict. No set of lofty appeals to "rationality" is likely to have a moderating effect. In fact, it is in those moments that the partisans discover that rationality is usually itself a political tool of one side or the other.

What is most deceptive about this analogy is its implication that local disputes are raised and settled like arguments among roughly equal individuals. In political disputes, the actors may be dramatically unequal. This interpersonal dynamic is irrelevant, for example, to the situation in which a gas consumer gets angry at an oil company.

DIFFERING EVALUATIONS OF URBAN SERVICE PERFORMANCE

The bulk of policymaking in American cities is not the result of rancorous conflict but is more conventional. The image that most Americans have of urban policies, in fact, is that they are dull and unimportant. Who wants to talk about sewers and garbage service? As one prominent local policy analyst says, "Local service delivery is the backwater of public policy analysis."[16] And, of course, compared with the magnitude of issues like inflation, national defense, and civil liberties, they do rank lower in the priorities of most citizens. But just let the garbage not get collected for a week and compare the stink raised on that subject with that raised over a controversial foreign policy decision. Most mayors know that garbage is even a better political mobilizer than insults to the flag.

Evaluating urban service delivery is not glamorous, just necessary. Broadly speaking, urban policies are evaluated in terms of two issues: Are the policy goals worthwhile? Do the policies actually achieve the goals? The political process answers the first question. A democratic politics allows continuous re-evaluation of the desirability of all public policy goals. But even when we can agree on the goals (there are few dissenters on the garbage collection issue), the second question produces some tough problems. A great many political controversies come down to differences as to the means of achieving goals. Is it better to have private or public garbage collection? Which choice is most efficient? Most inexpensive? Most equitable? As not all the answers to these questions would point the same direction, there is a politics of evaluation as well as a politics of goal setting.

Four major concerns appear to occupy the attention of those evaluating urban policy: the concern for (1) efficiency, (2) the role of bureaucracy, (3) equity, and (4) the fragmentation of local authority. Many would argue that these studies put too much emphasis on public service criteria and not enough on concern for democratic accountability, but to date that accurately describes evaluation studies. That these are questions to which there are no simply technical answers will be

---

[16]Richard Rich, "The Political Economy of Urban-Service Distribution," in Richard Rich, ed., *The Politics of Urban Public Services* (Lexington, Mass.: Lexington Books, 1982), p. 1.

made clear as we conclude this section by describing once again the differing perspectives of neoconservative, liberal, and radical policy evaluators.

The Concern for Efficiency

Politically active neoconservatives have made the call for "fiscal conservatism" and "efficiency" their own. And while there is little doubt that it was a popular and effective campaign theme in the late 1970s and early 1980s, there is no reason to associate that concern exclusively with neoconservatism. Bob Filner, the president of the San Diego School Board, a civil rights activist, and former aide to archtypical liberal Hubert Humphrey, made his local reputation by being the consummate fiscal conservative in 1981 and 1982. Efficiency and economy in government make good campaign themes because there is really no opposition: no "Citizen's Coalition for More Waste and Inefficiency" to offend. But efficiency does become an issue when policies seek to maximize several goals at the same time.

For example, the San Diego public schools have sought to expand voluntary integration by creating "magnet schools" in racially unbalanced districts. These schools used funds from a variety of sources to create particularly attractive curricula—a school for the performing arts, an advanced math-science program, foreign language–based programs—to attract majority and minority populations into each others' schools. One of the support activities for the voluntary integration program involved providing bus transportation. To encourage participation in the program, every effort was made to pick up children at a point as close to their homes as possible and at the time they desired and to provide as short a ride time as possible. The result was that school bus routes became a nightmare for an efficiency expert. Routes crossed and recrossed each other, empty buses moved from one area of the city to another at odd hours, schedules had to change as children were added to or dropped out of the programs. In other words, efficiency is but one evaluative standard. To critique the inefficiency of the bus routing process in San Diego was to miss the point that inefficiency was the price of service to a higher goal.

Efficiency is but an aspect of the larger concern for rationality as the basis for managing conflict. As with efficiency, everybody agrees that it is desirable. But when it comes to using it as the singular standard for evaluating policy, it often is inadequate by itself. Why that is so becomes clearer as we specify more precisely what is meant by rationality. Not an end in itself, but a tool for analysis, rationality involves five fundamental processes: (1) identifying the problem, (2) identifying the goal, (3) ranking goals according to relative importance, (4) assessing all the costs and the benefits of each set of alternatives to achieving the goal, and (5) selecting the package of goals and associated policies that provide the most benefits at the lowest costs.[17] In other words, rationality is the basic orientation of neoconservatism.

An illustration of the uses of rational assumptions is the mode of policy evaluation called "cost-benefit analysis." The effort is to provide a quantitative assessment of the costs and benefits of a number of policies so that the one with the best cost-to-benefit ratio can be selected. Fugii's analysis of a variety of proposals to treat heroin use make a good illustration.[18] After calculating the ratios of such alternatives as legalization, heroin maintenance, methadone maintenance, detoxification, imprisonment and vigorous law enforcement, and civil commitment, he concluded that heroin or methadone maintenance would be the most efficient choice.

Rational approaches have also provided a number of proposals for budgeting. Both the planning-programming-budgeting system (PPBS) and zero-base budgeting (ZBB) are variations on the same pattern. PPBS enjoyed a brief period of political favor when it was used extensively by Robert McNamara in the Department of Defense during the 1960s and Lyndon Johnson instructed its widespread use within the federal government. A number of state and local governments also adopted such procedures at the same time. The effort of PPBS was laudable, namely, to undercut the traditional budgetary pattern that contained information only about money put into the program and lent to the incremental growth of government expenditures. The method of PPBS was to put the budget in such a form that the outputs of each agency could be assessed. This meant (1) defining expenditures in terms of programs, (2) defining the outputs of each program in such a way as to allow precise measurement, (3) providing similar measurements of inputs into the program, (4) computing the costs of alternative combinations of inputs and their effects on the value of output levels, and (5) calculating the best cost-benefit ratios of each combination of inputs and outputs, recommending the best package for funding.

However appealing the logic of this procedure, the program often founders on its own cost-benefit ratio. The procedures are so elaborate and time consuming that it requires a substantial increase in the number of personnel working on the budget. A number of critics charge that the program tends to increase the size and control of certain elements of the bureaucracy and produces very few cost savings.[19]

[17]Charles Lindblom, *The Policy–Making Process* (Englewood Cliffs, N.J. Prentice-Hall, 1968), p. 13.

[18]Edward Fugii, "Public Investment in the Rehabilitation of Heroin Addicts," *Social Science Quarterly*, Vol 55 (June 1974), pp. 39–51.

[19]See the study of the zero-base budgeting experiment in the Department of Agriculture under Jimmy Carter as well as other criticisms of the approach in Leonard Merewitz and Stephen Sosnick, *The Budget's New Clothes: A Critique of Planning-Programming-Budgeting and Benefit-Cost Analysis* (Chicago: Markham, 1971).

The Concern for Bureaucracy

Expanding the power of bureaucracy has consistently been an unintended consequence of urban reform. Writing prior to the New York City fiscal crisis, Theodore Lowi observed that the bureaucracy of the city was its "new machine" and concluded that "the legacy of reform is the bureaucratic city-state."[20] Both neoconservatives and radicals tended to agree that these new machines were relatively insulated structures of power in that each agency is a crucial actor in shaping policies, yet the leadership in each agency is "relatively self-perpetuating and not readily subject to the controls of higher authority."[21]

Neoconservatives emphasize that many of the deficiencies of bureaucracy are the result of their monopolistic character. They are instances of what Hirschman calls "lazy monopoly," because competition does not spur them to higher performance levels. Even would-be strong mayors and managers fail to make a substantial difference. As Greenstone and Peterson note, "too effective an iron hand may actually invoke charges of 'dictatorship' and 'one-man rule.' "[22] Careful study of the effect of the bureaucracy on urban service delivery is relatively recent and inconclusive. Two interpretations are most common: the "decision-rule" hypothesis and the "bureaucratic discretion" hypothesis.

Decision-Rule Hypothesis.   Originally examining budgetary decision making, a number of studies discovered a remarkably high degree of predictability in budgetary decisions from one year to the next. The pattern was described as "incrementalism" and was also found in studies at state and national levels.[23] Once again, as a result of observations made in a time period in which budgets were experiencing long slow growth, it was discovered that administrators made marginal adjustments in their requests but that most of the budget was taken as a given to be added to rather than justified in any comprehensive way. Within the process, it was discovered that certain simple decision-making rules evolved that collectively could be used to predict expenditure patterns. John Crecine, for example, built an elaborate simulation model based on a number of such rules and predicted with great accuracy the actual expenditures of Detroit, Cleveland, and Pittsburgh.[24]

---

[20]Theodore Lowi, "Machine Politics—Old and New," *The Public Interest* (Fall 1967), pp. 86–87.

[21]Ibid.

[22]J. David Greenstone and Paul Peterson, *Race and Authority in Urban Politics* (New York: Russell Sage, 1973), p. 215.

[23]Otto Davis, M. A. H. Dempster, and Aaron Wildavsky, "A Theory of the Budgetary Process," *American Political Science Review*, Vol. 60 (September 1966), pp. 529–547; Ira Sharkansky, *Routines of Politics;* and John Crecine, *Governmental Problem Solving: A Computer Simulation of Municipal Budgeting* (Chicago: Rand McNally, 1969).

[24]Ibid.

The decision-rule studies support the view that the crucial decisions in the budgetary process are internal to the bureaucracy. Outside forces such as citizen attitudes, group pressures, and broader political considerations have little impact. This would mean that public bureaucracies behave in a highly structured, routinized, and deterministic fashion in making their decisions.

Bureaucratic Discretion. Apparently contradicting this picture of urban bureaucratic behavior are studies of the range of choice open to administrators at all levels as to whether and how to enforce the rules. For example, studies of the police and welfare bureaucracies show that individuals have a very broad range of discretion.[25] This is why Dallas police wrote twenty-four times as many traffic tickets as did Boston police in the same year even though the two cities are of comparable population. The best explanation was found to be differences in the attitudes of the police chiefs toward the traffic control function. Sometimes designated collectively as ''street-level bureaucrats''—the police, welfare workers, lower court judges, parole officers, and so on—have and use considerable independence in the application of public policy.[26]

These two images of the bureaucracy are not easily reconcilable. In one, the bureaucracy is portrayed as rigid, highly structured by its decision rules, closed to the external political process, and quite predictable. In the other, the bureaucracy is pliable, enjoys considerable discretion, and is idiosyncratic and decisions are not easily predicted. Part of the explanation is that the decision-rules image derives from studies of the budgetary process in a time of growing revenues. The stability of the situation and the quantitative clarity of money probably make routinization of allocative processes easier than in some other policy areas. The greater the clarity of the situation, the less discretion a bureaucrat needs. At the other extreme is the unpredictability of a police officer's encounters—from a sober high-class hooker to a drunken banker. Ambiguity makes discretion necessary.

The patterns of bureaucratic behavior have been affected by fiscal crisis and the need to retrench, but there is no great clarity yet as to how. It appears that two responses occur simultaneously. In one, the upper-level administrators begin to anticipate the reactions of those they believe have power over them. This is perhaps how what Stone called ''systemic power'' (Chapter 6) might have a magnified impact in periods of fiscal stress. But at the same time, the prospect of

---

[25]John Gardiner, ''Police Enforcement of Traffic Laws,'' and Martha Derthick, ''Intercity Differences in Administration of the Public Assistance Program,'' both in James Q. Wilson, ed., *City Politics and Public Policy* (New York: John Wiley & Sons, 1968), pp. 151–172 and 243–266. Also, see Kenneth Davis, *Discretionary Justice* (Baton Rouge: Louisiana State University Press, 1969).

[26]The concept ''street-level bureaucrat'' is from Michael Lipsky, ''Toward a Theory of Street Level Bureaucracy,'' in Willis Hawley, et al., eds., *Theoretical Perspectives on Urban Politics* (Englewood Cliffs, N.J. Prentice-Hall, 1976), Chap. 8. Also see Lipsky, *Street Level Bureaucracy: Dilemmas of the Individual in Public Services* (New York: Russell Sage, 1983).

cutting back gives comprehensive decision-making power over those people and programs under the bureaucrat's control. Now administrators have strong arguments to assure the compliance of their subordinates. Budget cutting, in other words, appears unlikely to curtail the powers of the bureaucracy.

The Concern for Equity

We Americans are ambiguous about our belief in equality. A strong part of our rhetorical heritage, we still have combined a belief in egalitarianism with such practices as slavery and persecution of ethnic and religious minorities and a belief that capitalism requires inequalities of wealth as "the mainspring in the economic watch." We also believe in inequality, that the talented should be left free to make their maximum contributions. No logic combines these contradictory patterns, but in our national experience, we seek to balance these contradictory ethics. Such balance is usually an act of politics. The delivery of urban services is a rather good indicator of the prevailing balance.

Most of us have a strong sense that there are inequities in the delivery of urban services. Claude Brown has one of the strongest when he says, "Harlem was getting f--ked over by everybody, the politicians, the police, the businessmen, everybody," and his illustration is a comment on urban performance: "We'd laugh about when the big snowstorms came, they'd have the snowplows out downtown as soon as it stopped, but they'd let it pile up for weeks in Harlem."[27]

Citizens can become intensely concerned about snow removal, as Mayor Jane Byrne discovered shortly after she became mayor of Chicago. Poor performance by city snow removal crews resulted in major public criticism. But usually such routine city activities result in little more than grousing. Inequities in educational policies, however, have produced the most heated and persistent contemporary controversies. Beginning at least with the historic decision in *Brown* v. *Board of Education* (1954), the courts have kept the school districts under continuing pressure to improve educational equality. The court told us that separate educational facilities for black and white students are inherently unequal. But the political turmoil that resulted from integration efforts led many to abandon integration as a goal and move to neighborhood control—in black neighborhoods that meant black control. The rancor of the Ocean Hill–Brownsville dispute in New York City in the mid-1960s was on exactly that issue, community control. It proved a disillusioning experience for many of the liberal integrationists of New York and in other cities that had similar controversies.

As with so many of the topics of this book, the 1970s was a period of turnaround, some would say "backlash," on the demand for greater equity and integration in education. Increasingly, coalitions whose major expressed concern

[27]Claude Brown, *Manchild in the Promised Land* (New York: Macmillan, 1965), p. 193.

is for quality of education—rather than equality in education—have ascended in power.

The most important piece of academic research done in the midst of these shifting winds was done by James Coleman. His book, *Equality of Educational Opportunity* (1966), set the tone and the issues in both public debates and for ongoing research.[28] The "Coleman Report," as it was popularly known, first drew a distinction between input equality and output equality in the measurement of the effect of educational systems. He argued that simply assuring input equality, that is, equal amount of money, numbers of teachers, and comparable facilities would not necessarily equalize education. In fact, he pointed out five different meanings of equal education: (1) equal facilities and teachers; (2) racial integration; (3) equal intangibles, such as prestige, alumni support, and morale; (4) equal educational outcomes given equal pupil capacities and backgrounds; and (5) equal educational outcomes given unequal pupil capacities and backgrounds. Coleman urges that the schools are failing to provide equality if judged by the standard of the last, and most rigorous, test. He maintains that "equality of educational opportunity implies not merely equal schools, but equally effective schools, whose influences will overcome the differences in starting points of children from different social groups."[29] In fact, Coleman found that initial pupil disparities actually widen over twelve years. Schools failed the equity test.

More recent criticisms argue that schools fail in tests of excellence as well. A Presidential Commission Report in 1983 warned that a "tide of mediocrity" was sweeping over public education. "Back to Basics" proved the basis of a successful campaign for State Superintendent of Public Instruction in California. Proposals for allowing tax monies to be turned back to parents to allow them to choose either public education or take their children to private schools (called the Voucher System) began to be taken more seriously. And proposals for comprehensive curricular and teacher training reform began to multiply. School controversies, in short, are the single best illustration of the concern over equity in urban performance.

Much of the concern for equity in schools and other urban services related to lack of equity between neighborhoods. Certainly that is what Claude Brown was emphasizing in remarking on the unreliability of snowplows in Harlem. It is relatively indisputable that public services are not equitably distributed, but it is not clear how that can be explained. Some allocative choices of government, for example, may result in inequitable service delivery unintentionally, accidentally, or in ways unintended by policymakers. Other inequities may be the result of lag between public sector response and private sector growth. It took several years for schools to be built in Scripps Ranch, California, for example, well after it had a large school-age population. But other inequities are less benign in their implications. Summarizing the literature that seeks to explain service inequities, Robert Lineberry distills three basic causes: what he calls the "underclass" hypothesis, the "ecological" hypothesis, and the now familiar bureaucratic "decision-rule" hypothesis.[30]

The Underclass Hypothesis.   The least benign of the proposed explanations of service inequities is exactly what Claude Brown wanted us to assume, namely, that Harlem gets lower levels of public service because its population is black and part of the American underclass. The essential point is that service preferences are consciously or unconsciously allocated so as to discriminate against certain groups and favor others. Lineberry finds three variations on this theme. First, racial discrimination is the central explanation. Second, social class, rather than race, is the cause. And, finally, the local "power elite" creates policies that favor themselves and their friends.

The Ecological Hypothesis.   Other explanations place less emphasis on deliberate discrimination. The ecological hypothesis essentially is that overt characteristics of a neighborhood other than race, class, or elitism determine the services it receives. Such ecological features of a neighborhood as its geography, age, and density sometimes dictate service levels. Or sometimes it is historical accident. Lineberry illustrates the point, noting that Brackenridge, San Antonio's major park, is located nearer to the richer than the poorer part of town. "There is nothing manipulative, mysterious or malevolent about this, however. The reason is a historical accident, involving the donation in the 1880s of a large tract of land by a wealthy benefactor." At the time, Lineberry notes, neither the rich nor poor were particularly proximate to the land. And by contrast, "Only a short hop up Interstate 35, in Austin, the opposite accident occurred, where the major park is closer to the poor than the rich."[31]

The Decision-Rule Hypothesis.   As explained more fully earlier, the decision-rule explanation is essentially that the level of urban services in a particular neighborhood is primarily determined by the need for bureaucracy to create a stable pattern of rules for itself to simplify its complex tasks, to save, and to protect its own time and resources.

In his own careful and elaborate study of public service delivery in San

[30]Robert Lineberry, *Equality and Urban Policy: The Distribution of Municipal Public Services* (Beverly Hills, Calif.: Sage Publications, 1977), pp. 57–67. Copyright © 1977 by Sage Publications. Reprinted by permission of Sage Publications, Inc.
[31]Ibid., p. 63.

Antonio, Lineberry verified no single one of these hypotheses. Within the great complexity of explanations for service inequities, Lineberry suggests that the decision-rule hypothesis has the strongest support. The result is "unpatterned inequality." But his research directly contradicts the underclass hypothesis, as his data show that "neither neighborhood ethnicity, nor political power, nor socio-economic status are very satisfactory predictors of service allocations."[32] As might be expected, not all research reaches these same conclusions, although this appears the prevailing interpretation.

The Concern for Fragmentation

In broader perspective, it may be that differences in local performance are more a consequence of the fragmentation of local governments than of the policymaking patterns within a particular government. When residents of a city become discontent with its performance, they may exercise their exit option if they have the resources. The cumulative effect of exiting is a pattern of residential segregation and the multiplication of political jurisdictions. The service inequities between these jurisdictions may be marked.

Using education once more as an example, the per child expenditures for schooling vary dramatically from district to district. Because schools are financed largely through the local property tax, the wealth of the district may affect the quality of education it offers. To be more concrete, in the early 1970s, relatively poor Baldwin Park, California, had an assessed valuation per child of $3,706, nearby Pasadena had $13,706, and the corresponding figure for Beverly Hills was $50,805. This is a revenue source difference in a ratio of 1 to 4 to 13. This is why the California Supreme Court held in *Serrano* v. *Priest* that these differences, coupled with state tax equalization formulas that did not much equalize, resulted in denial of the constitutional guarantees of "equal protection" under the laws.[33] But the California court is widely recognized to have been a liberal, socially conscious court in that period. So, even though other school systems throughout the country exhibit similar disparities in per child educational expenditures, the Supreme Court in *Rodriguez* v. *San Antonio Independent School District* refused to uphold such an interpretation.[34]

Meanwhile, studies of the politics of the creation of new governmental entities make it clear that the motive of the exiters is precisely to take advantage of available inequities. Gary Miller's study of the multiplication of small jurisdictions south of Los Angeles in the mid-1950s finds that exit was a "quiet" tax revolt. "Middle-class homeowners, motivated by the same frustrations that were

[32]Ibid., p. 183.
[33]*Serrano* v. *Priest*, 96 Cal. Reptr. 60 (1971).
[34]411 U.S. 1 (1973)

behind Proposition 13, responded to their frustrations through their choice of residential communities.''[35] This interpretation, if it is accurate, substantially contradicts much of the traditional literature on urban consolidation and also the approach of public choice theorists, as well as other neoconservatives, who make the concern for ''efficiency'' their central standard of evaluation. This is because Miller's study (done, not so incidentally, in close association with the perspective of the Ostroms, see Chapter 2) emphasizes that both consolidated local governments and fragmented local governments are based on systematic bias—''but toward different societal groups.''[36]

IDEOLOGICAL DIFFERENCES OVER URBAN PERFORMANCE

Each ideological perspective combines the foregoing concerns in differing ways to reach its own evaluation of the status of urban performance. Neoconservatives tend to put efficiency at the core of their evaluation. By that criterion, there is much to criticize in urban policy, particularly in those services in which the government has a monopoly. The proposed solutions are fundamentally to streamline the governmental process by cutting costs and subjecting continuing programs to careful cost-benefit analysis—getting ''more bang for fewer bucks.''[37] The monopoly of government can best be broken by encouraging private suppliers of the same goods. The school voucher system is a good illustration, as it would encourage the growth of private schools and would make the ''lazy monopoly'' of the public schools work harder to be competitive.

Government itself should continue to respond to what we called the New Reform in Chapter 6 by becoming more businesslike. This means, among other things, bureaucratic reform designed to increase the productivity of agencies and individual bureaucrats. The concern for bureaucracy has proved very difficult for neoconservatives. They have historically had a kind of ''tarbaby'' problem with it. The more they try to minimize it, the more power it develops. So the older reform movement made managers and planners more important and ushered in their current concern for the importance of bureaucratic decision rules as the locus of disproportionate governmental power. Even the new reform era finds cost-cutting and cost-benefit approaches adding to the power of some bureaucrats.

Neoconservatives are less concerned with the problems of equity in service delivery. Pressed too far, they contend, the concern for equity undermines initiative and ignores the rights and inhibits the contributions of the best among us. The

---

[35]Gary Miller, *Cities by Contract* (Cambridge, Mass.: MIT Press, 1981), p. 8.

[36]Ibid., p. 9.

[37]Jeffrey Straussman, ''More Bang for Fewer Bucks? Or How Local Governments Can Rediscover the Potentials (and Pitfalls) of the Market,'' *Public Administration Review* Vol. 41 (January 1981), pp. 150–156.

right to exit if urban services are inadequate is important and should be protected. They are thus somewhat ambivalent about metropolitan fragmentation. Viewed from the standpoint of efficiency, a larger consolidated metropolitan authority would be preferable. But viewed from the perspective of a resident, it is best to allow those fragmented governments to protect their chosen style of life.

Liberals exhibit a desire to balance the concerns for efficiency and equity. Few liberals are hostile to the neoconservative goal of improving the cost-benefit ratios of urban services., But there is a greater willingness to deal with bureaucracy as necessary, if potentially problematic. Liberals occasionally defend urban bureaucracies as a repository of expertise and a location for the common citizen within the governmental structure.[38] But more commonly they acquiesce in neo-conservative reforms.

Liberals have put strong emphasis on achieving relatively greater equality in the actual distribution of public services. The New Deal era saw liberals at the forefront of efforts to integrate schools and improve the lagging delivery of services in the urban ghettos. But their analysis seldom moved to fundamental criticism of the capitalist system. They remained content to allow government to continue in the role of equalizer. Certain liberals have become more critical of some of the effects of capitalism, and particular businesses, as the regional shift from Snowbelt to Sunbelt has emerged. Richard Morris, for example, blames the spread of delapidated urban housing on collusion between the federal government and mortgage lenders engaged in "redlining"—the lender practice of refusing to make a loan on properties in inner-city neighborhoods. "Behind redlining lies the federal government. In 1975 Washington channeled 29% of its loan insurance to three states—Florida, California and Arizona—which had together, 15% of the country's population . . . [this] led the way for the bank redlining of American cities."[39] Liberals, too, are ambivalent about the problems of metropolitan fragmentation, and in much the same terms as are the neoconservatives.

Radical political economy places a much stronger emphasis on equity than do any of the other concerns. They doubt that the patterns of service delivery that lead to great disparities between rich and poor can be sufficiently minimized within a capitalist system, and they doubt the findings that urban service delivery results in "unpatterned inequities." The inequities are all too patterned. And contrary to neoconservative protests about the urban bureaucracy, some radical analysis suggests that bureaucracy functions to serve the dominant class interests.

Richard Rich makes that point in re-evaluating the growing consensus that bureaucratic decision rules, rather than class-based biases, are the more important determinant of service inequities. He begins with a summary reformulation of the nature of the state in a capitalist society.[40] Two assumptions are most important, he

[38]Norton Long, *The Polity* (New York: Rand McNally, 1962), Chap. 5.

[39]Richard Morris, *Bum Rap on America's Cities* (Englewood Cliffs, N.J. Prentice-Hall, 1978), p. 12.

[40]Rich, "The Political Economy of Urban Service Delivery," pp. 1–6, 3.

says. The first is that the state evolved because of the need for a nominally separate institution to legitimate economic power and mediate the conflicts created by economic decisions. Second, state action serves two broad purposes: to make it possible to accumulate and circulate capital and to maintain social control so as to allow for production and to reproduce the economic classes.[41] If the state is, indeed, set up to serve these central functions, then the dominant classes have "every reason to be content to leave the calling of individual plays to bureaucratic umpires."[42] In fact, it is to the great advantage of an elite to have routine distributional decisions made by bureaucrats using "technical" rules. "This tends to depoliticize . . . and, in a society valuing professionalism and scientific management, to legitimate the social relations sustained by the resulting service-delivery patterns."[43]

Concerning governmental fragmentation, radicals are inclined to regard it in class terms. The exit of those who can exercise options is usually to escape the financial obligation to help the lower economic classes. For many radicals, the most crucial politics of urban performance may be the politics surrounding the processes of metropolitan fragmentation. This is because the boundaries determine the fiscal capacities of local governments to provide for local services.

SUMMARY

Governments exist to regulate conflicts by making public policy. Those policies are subject to conflict along the lines we have been systematically tracing throughout this book. Neoconservative evaluation of urban policy performance differs from that of liberal and radical.

To provide a broad synthesis and comparison of the policy effects of American local govenment, we reviewed the "performance" or outcomes of a number of urban policies. What we found was a mixed picture. American cities perform well on such indicators as availability of public works, availability of shopping facilities, and moderate taxation but perform poorly in areas like infant health care, racial inequities, and employment. Obviously, such judgments rest on some criteria of evaluation. Recent evaluation studies have tended to focus on (1) the concern for efficiency, (2) the concern for bureaucracy, (3) the concern for equity, and (4) the concern for the effects of governmental fragmentation. The concern for democratic accountability is not absent from these criteria but, especially to liberals and radicals, are inadequately traced.

[41]Citing J. Hirsch, "The Apparatus of the State, the Reproduction of Capital and Urban Conflicts," in M. Dear and A. Scott, eds., *Urbanization and Urban Planning in Capitalist Society* (New York: Methuen, 1981), pp. 593–607.

[42]Rich, "The Political Economy of Urban Service Delivery," p. 7.

[43]Ibid.

CHAPTER 8

*Summary
and Conclusions:
Directions
in Urban
Political Economy*

The single most important force transforming America and the world is advanced, multinational capitalism. It does not seriously overstate to call that impact revolutionary. That much is the common understanding of all three of the ideological positions we have been tracing throughout this book. It is also well agreed that multinationalism is the most important force reshaping the cities of America. But as with all profound change, its implications are as yet only dimly perceived and its extent, meaning, and value disputed. One of the disputes is over the degree to which the current generation of humans can or should seek to control these deeply imbedded forces of change.

Translating this understanding into personal terms, we are left with the recognition that there are two basic modes in which we will be able to make whatever impact is possible. First, we can allow our broad analysis of these issues to inform the many mundane daily decisions we make—on the job, in conversations with friends, as we choose what to buy and at which stores, how we relate to others, what values we stand for. The decision to eat at McDonald's rather than at George's family-owned corner deli is to some minor degree a political one. Second, democracy is the product of a long past revolution, but it continues to provide the means, as Thomas Jefferson liked to emphasize, for each generation to take control of its destiny. Democratic politics provides the means for continuing peaceful revolution.

Politics is the method we use to control, at least to affect, those broad forces. If politics occasionally gets a bad name, as it has in recent history, that is as it should be. A force so important should be carefully watched. But democratic politics will not be permanently impaired or constrained. In praising America, the visiting Frenchman André Gorz put it this way: "typical Americans start from the premise that the country belongs to them, that it will be what they make it, and that it is up to them and not the authorities to change life." That is why he concludes, "the American Revolution is not over."[1]

TRENDS

The politics of cities is but a small part of the total political economic process that is transforming us so fundamentally. But it marks an important arena within which we either perceive accurately and act intelligently in response to those forces or we fail to mesh and accelerate our alienation and irrelevance. More than that, in its impact on the city, we see quite clearly the consequences—strengths and weaknesses—of contemporary capitalism. The city, as always, reflects the tendencies of the culture in highlight.

In describing the central trends within cities, then, we are seeking to find our connections with a larger world. We must be strong localists to be truly cosmopolitan. What we find can be stated loosely as a number of trends. First, as just suggested, economic integration is internationalizing our concerns. Clearly, the city and the neighborhood are losing additional capacities for self-governance as this happens. This loss is not necessary, but it occurs because localism is a weak value among Americans and because of that, localistic concerns are consistently overpowered.[2] A number of urbanists, in fact, urge that more neighborhood "advocacy" become a part of local and even national policies.[3]

The movement of capital and jobs to the Sunbelt is the domestic implication of the pattern of multinational development. Businesses seeking lower costs of production and access to cheaper resources and cooperative local governments have found those advantages in Texas just as they may find them in Latin America. Here, once again, neoconservative explanations of "convergence" do not differ

[1]André Gorz, *Ecology as Politics* (Boston: South End Press, 1980), p. 215.
[2]The literature on neighborhood organization strongly suggests this. See Richard Rich, "Dilemmas of Citizen Participation in the Neighborhood Movement," *Urban Affairs Quarterly*, Vol. 17 (March 1982), pp. 387–392.
[3]See Pierre Clavel and Harvey Jacobs, "Planning and National Urban Policy," *Public Administration Review*, Vol. 41 (January–February 1981), pp. 87–92.

markedly in their description of this process from the radical explanation of "uneven peripheral development." But the prescriptions are nearly opposites. Neoconservatives and liberals appear ready to allow the forces of production to lead and, in fact, would discourage interference in "free market" decision-making patterns. Citizen input is mostly a bother in this formulation, and the politics of the bureaucracy is seen as insidious and dangerous. For the neoconservative, the basic strategy requires a transition for the politicized 1960s in the direction of depolitization. Fiscal scarcity in the public sector, symbolized by the New York fiscal crisis and Proposition 13, has led to a New Reform era that, like the old reform era, institutionalizes the biases of business. The leading consequences have been curtailed powers of the local governments, expansion of business control over those institutions, and a degree of depolitization of urban neighborhoods.

Radicals see the contemporary period as a short moment in the accumulation of contradictions that produce periodic "crises" in capitalist development. Class conflict is inevitable and will become more sharply defined and intense as the have-not's grow in number and in the consciousness that they are being exploited. Along with liberals, radicals expect that the corporate phase of capitalism will overextend and discredit itself as it increasingly demands the subordination of other human values.

A second underlying development that deserves attention is the continuing mobility of the American population, long after the presumed closing of the frontier. The right of both businesses and individuals to change place is held by most Americans with little question, but it appears a concern with a future. The leading reasons for re-evaluation of our mobility will be economic. Plant and operations relocation is an expensive activity. Unlimited right of exit creates social and economic problems that are expensive to solve. The mounting concern for a national policy on plant relocation may, therefore, prove attractive to a number of business leaders as well as to the unions and a coalition of interests seeking to minimize the economic losses in the Snowbelt. Such a coalition would make it possible for the first time to consider realistically the long-discussed dimensions of a national urban policy. One of the unintended consequences of this set of policies would be increasingly stable neighborhoods. In turn, more stable neighborhoods would contribute further to what Fainstein and Fainstein have described as convergence between American and European cities.[4]

There appears little likelihood that an intelligible national urban policy, meaning a framework for city policymaking defined in Washington, D.C., will be developed in the near future. As neoconservatives have gained political power, concern for urban policy "has been subordinated to national economic policy."[5]

[4]Norman and Susan Fainstein, eds., "Restructuring the American City: A Comparative Perspective," in *Urban Policy Under Capitalism* (Beverly Hills, Calif.: Sage Publications, 1982), pp. 161–189.

[5]John R. Logan, "Symposium: Urban Theory and National Urban Policy," *Urban Affairs Quarterly*, Vol. 19 (September 1983), p. 3.

The Reagan administration began to implement what it called the "New Federalism" in the early 1980s, the basic aim being to dismantle the social programs implemented in the 1960s, particularly the remnants of the War on Poverty and the later Model Cities Program. And, as Richard Child Hill notes, the New Federalism is "part of the conservative alternative agenda to redress the perceived failures of liberal, neo-Keynesian economic policy."[6]

More specifically, the New Federalism aims to (1) contract the welfare state while expanding defense expenditures; (2) change tax policy to shift resources from smaller businesses and poorer citizens to larger corporations and the more affluent; (3) within this pattern, decentralize federal authority and fiscal responsibility for a number of programs; (4) ease government regulation of business in such areas as environmental impact, workplace health and safety standards, economic concentration, and civil rights; and (5) encourage urban economic development that emphasizes government incentives to private parties. Such mechanisms as the urban enterprise zones, excluding some from the minimum wage requirements, and the effort to "reprivatize" some governmental services all aim to shift authority to the private sector.

Thirdly, although political office still disproportionaly belongs to white males, there have been substantial changes in the patterns of representation in city governments. Women and blacks have made impressive gains. Particularly worth attention will be the impact of new black mayoral leadership in industrial snow belt cities such as Chicago, Philadelphia, and Detroit. Up to the contemporary period, the conventional wisdom of political scientists has been that black mayors have operated within the same constraints as white mayors and have made only marginal differences. But the need to face the challenges of economic transitions, even if that is actuated by fiscal decline, may give black mayors of the 1980s considerably more capacity to reshape urban policies.

Fourth, the struggle between political coalitions of those holding a private city image and those whose vision is more like the bureaucratic city image provides the most synthetic outline for understanding local politics. Much of the analysis done to date suggests that the private city image is ascendent in the 1970s and 1980s and that even the substantial power of the bureaucracy is being effectively constrained within terms acceptable to the members of the private city coalition. The New Reform describes a package of changes being relatively successfully pressed by that same coalition. But, as with the old reform, the effect is not to undercut the power of the bureaucracy but to make it more responsive to the dominant coalition's preferences.

The other effects of the New Reform are generally in the direction of imposing business methods, institutional forms, and, indeed business people on local government. Neoconservatives will find this to be progressive change. But

---

[6]Richard Child Hill, "Market, State and Community: National Urban Policy in the 1980's," *Urban Affairs Quarterly*, Vol. 19 (September 1983), p. 7.

others are not so sure. There is skepticism on the left about the breadth of understanding of business leadership and some doubt that business people are equipped to deal with the ambiguities of democracy. A newspaper account of Lee Iacocca's much admired leadership style within financially troubled Chrysler Corporation contained a variety of testimonials from his peers, but none so provocative as the comment of the former governor of Florida, Claude Kirk, that "If there's any job [Iacocca] should be given, it's as emperor." He continued "We deserve that kind of leadership but we'll never get it. Why should he subject himself to the ridiculous problem of trying to win over some public-employee union delegate from Illinois to get to be President of the United States?"[7]

Finally, the conflicts over urban performance that have characterized capitalism since its industrial stage seem likely to continue. Essentially, what that means is that in the trade-off between efficiency and equality, our policies will continue to reflect preference for those who already have wealth and power— called the "systemic" basis of power by Stone.

IDEOLOGICAL CONFLICTS IN RETROSPECT

Reflecting on these trends, what emerges as the central point is simply that neoconservatism is ascendant in the 1970s and 1980s. Whether viewed as a personal ethic, as a creed, or as a method, it is the viewpoint of the period. Whether we endorse or oppose neoconservatism is irrelevant. We all profit from understanding that we are in a period that, more clearly than most, is testing the viability of a relatively coherent set of principles. That way we can learn from both successes and failures. To deny ideological relevance is to stay in the muddled middle and remain uncertain as to what our history teaches us. It is worth noting that as neoconservatism ascends, so does the relevance of radical criticism and alternative. This, too, makes it possible to learn from the clear presentation of oppositions.

Liberalism is appealing to those of us who are uncomfortable with conflict and unsure whether we can face the lessons of history squarely. It is more a practical compromise stance than an ideology, in fact. But liberalism retains a strong appeal. It has been our "public philosophy" since the New Deal. And pluralism, its methodological articulation, provides a plausible, though superficial, description of the total, complex process of politics.

Finally, let me recognize that there will be a great many who will be quite unsatisfied with this conclusion—those who want a ringing renunciation of one or the other ideological positions developed here may be tempted to find cowardice in my effort at even-handedness. I emphatically deny that and demand instead the

[7]*Los Angeles Times*, April 10, 1983, p. 18.

recognition that there is little to gain from premature renunciation except personal catharsis. The acceptance or rejection of ideas is finally a prerogative of ongoing experience, not of an academic—or any other—scribbler.

In the meantime, respect for differences is preferable. I would insist that politics, more than rationality, is the chief vehicle of such fundamental respect. Democratic politics, better than any rationalistic mode of analysis or any strong leader assures us that we will be faced by the realities our intellectualizations have overlooked. In other words, it is part of the poetry of politics that those people who are precisely the ones who need to hear each other find themselves in direct conflict. All parties will learn more from that experience of taking one another's differences seriously than by rationalistic screening, renunciation, or premature compromise.

But all this tolerant sounding talk too easily masks the need for practical students and citizens to take firm stands even in the face of uncertainty. Academicians can take lifetimes contemplating alternatives. That is one of the reasons the phrase "merely academic" means something like irrelevant. So, finally, this book boils down to a multiple-choice question. Just fill in the correct box and send it to the president, governor, mayor, this author, and the publisher.

The right approach to political economy is

1. Neoconservatism
2. Liberalism
3. Radicalism
4. All of the above
5. None of the above

We should then spend the rest of our lives in serious discussion and reflection as to whether we passed or failed.

Index